MODERN NOVELISTS

General Editor: Norman Page

MODERN NOVELISTS

Published titles

E. M. FORSTER   Norman Page
WILLIAM GOLDING   James Gindin
MARCEL PROUST   Philip Thody
SIX WOMEN NOVELISTS   Merryn Williams
JOHN UPDIKE   Judie Newman
H. G. WELLS   Michael Draper

Forthcoming titles

ALBERT CAMUS   Philip Thody
JOSEPH CONRAD   Owen Knowles
FYODOR DOSTOEVSKI   Peter Conradi
WILLIAM FAULKNER   David Dowling
F. SCOTT FITZGERALD   John S. Whitley
GUSTAVE FLAUBERT   David Roe
JOHN FOWLES   Simon Gatrell
GRAHAM GREENE   Neil McEwan
HENRY JAMES   Alan Bellringer
JAMES JOYCE   Richard Brown
D. H. LAWRENCE   G. M. Hyde
DORIS LESSING   Ruth Whittaker
MALCOLM LOWRY   Tony Bareham
GEORGE ORWELL   Valerie Meyers
BARBARA PYM   Michael Cotsell
MURIEL SPARK   Norman Page
GERTRUDE STEIN   Shirley Neuman
EVELYN WAUGH   Jacqueline McDonnell
VIRGINIA WOOLF   Edward Bishop

MODERN NOVELISTS
MARCEL PROUST

Philip Thody

St. Martin's Press
New York

First published in the United States of America in 1988

Printed in Hong Kong

Library of Congress Cataloging-in-Publication Data
Thody, Philip Malcolm Waller, 1928–
Marcel Proust
(Modern novelists)
Bibliography: p.
Includes index.
1. Proust, Marcel, 1871–1922—Criticism and
interpretation.   I. Title.   II. Series.
PQ2631.R63Z935   1988   843′.912   88–4598
ISBN 0–312–02088–0

Contents

Acknowledgments

I am grateful to Chatto and Windus, Random House Publishers and the Marcel Proust estate for allowing me to quote from Terence Kilmartin's 1981 translation of *Remembrance of Things Past*.

Annette Torode typed the many versions of my manuscript with exemplary care and good humour. Gwilym Rees made his accustomed and invaluable contribution to the accuracy and readability of what I had written. Any mistakes are entirely my own.

My thanks also go to the British Tax-Payer who provided the customary one hundred per cent subsidy without which this book – like my others – would never have been written.

General Editor's Preface

The death of the novel has often been announced, and part of the secret of its obstinate vitality must be its capacity for growth, adaptation, self-renewal and even self-transformation: like some vigorous organism in a speeded-up Darwinian ecosystem, it adapts itself quickly to a changing world. War and revolution, economic crisis and social change, radically new ideologies such as Marxism and Freudianism, have made this century unprecedented in human history in the speed and extent of change, but the novel has shown an extraordinary capacity to find new forms and techniques and to accommodate new ideas and conceptions of human nature and human experience, and even to take up new positions on the nature of fiction itself.

In the generations immediately preceding and following 1914, the novel underwent a radical redefinition of its nature and possibilities. The present series of monographs is devoted to the novelists who created the modern novel and to those who, in their turn, either continued and extended, or reacted against and rejected, the traditions established during that period of intense exploration and experiment. It includes a number of those who lived and wrote in the nineteenth century but whose innovative contribution to the art of fiction makes it impossible to ignore them in any account of the origins of the modern novel; it also includes the so-called 'modernists' and those who in the mid- and late twentieth century have emerged as outstanding practitioners of this genre. The scope is, inevitably, international; not only, in the migratory and exile-haunted world of our century, do writers refuse to heed national frontiers – 'English' literature lays claim to Conrad the Pole, Henry James the American, and Joyce the Irishman – but geniuses such as Flaubert, Dostoevski and Kafka have had an influence on the fiction of many nations.

Each volume in the series is intended to provide an introduction
to the fiction of the writer concerned, both for those approaching
him or her for the first time and for those who are already familiar
with some parts of the achievement in question and now wish to
place it in the context of the total *œuvre*. Although essential
information relating to the writer's life and times is given, usually
in an opening chapter, the approach is primarily critical and the
emphasis is not upon 'background' or generalisations but upon
close examination of important texts. Where an author is notably
prolific, major texts have been selected for detailed attention but
an attempt has also been made to convey, more summarily, a
sense of the nature and quality of the author's work as a whole.
Those who want to read further will find suggestions in the select
bibliography included in each volume. Many novelists are, of
course, not only novelists but also poets, essayists, biographers,
dramatists, travel writers and so forth; many have practised
shorter forms of fiction; and many have written letters or kept
diaries that constitute a significant part of their literary output. A
brief study cannot hope to deal with all these in detail, but where
the shorter fiction and the non-fictional writings, public and
private, have an important relationship to the novels, some space
has been devoted to them.

NORMAN PAGE

To Florence, Bill and Martin Johnson

1

The Book, the Memories and the Man

There are three ideas about Marcel Proust which it is useful to discuss before trying to bring out the full range of his achievements as a novelist. The first, which is well founded, is that Proust was a highly prolific writer whose major and most important work, *A la recherche du temps perdu* (1913–27), best known in English as *Remembrance of Things Past*, is very long. The second, which is not true, is that his book is mainly about the experience of involuntary memory, exemplified by the moment in which his whole past came flooding back to him when he tasted a mouthful of tea and cake. The third, which is potentially misleading, is that *A la recherche du temps perdu* is principally to be admired for its poetic recreation of the Narrator's childhood and early adolescence.

A la recherche du temps perdu is a very long novel. With some 1 240 000 words, it is twice the length of Tolstoy's *War and Peace*. You could fit one of Proust's own favourite novels, George Eliot's *The Mill on the Floss*, into the first of the three volumes in which the work is now most readily available, and still have room for the complete works of the playwright whom he mentions most frequently, Jean Racine. Admittedly, *A la recherche du temps perdu* has some formidable rivals, in the twentieth century as well as in the nineteenth. Balzac's *La Comédie humaine* contains some 4 700 000 words, and Zola's *Les Rougon-Macquart* well over 2 500 000. By 1985, the published work of Alexander Solzhenitsyn covered more than 6200 pages, as against the 3314 of the 1954 standard French *Pléiade* edition of *A la recherche du temps perdu*. But Proust also wrote a great deal else in addition to *A la recherche du temps perdu*. Between 1896 and 1899, he composed a long novel to which his literary executors later gave the title of *Jean Santeuil*. He never actually finished it, and it needed a happy accident for it to

1

be discovered and published some thirty years after his death, in 1952. But it nevertheless runs to some 700 pages, which is only slightly less than the various essays and reviews first collected in book form in 1954 under the title of *Contre Sainte-Beuve* (*By Way of Sainte-Beuve*).

It is true that Proust published relatively little during his lifetime. Only nine of the fifteen volumes in which it was customary to read *A la recherche du temps perdu* before 1954 appeared before his death in 1922. Apart from them, he was known in the fashionable rather than the literary world for a slim volume of essays, sketches and poems, *Les Plaisirs et les jours*, which came out in 1896, when he was twenty-five, and for a collection of very clever parodies, *L'Affaire Lemoine*. This was published in 1919 with a number of other sketches to which he gave the title of *Pastiches et mélanges*. Proust also devoted a great deal of time to translating Ruskin. His translation of *The Bible of Amiens* came out in 1904, of *Sesame and Lilies* in 1906, and he was certainly one of those authors who practised with the greatest enthusiasm the old Latin adage, *nulla dies sine linea* (Let no day pass without writing a line). He was so indefatigable a letter writer that his complete correspondence is still in the process of being published. Thirteen volumes have brought us up to 1914, the year after the first two volumes of *A la recherche du temps perdu* – *Du côté de chez Swann* (*Swann's Way*) – appeared on 8 November 1913. The whole collection will probably fill some twenty-three volumes, and give some justification to Samuel Beckett's description of Proust as 'the garrulous old dowager of the Letters'.[1] If you decide to read everything he wrote, you will need to set aside a couple of years. They will be well employed, and you will never see things in quite the same light again. Alternatively, like him, you can be an insomniac. In that case, you might do it in eighteen months. It will still be worth it.

Proust is certainly best known for his description of the way in which a chance physical sensation brought the whole of his past flooding back to him. But this experience of 'involuntary memory' occupies a relatively small part of the three thousand or so pages of *A la recherche du temps perdu* and has only an indirect relationship to his analysis of jealousy, his discussion of homosexuality, and his account of how snobs and social climbers behaved in late nineteenth- and early twentieth-century France. It has virtually nothing to do with his portraits of aristocrats, artists, diplomats, doctors, hotel keepers, journalists, military men, servants, society hostesses and university teachers. He is nevertheless so well known for his originality in describing the incident of the 'petite madeleine', the small cake dipped in tea which brings the Narrator's past back to him, that no account of his work can begin without it.

One day, when he comes home tired and depressed, the Narrator in *Remembrance of Things Past* allows himself to be persuaded by his mother to eat 'one of those squat, plump little cakes called "petites madeleines", which look as thought they had been moulded in the fluted valve of a scallop shell'. He soaks a morsel of it in warm tea, raises a spoonful to his lips, and is suddenly invaded by an exquisite pleasure, an all-powerful joy, which infinitely transcends the taste of the tea and cake. He takes a second mouthful, then a third, only to find that 'the potion is losing its magic'.[2] He turns his attention to what he feels lies within himself, tries to shut out everything which might distract him, and is suddenly rewarded with an explanation for his bliss.

The taste, he recognises, was that of the little piece of cake which his aunt used to give him when he was a child and went to see her in her bedroom on Sunday mornings before going to mass. The sight of the 'petite madeleine' had meant nothing to him. He had often seen such cakes in pastry-cooks' windows, and his visual memory of them had been overlaid by innumerable other events. But by some strange accident, the precise physical memory of the sensation provided by the little cake dipped in tea had remained intact. The bliss with which he had been filled by the tea and cake offered him by his mother stemmed from the fact that they exactly recalled the childhood memory which had been dormant for so many years.

The incident of the 'petite madeleine' is nevertheless not the only example in *A la recherche du temps perdu* of the experience of involuntary memory. This experience can take place only if you are not deliberately trying to remember something, and this is precisely what happens about half-way through the book when the Narrator bends down in a hotel bedroom in order to unlace his boots. His whole being is suddenly filled with 'an unknown, a divine presence'. He is shaken with sobs and tears stream from his eyes. The exact reproduction, at a moment when he was least expecting it, of the way in which his grandmother had bent down to help him undo his boots when they first arrived at the same hotel a number of years before has done more than bring back to him the 'tender, preoccupied, disappointed face' which she had often showed him when she was alive. It has also brought fully home to him, in a way that his more conscious efforts to grieve for her had never done, just how much he loved her and how irreparable a loss he has suffered in her death. Until that moment, it was almost as though he had not fully realised that she was dead.[3]

There is a sense in which the Proust who described the experience of the 'petite madeleine' was writing as an essayist, a philosopher or a poet rather than as a novelist. Indeed, in *Contre Sainte-Beuve*, he had originally tried to deal with the experience in essay form, and no reader of *A la recherche du temps perdu* can fail to be struck by the similarities between the taste which brings Proust's childhood back to him and the way Baudelaire, in *La Chevelure*, describes how he is made to see a tropical seascape by the smell of his mistress's hair. The circumstances in which the Narrator of *A la recherche du temps perdu* suddenly realises, through the grief which invades him in his hotel bedroom, that he is still the same person who enjoyed so perfect and loving a relationship with his grandmother, are therefore especially important because they remind us that Proust was writing a novel. He was, in other words, describing our relationship with other people as well as our private experience of ourselves. One of the central themes in *A la recherche du temps perdu* is the contrast between the secure, morally authentic world which the Narrator has known as a child, incarnated in what he calls 'les vertus de Combray', and the glamorous but totally meretricious world which he meets when he rises in society and mixes with the aristocrats in the fashionable Faubourg Saint-Germain. For just as the total indifference to his wife's happiness with which the Duc de Guermantes pursues his various mistresses contrasts with the kindness and consideration the Narrator's parents show towards each other, so the attitude which Proust's real or would-be aristocrats adopt towards death stands out in contrast to 'les vertus de Combray' by its complete heartlessness and superficiality. For the Guermantes, who are joined in this as in other ways by the ambitious Madame Verdurin, the death of a friend or relative is merely a tiresome interruption to the social round. The idea that anyone might feel the grief that shakes the Narrator with such uncontrollable sobs as he realises that the most perfect human being he has ever known has gone for ever is totally alien to them.

It is because *A la recherche du temps perdu* is a novel about human emotions and social attitudes that it can be misleading to see it as centred principally around the privileged access to the world of his childhood which is bestowed upon the Narrator by the taste of the 'petite madeleine'. There are, however, times when the Narrator speaks in terms which might well lead to such a misinterpretation of his own created world, and this is especially so at the end of the novel. For in addition to being the first book to talk in such detail and at such length about the experience of involuntary memory, *A la recherche du temps perdu* is also the first novel in world literature – apart from *Tristram Shandy*; as usual a Yorkshireman came first – to have as one of its main themes the story of how it came to be written. The Narrator's decision to spend the rest of his life writing this book comes after three further examples of the phenomenon of unconscious memory, which occur one after another in the closing volume of the novel, *Le Temps retrouvé* (*Time Regained*). Like the 'petite madeleine' episode, they are based upon accidental physical sensations which bring the whole atmosphere of the past back to life. But unlike the 'petite madeleine' incident, these also lead somewhere: to the decision on the Narrator's part to write *A la recherche du temps perdu*, the book which the reader then discovers to be the one which he is on the point of finishing reading.

On his way to a reception at the house of the new Princesse de Guermantes, the Narrator steps on an uneven paving stone in a Paris courtyard and is overwhelmed by an inner vision of profound azure and dazzling light. Without his anticipating what is going to happen, the movement underfoot of the Paris paving stones has reproduced another memory which has been dormant and unnoticed for years, that of an identical sensation which he felt when he stood upon two uneven paving stones in the baptistery of St Mark's, Venice. The sound of a spoon hitting accidentally against a plate as he waits to go in and greet his hostess brings back an entirely different sensation of heat, this time 'combined with a whiff of smoke and relieved by the cool smell of a forest background'.[4] It has reproduced the moment when, looking through the window of a railway carriage at a row of trees, he had heard a workman tapping the wheels of the train.

A manservant hands him a starched napkin on which to wipe his mouth, and he is immediately transported back to the moment when he stood drying his face on a similarly starched towel before the window of his hotel at Balbec, in Normandy. This napkin has unfolded for him what he calls 'the plumage of an ocean green and blue like the tail of a peacock'.[5]

What the Narrator then realises is that although these 'fragments of existence withdrawn from Time' have given him the only genuine and fruitful pleasure he has ever known, they are essentially fleeting and unpredictable. The only way in which he can recapture them is by the creation of a work of art in which they are given permanent form. They have to be rescued from contingency by the perfection of the language used to describe them, by 'les anneaux nécessaires d'un beau style' (the necessary links of a well-wrought style) in which they will then be held prisoner. But this recognition of the supreme role which art can play in enabling him to give sense to his experience goes hand in hand with a recognition that these moments of escape from time are too pure, precious and intense to exist alone. They will need to be set, like jewels, in the 'less pure' material provided by the more ordinary memories which his conscious mind has retained of people, places and events, and it is the vocabulary which Proust uses to describe these settings that lies at the origins of the second and third of the beliefs which I mentioned at the beginning of this chapter.

For Proust does make his Narrator describe his conscious memories in slightly condescending terms. They are, the Narrator says, 'not altogether to be despised' in the role which they will play in enabling him to 'enshrine in a less pure matter' the moments of pure bliss provided by involuntary memory. The truths which he extracts from his examination of social change are merely suitable to 'cement together' the more poetic sections of his work, and Proust's use of such words clearly invites the reader to adopt a particular attitude towards the contents of *A la recherche du temps perdu*. He is to see the 'splendour in the grass' experience reproduced through involuntary memory as being on a higher plane than the analytical and comic passages describing how adults behave in their relationships with one another.[6]

One of the advantages of trying to look at Proust primarily as a novelist is that it draws attention to the value of the less lyrical parts of his work. The novel is the most flexible of all literary genres. It has nevertheless produced its best effects when used for three main purposes: telling stories, presenting characters and analysing society. It is, of course, capable of almost infinite expansion, and Proust himself made a major contribution to its development by showing that it did not need to be tied down to a specific style of story-telling. One of the publishers who refused to accept *Du côté de chez Swann* when Proust was first trying to place it in 1912 did so on the grounds that he might be a bit stupid but could not understand why an author needed to spend thirty pages describing how he turned over in bed at night before going to sleep.[7] But once the appearance of *Du côté de chez Swann* in 1913, and more especially the tremendous success of the next three volumes, *A l'ombre des jeunes filles en fleurs* (*Within a Budding Grove*), in 1919, had shown that the general reading public was less blinkered, the novel itself had taken a major step forward as an art form. Proust is certainly one of the greatest of writers in the revolutionary and experimental tradition of the European novel. But it is both possible and profitable to study him as a novelist working within a set of more established traditions. In his analysis of love, he is often in the same line of country as Stendhal, Laclos or Constant. His portrait of family life so reminded his first French readers of Dickens and George Eliot that they occasionally dubbed him an 'English novelist'. His social comedy makes us think of Thackeray, Wilde, Saki, Evelyn Waugh or Anthony Powell, and even – at times – of P. G. Wodehouse.

It is true that his passionately held conviction, expressed in the closing pages of *Le Temps retrouvé*, that 'real life, life at last laid bare and illuminated – the only life in consequence which can be said to be really lived – is literature'[8] meant that Proust had less enthusiasm for the ordinary stuff of lived experience than writers such as Balzac, Dickens or Zola. But he did, in December 1902, write to Antoine Bibesco about how 'a thousand characters for novels, a thousand ideas', urged him to give them body 'like the shades in the *Odyssey* who plead with Ulysses to give them a little blood to drink to bring them back to life',[9] and enough of this ambition remained to make him into a novelist who wrote about other people as well as about himself, who analysed the society in which he lived, and who told stories. Indeed, if one takes Proust at his own word and looks at *A la recherche du temps perdu* as what he calls 'the story of a Vocation', it has both a clear narrative line and a happy ending. What it tells us is how a small boy grew up to be a writer.

In this respect, Proust also creates one of the most powerful and tempting and potentially dangerous myths in modern literature. For what he shows us is how a man who has made a mess of almost every relationship in which he has been involved nevertheless manages to give meaning to his life by writing a book. It is an example which Michel Butor followed in 1957 with *La Modification*, and is a dream whose appeal coincides most intensely with those moments at which we are most aware of our own inadequacies. As in its description of the phenomenon of involuntary memory, *A la recherche du temps perdu* gives to the realisation of this dream 'a local habitation and a name'. It sets the development of the Narrator Marcel's vocation against the atmosphere of late nineteenth- and early twentieth-century France. But precisely because it both does and does not tell the story of Marcel Proust the man, any study of *A la recherche du temps perdu* has to include at least a glance at the person who wrote it.

The taking of such a glance would not have pleased Proust himself. In 1909, in his draft for an article attacking the importance which the French literary critic Sainte-Beuve gave to an author's private life in any assessment of his work, he stated categorically that 'a book is the product of a different *self* from the self we manifest in our habits, in our social life, in our vices'.[10] If we want to understand the genuinely creative part of our personality, he argued, we must look for it nowhere but in ourselves.

There is a good deal to be said for this idea, and the appearance of *Contre Sainte-Beuve* in 1954 had a very happy effect on Proust's posthumous reputation. For this was just when the structuralist movement was beginning in France, and critics were delighted to find that they had so eminent a predecessor for the view which Roland Barthes expressed in 1968 when he proclaimed that the author as individual was dead and that a work of literature has 'no origins but language itself'.[11] The problem of applying this idea to Proust is that he so often gives the appearance of being one of the most autobiographical novelists ever to put pen to paper. Like the Marcel of *A la recherche du temps perdu*, he was a rich, male, neurotic, unmarried member of the French upper middle class. The very starting point for the incident of the 'petite madeleine', as *Contre*

Sainte-Beuve tells us, lies in the moment when the real Marcel
Proust tasted a mouthful of tea and toast offered to him by his
housekeeper and realised that it brought back to life the days
when his grandfather used to give him a piece of rusk. The
incident in *Le Temps retrouvé* in which he is reminded of Venice by
the uneven paving stones in a Paris courtyard was also based on
personal experience, as was the effect of hearing a spoon catching
against a plate. Like the Narrator Marcel, Proust suffered from
asthma, had difficulty in sleeping, was a middle-class boy who
managed to make himself extremely acceptable to the aristocratic
high society of late nineteenth-century France, and saw genuine
value only in the writing of books. Admittedly, there are anecdotal
differences between Proust and Marcel. The latter keeps falling in
love with girls, and claims at one point in the novel to have
enjoyed the 'ephemeral favours' of fourteen attractively nubile
ones during a single summer holiday in Normandy.[12] Proust, in
contrast, was a homosexual, and it is open to question whether he
ever had even the somewhat incomplete sexual relationships with
women which the Narrator has with Gilberte Swann and
Albertine Simonet.[13] Proust's mother was Jewish, but there is no
question of the Narrator's family being anything but Gentile and
even Christian. At no point in *A la recherche du temps perdu* do we
discover the Narrator's surname. But there are so many other
similarities that it would come as no surprise to find out that it
happened to be Proust.

Like his creator, the Marcel of *A la recherche du temps perdu* never
has to work for a living. His father, like the hero's father in
Proust's first attempt at fiction in *Jean Santeuil*, is a higher civil
servant. But there is inherited money in the world of *A la recherche
du temps perdu* as well, and the Narrator receives a large enough
legacy from his eccentric Aunt Léonie to offer his adored Albertine
the bribe of a yacht and a Rolls-Royce if she will agree to stay with
him. In 1914, Proust was in a position of being able to make a
similar offer to his chauffeur, Alfred Agostinelli. By selling his
shares in the Royal Dutch and Suez Canal company, he managed
to raise the 27 000 francs necessary to buy him an aeroplane, and a
note in Philip Kolb's invaluable edition of the *Correspondance*
points out that this was almost exactly the same price as a Rolls.[14]
It is also pleasant to know that his father, Dr Adrien Proust, did
not depend exclusively on his fees or his salary to ensure a high
standard of living. When, at the age of thirty-seven, on 20 August

1870, he married the twenty-two-year-old Nathalie Weil, she brought him a dowry of 200 000 francs. The purchasing power of the sum which thus came to a man who had been the equivalent of a Senior Registrar since 1863 can be judged from the fact that the couple paid 2500 a year for their first Paris apartment.[15]

Marcel was born on 10 July 1871 and was followed by his brother, Robert, on 24 May 1873. After that, at a period when the British medical profession considered all artificial methods of birth control as injurious to the health of the working class, Dr Adrien Proust and his wife had no more children. In *A la recherche du temps perdu*, Proust goes one better and makes the Narrator Marcel an only child. Fond though he was of Robert, and devoted as he was later to be to his niece, the present Madame Mante-Proust, he behaved in a literary context like the Turk in Pope's *An Epistle to Dr Arbuthnot*. He brooked no brother near the throne.

Robert was a more conventional child than Marcel, and grew up to be almost as distinguished a doctor as his father. He remained on good terms with his brother, and in 1920 was entrusted with the task of formally bestowing on him the insignia of the Legion of Honour which Marcel had just been awarded. Proust, as was very often the case, was too ill to leave the cork-lined, fumigated room in which he spent the last fifteen years of his life. He was already, like the Narrator of *A la recherche du temps perdu*, 'the strange human who, while he waits for death to release him, lives behind closed shutters, knows nothing of the world, sits motionless as an owl, and like that bird can see things at all clearly only in the darkness'.[16] No other novelist takes us quite so far as Proust into the world of the invalid. Before the middle of the second paragraph of *Du côté de chez Swann*, we are already presented with the experience of a sick man lying in a hotel bedroom, rejoicing that the light he can see coming in under the door is a sign of morning. But, alas, he is wrong. 'The ray of light beneath the door is extinguished. It is midnight; someone has just turned down the gas; the last servant has gone to bed, and he must lie all night in agony with no one to bring him relief.'[17]

Proust suffered his first attack of asthma in the spring of 1881, at the age of nine. It remained with him throughout his life, and helped to provide an excuse for his failure ever to take a job and earn his own living. It did not prevent him from going to school, and he had quite a distinguished academic career at the Lycée

Condorcet. In 1889, he found he was well enough to take advantage of the arrangement whereby young men who were going to be students could avoid the normal three years of compulsory military service introduced as a result of the falling French birth rate and the defeat of France by Prussia in 1870 and serve for one year as volunteer officers. He completed his training, and left behind him one of the great mysteries of French literary history: the identity of the officer who was placed sixty-fourth to Proust's sixty-third when they completed their initial training on 14 November 1890.

Proust then studied at the Ecole des sciences politiques, and in the Faculties of Arts and Law at the University of Paris. He took degrees in both subjects, and competed in June 1895 for a post as librarian at the Bibliothèque Mazarine. He was placed third out of three candidates, and proved neither an assiduous nor a successful librarian. Although his immediate superior once commented that 'Monsieur Proust seems to me to enjoy excellent health', the dust from the books irritated his throat and he was, in any case, far more interested in becoming a writer. His father was apparently convinced that young Marcel would eventually be elected to the Académie française, and was wrong only in his confidence in that institution's ability to recognise original talent when it saw it. Even if he had lived to be eighty, instead of dying on 18 November 1922 at the age of fifty-one of a combination of asthma, bronchitis, protein and vitamin deficiency and systematic under-nourishment, it is doubtful if Proust would have made it. He was too original.

Dr Adrien Proust's own conviction that Proust's asthma was of nervous origin, and might well therefore be overcome with a little more will power, did not make him press his son too hard to take a job. Proust was consequently free to lead what must have seemed to his hard-working father an almost unbelievably butterfly existence. While Adrien Proust indefatigably pursued his own career as one of the leading specialists in world health, prefacing in November 1900 the 1245 pages of the third edition of his *Traité d'hygiène*, and risking his own life by going to Marseilles during an outbreak of the plague, Proust devoted his energies to making himself acceptable to the more fashionable reaches of Parisian aristocratic society.

The appearance in June 1896 of *Les Plaisirs et les jours*, with illustrations by the well-known hostess Madeleine Lemaire and a preface extracted with some difficulty from Anatole France, in which he described the twenty-five-year-old Proust as 'a depraved Bernardin de Saint-Pierre and an innocent Petronius', consequently seemed for a long time to fit better into his social than into his literary career. The book was published in a luxury edition at fifteen francs a volume, at a time when most books cost only three, and by June 1918 had sold only 329 copies. When André Gide made what he later recognised was the greatest mistake of his literary career and turned down the first volume of *A la recherche du temps perdu*, *Du côté de chez Swann*, for the *Editions de la Nouvelle Revue française* in 1912, it was because he thought of Proust as an elegant dilettante. Proust solved the problem by using some of his considerable fortune to pay to have the book published himself – Gide had done the same for his own early work – and became one of the *NRF* writers only when the opportunity to read *Du côté de chez Swann* in its entirety made Gide change his mind. Proust subsequently endeared himself to the publisher of the *Nouvelle Revue française*, Gaston Gallimard, by never asking him for any advance on royalties.[18]

Les *Plaisirs et les jours* – also published at Proust's own expense – has a slightly frivolous *fin de siècle* aestheticism about it. We are in the world of Oscar Wilde or even Aubrey Beardsley, with a strong touch of Huysmans and only an occasional hint of Mallarmé. It is only in retrospect that the almost constant equation of sex with guilt looks forward to the treatment of homosexuality in *Sodome et Gomorrhe* (*Cities of the Plain*), or that the remark about 'the contrast between the immensity of our past love and the absolute nature of our present indifference' can be seen as a harbinger for Proust's great theme of the transient nature of the self. You also need to know about Proust's treatment of insomnia in *A la recherche du temps perdu* to see the promise concealed in the apparently simple remark about how sleeping pills make you sleep without being aware that you are doing so, and the same is true of the other themes which are given their first, tentative expression in *Les Plaisirs et les jours*. Indeed, Proust himself felt so unsure of the acceptability of some of his ideas that he omitted from one of the articles reprinted from *La Revue blanche* a remark about Lesbianism which showed how preoccupied he already was with what was to become one of the major themes of *A la recherche du temps perdu*. Lesbianism was, he wrote, an affliction of such obviously nervous origin that no moral judgement could ever be applied to it.[19] The Narrator of *A la recherche du temps perdu* has a different attitude. Whenever he asks Albertine if she has 'fait le mal' (been wicked, sinned, done wrong), what he wants to know is whether or not she has had sexual relationships with other women. In addition to taking you into the world of the invalid, *A la recherche du temps perdu* also shows you what it is like to suffer from a number of emotional and sexual obsessions.

Proust was destined to become the patron saint of all insomniacs, and his letters to his mother are full of attempts to reassure her that he is trying to go to bed early and to sleep naturally. His habit of sleeping during the day so that he could work at night had clearly begun as early as 1899, when his friend Reynaldo Hahn made the most elaborate arrangements to ensure that a registered letter which he was sending him should be addressed to his concierge in order that it did not wake him up, and it is in this and other peculiarities of his domestic life that one of the reasons for his insistence on not confusing the writer who creates with the man who lives is most probably to be found. For in December 1903, when he was thirty-two and still living at home with his parents, he wrote a long letter to his mother describing how he had failed to keep his resolution of sharing her life to the point of sleeping at the same time as she did. He had indeed, he explains, gone to bed at one-thirty in the morning. But he had needed to get up to go to the loo, and had not been able to find the safety pin which was essential to hold his underpants firmly enough across his stomach to enable him to sleep in comfort. The time he had spent searching in his dressing room had brought him only a heavy cold. No wonder that he explained to Anna de Noailles, shortly after his father's death in December 1903, how fully he realised that he had been the one black spot on his parents' happiness.[20]

Not all Proust's life quite came up to this standard of inadequacy. He was not lacking in physical courage; on 6 February 1897 he fought a duel with a journalist called Jean Lorrain. Pistols were the weapons used, the motive being an ironic review of *Les Plaisirs et les jours* in which Lorrain had hinted at an unnatural relationship between Proust and his friend Lucien Daudet. In January 1898, Proust was one of the first signatories of the letter which Emile Zola wrote to *L'Aurore* in order to protest against the irregularities in the trial of Captain Alfed Dreyfus, the Jewish artillery officer falsely accused of passing military secrets to the Germans, and he was one of the most assiduous in collecting signatures in support of Dreyfus's rehabilitation. Proust lived at a time when the French were going through one of their periodic bouts of anti-semitism, and *A la recherche du temps perdu* is most instructive on this peculiarity of their national behaviour. He had a very wide circle of friends, and the ease with which the Narrator in *A la recherche du temps perdu* moves into the most exclusively aristocratic society is only a slight idealisation of Proust's own social career. He may, as André Gide suspected, have sometimes exaggerated the seriousness of his various illnesses in order to provide himself with the time and isolation in which to write, but a reading of his letters leaves no doubt but that he was a very sick man. But in writing his novel, he rose above his illness. For he used it not only as an excuse for the necessary isolation of the writer, but as an instrument through which he perceived the world.

The great disadvantage of the Sainte-Beuve style of literary criticism – apart from Sainte-Beuve's own notorious inability to do what he thought a competent critic ought to do and spot the good writers among his contemporaries – is that it confuses literary judgements with personal ones. Proust had an understandable reluctance to be judged by the kind of criteria which lead critics to say that Verlaine's love poetry has no value because he turned out to be such a rotten husband. He knew how vulnerable the life he lived made him to this kind of reductionism and wished to avoid the accusation that any book he wrote was unsatisfactory as a work of art because it was so clearly about his own problems. This is one reason why he made the initially surprising claim that 'a book is the product of a different *self* from the self we manifest in our habits, in our social life, in our vices'. He was not denying its autobiographical origins, or trying to insist that there was nothing in common between himself and his Narrator Marcel. He was saying that he wrote the book with a part of his personality that the world could not see.

The poetic recreation of his own childhood in the first section of *Du côté de chez Swann*, with its subtitle of Combray, was nevertheless so obviously autobiographical that in 1971, the centenary of Proust's birth, the small town of Illiers decided to change its name. Since it was there, some eighty kilometres south of Chartres, that Marcel Proust had spent his holidays in the 1870s and immortalised in *Du côté de chez Swann*, the authorities officially decided that this town would be known as Illiers-Combray. This was an excellent decision, and did a great deal for the tourist trade in what in other ways is not an outstandingly interesting part of France. In no other French provincial town are there quite so many shops selling 'petites madeleines'. But it has tended to distract attention away from the fact that *A la recherche du temps perdu* is as much a novel as a kind of autobiography. For although Proust's treatment of the theme of jealousy has an equally clear starting point in his own experience, his reputation as a writer and thinker can only benefit if the Marcel of *A la recherche du temps perdu* is seen as a character in a novel rather than an autobiographical figure for whom the reader is expected to feel the same kind of sympathy and admiration which are evoked by Proust's recreation of the idyllic side of childhood.

This is not the only advantage of looking at Proust primarily as a novelist. The Narrator in *A la recherche du temps perdu* mentions his 'complete egoism',[21] and you can see what he means. It is unusual for him to be interested in anyone but himself, so that if one reads *A la recherche du temps perdu* primarily as the 'story of a Vocation', the almost complete absorption of the main character in his own problems and ambitions does lead him to forfeit a good deal of the sympathy of any reader who does not share his view that all activities in life except the writing of books are ultimately valueless. Admittedly, he expresses considerable guilt at the unhappiness which his inadequate and self-centred life-style has caused to those dearest to him. He also confirms the importance of 'les vertus de Combray' by writing of his grandmother that no masterpiece, past, present or to come, would have had the slightest value in her eyes compared to his happiness.[22] But he is so self-centred that if you treat *A la recherche du temps perdu* as a kind of autobiography, the triumphant story of how the Narrator came to make sense of his experience through art, its concern with only one person's salvation does give off a slight air of self-indulgence.

If, however, you look at *A la recherche du temps perdu* as a novel, some of these defects tend to disappear. There is no reason, just because a novel is written in the first person singular, for the reader to feel obliged to accept the narrator as hero. Neither does he always have to regard the narrator's point of view as the only one which is valid. Indeed, in the case of André Gide's *L'Immoraliste*, any reader who did so would be missing the whole point of the book. In James Hogg's *Confessions of a Justified Sinner*, the person telling the story is made to condemn himself out of his own mouth, and there are times when the Narrator of *A la recherche du temps perdu* comes very close to doing this. He certainly shows himself sufficiently limited as a person for the reader to be able to profit from adopting a different frame of reference from that of the Narrator.

This is especially true if you look at the role played in *A la recherche du temps perdu* by Odette de Crécy and Albertine Simonet. Since Swann's love affair with Odette, like Marcel's with Albertine, is told entirely from the man's point of view, the reader's initial tendency is to look at the two women only through the man's eyes. But you do not need to shift the angle of vision very much to see how Odette or Albertine felt about things. I try to do this in Chapters 2 and 3, and also suggest in Chapter 3 that certain sections in *Du côté de chez Swann* become even more interesting if you also try to imagine how Marcel's parents must have felt. As Michel Tournier observed, 'in any novel, the author writes one half and the reader the other'.[23] One of the advantages of Proust's mode of narration is that it positively invites the reader to do this, and thus to put into practice the remark which X. Trapnell makes in the eleventh volume of Anthony Powell's somewhat Proust-like *A Dance to the Music of Time*. For he says in *Temporary Kings* that reading novels requires almost as much talent as writing them,[24] and his comment also draws attention to an aspect of *A la recherche du temps perdu* which explains why it sometimes makes an even greater appeal to the literary critic than it does to the more conventionally minded reader: it is a book about literature itself.

Because novels have traditionally described people's private lives, they have inevitably involved the presentation of the moral and social values by which these people have tried to live. In *A la recherche du temps perdu*, the reader is invited to admire two main sets of values: the steadiness of domestic affection embodied in 'les vertus de Combray'; the ethic of the artist which inspires the Narrator's attempt to recapture past time through art. But not all Proust's characters – or all his readers – are fortunate enough to be able to practise these virtues. They have to organise their lives differently, and there is no compulsion upon the reader to judge either them or himself by the standards which Proust regards as self-evidently true. The reader is always free to step outside the immediate value system of the novel, just as Ernest Renan did when he stepped outside the framework of *Madame Bovary* and said that we should not despise Monsieur Homais. Without him, he added, we should all be burned, and it is easy to see what he meant. The intolerance which gave rise to the Inquisition is sometimes best countered by an equal if opposite intolerance, that of the ferocious anti-clericalism of Flaubert's pompous provincial chemist.

The mere possibility of seeing any virtue in Homais would, of course, have made Flaubert bellow with indignation, and Proust would probably not have rejoiced in the suggestion that Albertine had rather a raw deal or that Odette de Crécy did remarkably well with the resources at her disposal. But part of the aim of literary criticism, as G. K. Chesterton once remarked, is precisely to say things that would have made the author jump out of his boots. It is also, as Roland Barthes argued more recently and in a more abstract vocabulary, to put forward 'une lecture plurielle' of a text – to try, in other words, to look at it in as many different ways as possible. I shall naturally try, in talking about *A la recherche du temps perdu*, to give an accurate account of what Proust was trying to do and how he saw the world. But I shall also try to suggest other ways of looking at *A la recherche du temps perdu*, not all of which involve underwriting Proust's own value system. Like a number of other twentieth-century writers – James Joyce, T. S. Eliot, Samuel Beckett – Proust shows remarkably little sympathy for the life-style of most of his readers. While they have wives, children, jobs and friends, dig the garden, go to church, worry about the mortgage or interest themselves in politics, Proust presents them with a world in which none of these activities has either any ultimate value or much immediate interest. There is, of course, no reason why he should. The wealth, variety, complexity and beauty of the experiences described in *A la recherche du temps perdu* are entirely self-sufficient. But at the same time as Proust presents us with this world, he also argues that its recreation through art is the only thing that matters. The challenge which his very articulate presentation of the doctrine of life for art's sake offers is not one which I myself can let pass without responding.

Proust's decision to write *A la recherche du temps perdu* in the first person also creates a number of more formal problems for the attentive reader, and a purist might even argue that he has not entirely mastered this particular mode of narration. Sometimes, his Narrator is totally omniscient, as when he tells us exactly how Swann feels about Odette or explains, in the last volume of *Le*

Temps retrouvé, that Swann's grand-daughter is going to marry a totally obscure literary man and thus lose the magnificent social position created for her by her parents.[25] At moments like these, he is granted the traditional privilege of knowing all that there is to know both about the distant past and the equally distant future. At other times, however, the situation is quite different. However hard the Narrator tries, he never finds out whether Albertine was a Lesbian or not, and he discovers the truth both about Charlus's homosexuality and about his masochistic tendencies only by a repeated and slightly disturbing readiness to act as a *voyeur*. If he did not have this tendency to peer through windows or watch through a crack in the door, then the implication is that neither he nor the reader would find out what is happening.

It would be churlish to criticise Proust for inconsistencies of this kind, just as it would be unkind as well perhaps as incorrect to argue that the length of the analyses of jealousy in *La Prisonnière* and *La Fugitive* show an obsessional mind which has not managed to bring its experience under control. *A la recherche du temps perdu* has a large number of different themes, and it is quite reasonable for each of these to be treated from a different point of view. When you are reading the novel, you quite easily make the adjustment from the semi-autobiographical Marcel who talks about Combray to the more impersonal Narrator who shows how the France of *La Belle Epoque* was destroyed by the impact of the First World War. You also learn to distinguish between the Marcel who acts as a mouthpiece for Proust's ideas on art and the Marcel who tells the story of how childhood traumas can determine adult sexual behaviour. If you also accept that this Marcel is to be seen as a character in a novel, rather than an autobiographical character who invariably invites and deserves your sympathy, then you are also more likely to be able to profit from what Proust has to say about the nature of human emotions.

2
Narration, Chronology and Technique

When you first read *A la recherche du temps perdu*, especially if you are thinking of it as a novel, it does not give the overwhelming impression of being a highly organised work of art. You move backwards and forwards in time, and there sometimes seems no immediate reason why one incident should come before another. *Un Amour de Swann*, for example, strikes you first of all as an episode which could be placed almost anywhere; since 1966 it has not lost either its appeal or its meaning by being available as a separate volume in paperback. There also seems to be no particular thread apart from the accidents of the Narrator's own experience linking the events together. It is hard to remember, in the middle volumes, which of the many parties he did go to first. Only when you follow out the implied injunction at the end of *Le Temps retrouvé* and set about reading the book again do you become more aware of what Anthony Powell calls 'secret harmonies', and see how the construction is subtler than you thought.

The first part of *Du côté de chez Swann*, *Combray*, begins with the Narrator describing how he used to go to bed early, how he would fall asleep, wake up again, and begin to think about the past. This leads on to the episode of the 'petite madeleine', to the famous description of the hawthorns in bloom and to the account of his childhood visits to Combray. We meet his mother, father, grandmother, great-aunts and great-uncles. We are given detailed descriptions of the church at Combray, and of the surrounding countryside. We learn the importance of the two directions in which one can go for a walk. There is Swann's way, *Du côté de chez Swann*, which takes you across the plain, and the Guermantes way, *Le côté de Guermantes*, which goes along the river. To the infant Marcel, whose experience the Narrator is recording, these two ways are so different that there seems no possibility of their ever coming together.

We then move backwards in time, to a period round about or preceding the Narrator's birth, and to the episode entitled *Un Amour de Swann*. The tone changes from the poetic evocation of the past to one of controlled irony as we meet the pretentious Madame Verdurin and her amiable, slightly henpecked husband. Much later in the novel, we discover that he is called Gustave, and it is only by an apparent accident that we discover that Madame Verdurin's first name is Sidonie.[26] We are, however, introduced to her guests, and especially to a lady of somewhat uncertain virtue, Odette de Crécy. Among her acquaintances is a rich Jewish man-about-town called Charles Swann, and we remember that one of the few visitors to call on the Narrator's grandparents at Combray was a man with the same name who always came alone. He had, we are given to understand, made an unfortunate marriage, and there is talk even now of his wife making a fool of him with a certain Monsieur de Charlus.

When he first meets her, Swann is not particularly attracted to Odette. He prefers plumpish, healthy-looking women and she has a kind of frail, languorous, Botticelli beauty which makes no immediate appeal to his senses. It is only when she happens not to be free on an evening when he is expecting to meet her that his feelings for her change. He worries that he might lose her and becomes hopelessly dependent on her presence. He also becomes intensely jealous of the relationship which she might be having not only with other men but also, perhaps, with other women. Madame Verdurin does nothing to relieve his anxiety, and positively encourages Odette's growing friendship with the Comte de Forcheville. It is only after Swann has lived through his jealousy and become virtually indifferent to Odette that he realises that he has wasted the best years of his life on a woman whom he did not really love and who was not his type.

The last chapter of *Du côté de chez Swann* takes us back to the Narrator. For a novel about time, *A la recherche du temps perdu* is curiously devoid not only of precise dates but also of any exact indication as to the age of the various characters. The Narrator now seems to be in his early teens – in *Combray* he appears to be about five or six – and is fascinated by the possibility of visiting Florence and Venice. But the very excitement of the idea makes him fall ill, and he has to stay at home in Paris. He is taken to play in the Champs-Elysées, where he meets and falls in love with Gilberte, Swann's daughter by Odette. We never discover when the marriage took place, or when Odette succeeded in her ambition of making Swann move from his bachelor apartments on the Quai d'Orléans to one of the smarter houses in the Bois de Boulogne. What we do realise is that Madame Swann has become a very different person from the slightly raffish Odette de Crécy of *Du côté de chez Swann*. She is now almost ostentatiously respectable, and one of the most elegantly dressed women in Paris. However, she is not yet accepted in the best houses.

The Narrator's unhappy passion for Gilberte Swann takes up the beginning of what were originally the next three volumes of *A la recherche du temps perdu*: *A l'ombre des jeunes filles en fleurs* (*Within a Budding Grove*). Both he and we are then absorbed in the social life of the Normandy seaside resort of Balbec to which he is taken on holiday by his grandmother. She is eventually compelled, after many hesitations, to acknowledge her earlier acquaintance with an old school friend, the Marquise de Villeparisis, who is staying at the same hotel. This is a useful indication of an important difference between Proust and his Narrator. Since Proust's mother was Jewish, her own mother would never have been educated at one of the convent schools which would have been the only institutions frequented by the French aristocracy. The Narrator's grandmother, however closely modelled she may have been in other respects on Proust's grandmother, Nathé Weil, is obviously a Gentile, if not necessarily a practising Christian.

Within the novel, this encounter is an important step on the Narrator's ascent into society. It enables him to strike up a friendship with Madame de Villeparisis's aristocratic nephew, Robert de Saint-Loup, and emerge from the social isolation which caused him so much initial embarrassment at Balbec. Later on, in Paris, Madame de Villeparisis's salon will give him his first opportunity of meeting other members of the aristocracy face to face. While he is still in Balbec, he encounters the Baron de Charlus, Robert's uncle, who behaves in a very strange way. He also becomes greatly attracted to a group of young girls who start off by seeming to belong to so indeterminate a social class that he thinks they must be the mistresses of professional cyclists. It is only gradually that the girl who is going to play so great a part in the Narrator's life, Albertine Simonet, takes on a distinct individuality.

With what were, when *A la recherche du temps perdu* was available only in fifteen separate volumes, books six, seven and eight, we enter more fully into the aristocratic world of the Guermantes. Both Madame de Villeparisis and Robert de Saint-Loup are members of this family, whose sonorous and golden-sounding name Proust borrowed from an actual village in the Départment de Seine-et-Marne, to the south-west of Paris. Later on in *Le côté de Guermantes*, the Narrator discovers with some surprise that the Baron de Charlus is the brother of the present Duke, and when he eventually comes to dine at the Guermantes table, he reflects that he has never before heard the phrase 'But that's one of our cousins' pronounced so frequently. After a brief stay with his friend Saint-Loup at the garrison town of Doncières, the Narrator comes back to Paris where his parents are renting an apartment in one of the wings of a very large private house belonging to the Guermantes. A series of both lucky and tragic coincidences, chief among them being the death of his grandmother, finally enables the Narrator to cross what he calls the magic threshold of the Guermantes doormat, and he becomes one of the most favoured guests of Oriane de Guermantes, whom he had first seen in the church at Combray.

With volumes nine and ten of the original fifteen-volume series, *Sodome et Gomorrhe*, we finally discover the truth about the Baron de Charlus: he is a homosexual. Homosexuality then becomes an increasingly dominant theme in the Narrator's continued discovery of the complex and comic life of Parisian high society. It is also, in his own private emotional life, the possibility that Albertine Simonet may prefer members of her own sex that causes the Narrator most anxiety. For he has now fixed upon her as the great love of his life, especially after the revelation that she has been a friend of the older Lesbian woman whom he saw, many years ago at Combray, acting out a scene of sado-masochistic sexuality with the daughter of the musician Vinteuil. It is also at this stage in the novel that the now ageing Monsieur de Charlus meets the great love of his life in the violinist Charles Morel, and their relationship, like the one between Swann and Odette or Marcel and Albertine, exemplifies the truth of the famous saying that in any love affair there is always one partner who loves while the other accepts to be loved.

The Verdurins are also spending the summer holidays in Normandy, at a house rented from the Cambremer family, and the growing hostility between the Baron de Charlus and Madame Verdurin begins to prepare us for one of Proust's best-known scenes of social comedy. For the Baron has decided to launch Morel as a musician deserving of all the admiration of high society, and to do so by inviting all his most aristocratic acquaintances to an evening concert given in Paris by Madame Verdurin. But both the Baron and his guests behave extremely rudely, totally ignoring Madame Verdurin and behaving as though it is Charlus alone who is giving the party.

This incident, like Madame Verdurin's rather successful revenge, in which she convinces Morel that he has become an object of public ridicule as a result of the fact that everybody sees his relationship with Charlus as an essentially sexual one, takes place in volume eleven of the original fifteen-volume series, *La Prisonnière*. This is the title of two volumes describing how the Narrator is so afraid that Albertine will be unfaithful to him that he keeps her as a prisoner in his apartment. The volumes were the last to appear before Proust's death in 1922, and have strained some readers' credulity. Officially, the Narrator's intention is to marry Albertine, but there is no mention of any preparation for a wedding. Critics who have gone against Proust's injunction in *Contre Sainte-Beuve*, and refused to separate the man from the author, have seen this episode as a transposition of Proust's relationship with his chauffeur, Alfred Agostinelli, who was seventeen years his junior. There is strong evidence for this view, both in Proust's letters and in the way the two affairs ended. In October 1914, five months after Agostinelli's death, Proust wrote to his friend Reynaldo Hahn: 'I really loved Alfred. No, that's not enough, I adored him. And I don't know why I write in the past tense for I still love him.'[27] Agostinelli ran away from Proust and was killed on 30 May 1914, in a flying accident. He had registered for lessons under the name of Marcel Swann. Albertine also runs away, and is killed in a riding accident. The grief which her death inspires occupies a good deal of what used to be volume thirteen, *Albertine disparue* (*The Sweet Cheat Gone*). This is now called *La Fugitive* (*The Fugitive*), and takes us to page 688 in the third volume of the *Pléiade* edition. As in the case of Swann's earlier passion for Odette, time brings about the gradual death of the Narrator's love for Albertine, and this leads Proust to point out once again how misleading it is for us to see ourselves as having just one personality. What Proust calls 'the general law of oblivion' ('la loi générale de l'oubli') causes the self which loved Albertine to die and to be replaced by another self, this time one preoccupied with more social matters.

These include the marriage of Robert de Saint-Loup to Gilberte Swann. Since he is a Guermantes, and since her father owned Tansonville, the property situated 'du côté de chez Swann', this marriage finally brings together the two apparently inseparable 'Ways' of the Narrator's childhood. Later on, this union finds its incarnation in Gilberte's daughter, Mademoiselle de Saint-Loup, whom the Narrator meets at the 'soirée chez la Princesse de Guermantes' in the last of the two volumes of *Le Temps retrouvé*. This section of the novel is not only important because of the description which it contains of the three incidents of involuntary memory which inspire the Narrator to write the book which the reader is about to finish reading. We also learn that Marie-Gilbert, who was Princesse de Guermantes in the earlier volumes, is dead, and that her place has been taken by the twice-widowed Madame Verdurin, whom the Duke has presumably married for her money. After the disappearance of Gustave, she married the Duc de Duras, who also died. The Duke has been ruined by the First World War. Oriane, Duchesse de Guermantes, who before the war dominated the aristocratic society of Paris by her wit and beauty, has deliberately sacrificed her position by mixing principally with artists and intellectuals. But this is not the only example of how Proust, like the Preacher in Ecclesiastes 9:11, proclaims that 'time and chance happeneth to them all'.

Another of the idols of the Narrator's childhood and early youth was the great tragic actress, La Berma. She has now fallen to the point where she is deserted by everyone she has invited to the party which she is giving in honour of her daughter and son-in-law. Both relatives leave her in order to come and beg the honour of being received by the new Princesse de Guermantes, and thus be able to listen to a recital by the new star of the Paris social and theatrical scene, Rachel. But Rachel, as we know, began life as a low-class tart whose services the Narrator was once offered for as small a sum as twenty francs. He declined them, but Robert de Saint-Loup, before his marriage to Gilberte, was as passionately and unhappily in love with Rachel as Swann ever was with Odette.

Like Anthony Powell's *A Dance to the Music of Time* (1951–75), the novel in English with the largest number of deliberate parallels with Proust's work, *A la recherche du temps perdu* also contains a number of characters whom we see at different stages in their career. As Proust observes, in a very Powell-like statement, 'One and the same man, taken at successive points in his life, will be found to breathe, on different rungs of the social ladder, in atmospheres that do not necessarily become more refined.'[28] This is especially true in *Le Temps retrouvé*, when the Baron de Charlus and Robert de Saint-Loup both turn up in a homosexual brothel. For Proust's account of the world of homosexuality makes an important point about its social implications. Those who cannot deny either their nature or their needs take their partners from a lower social class. Those who, like Charles Morel, are able and willing to fit in with other people's preferences, tend to rise in society.

Yet although it is more common for people in *A la recherche du temps perdu* to rise, they do not always do so through sex. The Narrator's young Jewish friend Albert Bloch, whose pretentious mode of speech owes something to Proust's own early affectations, ends up by becoming quite a well-known writer. His metamorphosis is helped by the fact that he changes his name to Jacques du Rozier, and he is not the only person in *A la recherche du temps perdu* whose literary success comes as something of a surprise. Among Albertine's friends at Balbec is a young man called Octave, nicknamed 'dans les choux' ('I'm a wash-out') because of his use of that expression when he went round what one hopes was the eighteen-hole golf course at Balbec in ninety-two.[29] Although his principal interests seem to be golf and gambling, he nevertheless startles the Narrator by the obvious genius which later shines through his work for the theatre. For this produces a revolution 'at least equal to that accomplished by the Russian ballet'.[30] He too has an affair with Rachel, before finally marrying Abertine's intellectual friend Andrée, and there is something agreeably Balzacian about the way Proust alludes to events of this kind without describing them in detail. It gives the impression that the adventures of the more central characters in *A la recherche du temps perdu* – the Narrator himself, Swann and Odette, Madame Verdurin, the Baron de Charlus – take place in a complex and extended society in which there are lots of other things going on all the time.

This old-fashioned belief in the independent reality of Proust's fictional world, and of the imaginary characters who inhabit it, was given a particular boost for English readers in 1958 by the publication of Pamela Hansford-Johnson's *Six Proust Reconstructions*. We are pleased but not surprised to find that the events of the Second World War have brought Swann to London to broadcast for the Free French on the BBC. Saint-Loup has joined de Gaulle, also in London. Bloch has escaped to America. Bergotte is in a concentration camp. The Guermantes, in character to the end, are preparing to drop the Narrator, who is now revealed, like Proust, to be half-Jewish. Monsieur de Charlus, who had earlier shown his undoubted physical courage by staying in Paris during the 1871 siege, has joined the Resistance, inspired in part by a fancy for a Gaullist footman. Monsieur de Norpois has offered Otto Abetz, Hitler's official representative in Paris, the choice between encouraging his master to become the Caesar of Britain or the Cromwell of Ireland. Madame Verdurin, whose house is full of the most charming and cultivated Germans, has convinced herself that it was she who inspired Hitler to write *Mein Kampf*.[31]

But although *A la recherche du temps perdu* can be read, as Derwent May has suggested, as a 'tremendous piece of gossip',[32] the remarks which Proust himself made about his work do not suggest that he would have been very happy to see it discussed in these terms. Although he did have a good deal to say about how he wanted *A la recherche du temps perdu* to be read, his comments do not give pride of place to the human interest side of the book. He even seems to have been rather hesitant about calling it a novel,[33] and it does initially seem to make most sense as a fairly free description of how Proust, or someone remarkably like him, came to be a writer. Taken in isolation, the passages of social analysis are brilliant. So, too, are the descriptions of the pathological state of mind which the Narrator works himself into about Albertine. But it is sometimes difficult, when you first read the novel, to see exactly where you are going. Events do, however, form a much more satisfying pattern when you read the novel for a second time, or even think back to how a particular character was first presented.

This is especially true of Charles Swann, whom we first see as a visitor to the Narrator's grandparents at Combray. If we remember the reference to the 'mauvais mariage' which prevents his visits being as frequent as they had been in the past, the whole of *Un Amour de Swann* takes on a different light. If we also remember, from *A l'ombre des jeunes filles en fleurs*, the refusal of the Narrator's mother to ask Gilberte about her mother if Gilberte should come to take tea with the Narrator, we can also see a slight shadow over the one person in the novel who is never laughed at or criticised. She is not strong in Christian forgiveness, or free from social prejudice. We might have thought so when, in *Combray*, she talks in very sympathetic tones to Swann about his daughter. But since her husband will not permit her to greet Madame Swann, she will not allow the name of Gilberte's mother to soil her lips.[34]

The reference in the first pages of *Combray* to the brilliant social life which Swann leads in Paris, and which has led him somewhat to neglect his right to be received 'by the most respected barristers and solicitors of Paris (though he was perhaps a trifle inclined to let his hereditary privilege go by default)',[35] also takes on a richer set of overtones from the knowledge we later acquire of the various levels of social acceptability in late nineteenth-century France. This also applies to the description in *Combray* of how Swann, a great connoisseur of the visual arts, combined a refusal to make any value judgements about a painting with a readiness to give exact details about the museum in which it could be found or about its date of composition. It is only later that we recognise the self-consciously low-key style of conversation regarded as desirable in the Faubourg Saint-Germain, and appreciate how the behaviour considered rather odd at Combray represented the height of elegance elsewhere.

Our first glimpse of Oriane de Guermantes, at the soirée Saint-Euverte in *Un Amour de Swann*, also takes on extra meaning from what we later learn both about her and about aristocratic behaviour in general. This is characterised, we are told, by an almost exaggerated anxiety to put your inferiors at their ease by constantly seeking to understate your own importance. As Princesse des Laumes – she becomes Duchesse de Guermantes only later, on the death of her father-in-law – Oriane is much the superior of the Marquise de Saint-Euverte. Indeed, she emphasises this fact in *Le côté de Guermantes* by rather pointedly not going to her garden party. But when she arrives – late – at the soirée in *Un Amour de Swann*, she deliberately sits at the back. She knows that she will, on being recognised by her hostess, immediately be led to the place of honour. When this happens, her modesty as well as her superiority is clear to all.[36]

'Our social personality', as Proust observes 'is the creation of the thoughts of other people', and this certainly applies to the difference between the way the Narrator's family at Combray tend to patronise Swann because they don't think he has many friends and his actual situation as one of the most elegant and sought-after quests in the Faubourg Saint-Germain. But people can also change with the passage of time, for when we meet Swann again, as we go forward in time to the Narrator's early teens, in the last part of *Du côté de chez Swann* and the opening chapters of *A l'ombre des jeunes filles en fleurs*, he has in fact become a different person. He is no longer the neurotic lover who wastes his life on a woman he knows to be worthless. His attitude to Odette is one of an almost detached benevolence. But he has also lost something of the modesty and discretion which made him so ideal a companion for the Guermantes. In his desire to help his wife in what is now an overwhelming ambition to establish a position for herself in polite society, he has become rather vulgar and pushing.

Occasionally, Proust's anxiety to show the character from as many different angles as possible creates a problem for his more pernickety readers. When the Narrator first meets Odette de Crécy, it is as 'la dame en rose' (the lady in pink) in the Parisian apartment of his great-uncle Adolphe. He is lost in admiration for so glamorous a creature, though conscious of the slight embarrassment which his presence causes to his bachelor uncle, whose life-style is so obviously alien to 'les vertus de Combray'. Indeed, by revealing that he has been introduced to Odette, he even brings about a serious family quarrel. His parents clearly disapprove of his being in the same room as a lady of such ambiguous charms, and he makes matters worse by then cutting his great-uncle in the street. The whole incident is beautifully handled, but is not easy to fit into the overall time scheme of *A la recherche du temps perdu*.

For at the time of this first meeting with Odette, the Narrator seems to be about eight or nine. He is too young to be allowed to go to the theatre, but old enough to venture out alone from his parents' house in Paris to find his own way to l'oncle Adolphe's apartment. But when Swann pays his evening calls in Combray, the Narrator is clearly much younger – about five or six – and the marriage to Odette has already taken place. It is therefore a little puzzling to know how she comes to be making an afternoon visit to an old admirer, and refusing his offer of a cigarette on the grounds that she smokes only those sent her by the Grand Duke.[37] Once married, Swann is understandably jealous of his wife's reputation. We are told this at least twice, and no nineteenth-century upper-class husband would in any case allow his wife to dress and behave like 'la dame en rose'. Odette may indeed have made Swann marry her, as Monsieur de Norpois explains in *A l'ombre des jeunes filles en fleurs*, by refusing him access to his daughter. But as Norpois also tells us, she acquired an angelic sweetness of nature once the marriage had taken place, and gave the lie to all those who predicted that she would make Swann's life a misery. This scarcely squares with afternoon visits to single men in their Paris apartments, even if one of the Baron de Charlus's later allegations suggests that not all was invariably sweetness and light in the Swann household. On one occasion, he says, 'she fired a revolver at him, and nearly hit me'.[38]

There are other minor problems in the characterisation and chronology of *A la recherche du temps perdu*, and it is difficult to decide whether they form part of a deliberate attempt to disorientate the reader and destroy his confidence in the reliability of traditional techniques of narration or are merely a result of the fact that Proust died before having the opportunity of seeing the whole of his novel through the press and checking over the proofs. For although Swann is described in the first volume as being quite happy for Charlus to keep an eye on Odette because he knows that nothing could happen between the two of them, there is a later scene in *La Prisonnière* in which Charlus insinuates that he slept with her before trying to get rid of her by introducing her to Swann.[39] But this apparent problem pales into insignificance by the side of Bloch's insistence in *A l'ombre des jeunes filles en fleurs* that Odette gave herself to him three times with enthusiastic and professional skill in a carriage on the Paris suburban railway.[40] For she is, by then, the almost ostentatiously respectable Madame Swann, and a possible explanation is that Proust is merely showing us how compulsive a liar Bloch really is. Charlus is also something of a mythomaniac himself, and while this may explain the discrepancy between his account of what happens and what we are told elsewhere in the novel, it does not free the conscientious reader from the need to choose how to interpret this aspect of *A la recherche du temps perdu*. If he follows the example of Gérard Genette, undoubtedly the best advanced French critic to read when you have finished going through Proust's novel for a second time, it is indeed all deliberate. Traditionally, events in the

novel were seen as true because the novelist said they were. He
ruled supreme, and presented the reader with a wholly consistent
universe in which a certain order reigned supreme because he said
it did. Proust's originality, argues Genette, is to have been the first
to destroy this illusion and present the reader with a fictional
universe which is as problematic and mysterious as the real one.[41]
Alternatively, you can say that these are all minor inconsistencies
which any competent copy editor could have ironed out in an
afternoon.

You also have to make something of the same choice when
confronted with some of the problems set by the chronology of *A la
recherche du temps perdu*. For there is something odd about the
implied mention in *Le côté de Guermantes* of the spectacular defeat of
the Russians in the Russo-Japanese war of 1905. This reference
occurs in a conversation which clearly pre-dates a number of
developments in the Dreyfus case which did not take place until
1898,[42] and there can be no question here of Proust using
inconsistencies in order to create character. If you think that he is
deliberately distorting chronology in order to show the falsity of
traditional concepts of time, then you will agree with Gareth H.
Steel, whose *Chronology and time in 'A la recherche du temps perdu'* is a
fascinating account of all the temporal markers in Proust's novel.
Mr Steel's argument is that since *A la recherche du temps perdu* is
'essentially hostile to the position of the "general reader" who
assumes that the time-scale of fiction is equivalent to the
time-scale of history', its final effect is to make this reader
'experience the catastrophic nihilism of a total disbelief in the
continuity of time'. Alternatively, you can take the more
forthright opinion of J. B. Priestley and simply say that there is 'no
major novel in which the time scheme is more muddled and
bewildering than it is in this one'.[43]

But even if you think that Proust is slightly cavalier in his
treatment of chronological time, this is more than outweighed by
his ability to show us how people change with the passage of years.
Odette, for example, becomes quite a different kind of person. She
still retains some of the basic silliness which first made her so
oddly attractive to Swann, but puts it to a better purpose. She also
adopts a new, fuller style of beauty, so much so that Swann,
seeking to remember what she was like as a younger woman,
prefers a little daguerreotype which showed a different conception
of her as a 'frail young woman with pensive eyes and tired

features' and which preserves 'a more Botticellian charm'.[44]

But Odette's new beauty, as the Narrator observes, is 'toute une époque' ('quite a period in itself'; the Tissot painting of *L'Ambitieuse*, on the front cover of this book, gives some idea of what she might have looked like); and it is no small pleasure, at the end of Proust's novel, to list her social triumphs. Not only has she achieved her ambition of becoming a fashionable hostess; she is also mistress to the Duc de Guermantes and has tamed the old reprobate in a way which Oriane herself never managed. She has made the best possible marriage – on social terms, at any rate – for the daughter she bore out of wedlock. Indeed, when she sees the fastidiously selective Madame de Sabran attending one of Gilberte de Saint-Loup's evening parties, she has some justification for feeling 'qu'elle avait été une bonne et prévoyante mère et que sa tâche maternelle était achevée' (that she had been a good and far-sighted mother and that her maternal task was accomplished).[45] The irony with which this triumph is presented nevertheless raises the question of the point of view from which the stories in *A la recherche du temps perdu* are told and how the reader can best look at them. If the book is seen as a self-justifying and self-congratulatory autobiography, in which we have to accept all the judgements made because the person telling the story is none other than the omniscient author Marcel Proust, a rather odd gap opens up between what we feel about Odette and what we are told we ought to feel. For at the end of *Le Temps retrouvé*, when she is the Duc de Guermantes's mistress, the Narrator describes her as being as 'médiocre dans ce rôle comme dans tous les autres' (commonplace in this role as in all her others) and says that although life had given her good roles 'she had not known how to play them'.[46] But we have already seen in *A l'ombre des jeunes filles en fleurs* that she was painted by Elstir in the intriguingly bisexual role of Miss Sacripant in 1872, and the events in *Le Temps retrouvé* are taking place well after the end of the First World War. She must therefore be nearer sixty than fifty, so her sexual attributes alone – she is also being unfaithful to the Duke – are somewhat out of the ordinary.

Neither is this the only aspect of her achievements for which the modern reader is tempted to feel a not wholly reluctant admiration. She was, we are told in *Du côté de chez Swann*, sold by her mother to a rich Englishman in Nice when she was still almost a child. This statement is repeated in *Sodome et Gomorrhe*, where she is referred to as 'a whore sold by her mother in her childhood', so we don't tend to forget it.[47] It is therefore not altogether surprising that she should have exploited any upper-class male with whom she came into contact. The alternative is to end up as one of those who, like 'Rachel quand du Seigneur' in her earlier incarnation, are offered by a madam in a brothel for as little as twenty francs. Odette has, admittedly, cleaned out her first husband, Pierre de Verjus, Comte de Crécy, to the last farthing. In *Sodome et Gomorrhe*, he turns up again in an Anthony Powell-type way, and the Narrator treats him to a series of expensive meals during which they indulge in their mutual passion for discussing the genealogical trees of the various members of the French aristocracy. It is then that we learn that the Comte de Crécy's title is quite a genuine one and this explains his expertise at genealogy. But he is not depicted as having any grudge against Odette. In the social world described by Proust, this kind of behaviour seems to have been par for the course. The Marquise de Villeparisis, as we shall see, ruined one of Tante Léonie's neighbours at Combray in a similar fashion, and the only reason Odette doesn't do the same for Swann is that he has a longer purse. As Maurice Bardèche observes in his *Marcel Proust, romancier*, the rate at which Swann subsidises her – 4000 francs a month in late nineteenth-century currency; the equivalent in purchasing power of £7000 or $9000 in the late 1980s – would have enabled Balzac to pay off all his vast debts within eighteen months. But Odette doesn't make all her lovers unhappy or milk them all completely dry. She has always, we are also told, been very accommodating to l'oncle Adolphe.[48]

The unnamed passer-by in the Bois de Boulogne who sees her in her full glory as the elegant Madame Swann clearly has quite agreeable memories of her as well. He had, he says, been in bed with her on the day that Maréchal Mac-Mahon was forced to resign as President of the Third Republic, and this reference to the events of January 1879 confirms the suggestion that she was no chicken when she met Swann. A reference to the state funeral for Gambetta on 6 January 1883 is a further indication of when their affair begins, and the events of *Du côté de chez Swann* do indeed take on rather a different light when seen from the point of view of Odette herself. A single woman in her late twenties who finds a rich man becoming neurotically dependent on her can scarcely be blamed for having taken advantage of the situation.

Proust may well not have wanted the reader to think this. There are times, as when *A la recherche du temps perdu* contains long discussions on the nature of art, when we are clearly expected to take as gospel truth whatever the Narrator tells us, and there are probably many readers who share his opinion of Odette. A reviewer in *The Times Literary Supplement*, for example, described her as 'the most commonplace of lying mopsies and a born torturer of the sensitive',[49] and it is true that she is prepared, in spite of being married to a Jew, to espouse the anti-semitism of Dreyfus's opponents if this enables her to rise in society. She was also, according to Charlus, illiterate to the point of being quite unable to spell, so it is improbable that she was able to offer Swann much intellectual companionship. But the phenomenon whereby a character in a novel escapes from the author and takes on a life of her or his own is not at all uncommon, and this is what I find Odette doing. Moved as I am by Swann's predicament, I am nevertheless pleased when Odette does rather better for herself either than the Becky Sharp of *Vanity Fair*, whom she resembles in some of her social disadvantages, or the Mildred of Somerset Maugham's *Of Human Bondage*, with whom she can be compared in two respects: her ability to twist a very sensitive man completely round her little finger; and the way she shows how we can be made to suffer most acutely by somebody whom other people see as very commonplace.

We are, of course, some way here from the 'petite madeleine'. But we are not too far from Proust's implied suggestion that we read *A la recherche du temps perdu* through twice if we want to see how it all fits together. For Odette and Swann are not the only characters who benefit from being approached from a number of different angles and seen in several contexts. The Narrator himself talks in *Le Temps retrouvé* about the 'different planes according to which time disposed his life' and of the 'three-dimensional psychology' necessary to an understanding of how our perception of people changes with the passage of time.[50] In one of the first mentions of the Baron de Charlus, we are told that Swann is quite happy to have him keep an eye on Odette. He knows – or thinks he does – that nothing can happen with him, and it is not until *Sodome et Gomorrhe* that we fully understand why. It is only very gradually that we come to appreciate that some of the social disgrace into which the Marquise de Villeparisis has fallen is due to her liaison with Monsieur de Norpois, and even then we receive total confirmation only in a footnote. The idea that the man whom the

Narrator sees as a pompous old bore should have behaved with such passion as to ruin the reputation of somebody who, after all, was born a Guermantes, is not without its charm; neither is the fact that this rather starchy old lady had, during an earlier incarnation as the Duchesse d'Havré, so bewitched Monsieur Sazerat that she had totally ruined him.

But it is not only people who change or develop with the passage of time. Societies do so as well, and *A la recherche du temps perdu* tells the story of how the old aristocracy of the Faubourg Saint-Germain is ousted by upstarts such as Madame Verdurin or Madame de Forcheville, *ci-devant* Odette de Crécy. When this change in her social position leads to Odette being referred to as having in another incarnation 'been married to an adventurer by the name of Swann',[51] we really do see how the whirligig of time brings in its revenges. For on his evening visits to Combray, Swann had often had a letter in his pocket from Twickenham, the residence in exile of the Comte de Paris, regarded by all the best people in the country as the sole legitimate ruler of France. One of Proust's most intriguing achievements is to present us with the aristocracy of late nineteenth-century France, and the high society over which it presides, as simultaneously quite fascinating and totally worthless. When the Princesse de Silistrie proclaims that if Saint-Loup marries the daughter of Odette and of a Jew, then it will be the end of the Faubourg Saint-Germain,[52] we are moved to simultaneous agreement and hilarity. We can see what she means and appreciate her standards. But since Gilberte Swann and Robert de Saint-Loup are rich, young and handsome members of what any outside observer would see as the same social class, her remark is almost in the same category as Lady Bracknell's view in *The Importance of Being Earnest* that being found in a handbag in the cloakroom at Victoria station recalled 'the worst excesses of the French Revolution'.

Proust's view of how people and societies change with time is nevertheless not limited to what he called the 'prodigieuse aptitude au déclassement' of French aristocractic society, the 'prodigious ease with which individuals move up and down the social scale'.[53] It is true that it is this which produces the most dramatic results, with the Narrator being greeted by the Duchesse de Guermantes as her oldest friend, and Odette being referred to at the same 'matinée chez la Princesse de Guermantes' as 'a great friend of my cousin Marmantes'.[54] For Robert de Saint-Loup's mother – for that is who Madame de Marmantes is – would never have even acknowledged the existence of either Odette or Madame Verdurin before the social cataclysm of the First World War, any more than Madame Bontemps would have been seen as anything but the wife of a very minor civil servant whose charms consisted of 'a fair, silky beard, good features, a nasal voice, bad breath and a glass eye'.[55] But Madame Bontemps becomes a very fashionable lady, just as the young violinist Charles Morel rises as a result of a combination of musical skill and sexual adroitness and becomes one of the most respectable men in Paris.

Neither is Proust talking solely about movements within the upper class. When we first meet Jupien, he is introduced to us quite anonymously as a waistcoat-maker who has his shop in the courtyard of the town house of Madame de Villeparisis. It is only on re-reading that you appreciate how quietly and skilfully Proust has introduced one of his most interesting middle-ranking players, for Jupien is later to perform a central role in Proust's depiction of homosexuality. Not only does he illustrate one of the more mysterious laws governing homosexual behaviour by instantly recognising the Baron de Charlus as a fellow practitioner. He is also made to express a moral as well as a social disapproval of the relationship between Robert de Saint-Loup and Charles Morel on the grounds that it was wrong for Morel to desert the Baron de Charlus for his nephew,[56] and thus to remind us of the inconsistencies of which we can all be guilty. A further strand to his complex character is revealed to us almost at the end of *A la recherche du temps perdu* when we see him looking after the aged and decrepit Baron de Charlus, after having earlier helped to supply some of the Baron's other needs by running a homosexual brothel. The social side of *A la recherche du temps perdu* is nevertheless not presented by Proust himself as the most important part of his novel. It does take up a lot of space, and it is as fascinating for the traditionally-minded connoisseur of fiction as it is for the historian and the sociologist. But the society which Proust analysed was, on his own showing, so completely worthless that the initial if unjustified reaction of readers might be to dismiss any study of it as a waste of time. It would be hard to say this of what is certainly a better-known side of Proust's work, his analysis of human emotions.

3

Freud, Childhood and the Unconscious

Although Proust did study German for four years at the Lycée Condorcet, there is no evidence that he ever read any of Freud's works, either in the original or in translation. The first translation to appear in French was *The Psychopathology of Everyday Life*, but this was not published until 1922. Dr Adrien Proust had originally been a specialist in nervous diseases, and it is possible that he may have heard mention of Freud's visit to Paris in 1885 to study under Charcot. But Marcel Proust's interest in things German seems to have been mainly in the music of Wagner, and the principal foreign influence on his work was certainly English. When, in 1899, he felt he was making little progress welding together the various aspects of his experience into a coherent work of art, he compared himself to the hapless Mr Casaubon from George Eliot's *Middlemarch*.[57] *The Mill on the Floss* was a book that moved him to tears, and the morally secure background in which the Narrator spends his childhood at Combray has strong similarity to the atmosphere in the early chapters of George Eliot's novel. Ruskin inspired him with an enthusiasm for mediaeval and Renaissance architecture, and strengthened his belief in the importance of the artist as a man who taught people how to see. Proust's hostility to materialism and lack of enthusiasm for industrialisation and applied science also have a distinctly Ruskinian ring, and it could be argued that he might well never have become a writer at all without the encouragement of Ruskin's ideas and example. But when you read *A la recherche du temps perdu*, it is the Freudian parallels that strike you first. The author who writes in *Du côté de chez Swann* about 'the vast, unfathomed and forbidding night of the soul which we take to be an impenetrable void',[58] also seems to have hit upon a very important Freudian concept, even if he has never read a word by Freud himself. This impression is even stronger if you look at what happens in the novel.

Thus at the very beginning of *Du côté de chez Swann*, even before the experience of the 'petite madeleine' and the section subtitled *Combray*, there is the episode known as 'le drame du coucher' (the drama of the good-night kiss). It is this which has the strongest Freudian overtones, and which led a reviewer in *The Times Literary Supplement* on 12 December 1940 to make the very accurate comment that Proust himself was 'superlatively well acquainted with the agonies of the mother fixation'. For every evening, when he is about to go to bed, the Narrator Marcel is heartbroken at the thought that he is going to be separated from his mother. His sole consolation is that she will come upstairs to kiss him goodnight before he finally goes to sleep, but this final kiss never lasts long enough. He would like to call her back and make her kiss him again, but is restrained by the fear of annoying her. This, he knows, will destroy the peace which her good-night kiss has bestowed upon him, and the insistence is on the calm provided by this reassurance of his mother's love rather than on any erotic overtones. But it is not hard to see how the incident could also be interpreted in Freudian terms. The male child, according to Freud's interpretation of the legend in which Oedipus killed his father and married his mother, wants to possess the mother sexually. Proust's explanation in terms of emotional reassurance strikes the thorough-going Freudian as either a wilful or an unconscious refusal to face the facts. Add the knowledge that Proust was also a homosexual, and the hunt is really on. Homosexuals, as any Freudian will tell you, prefer men because they see every woman as a reincarnation of their mother. Because they were taught in their childhood that they could not have her, they are put off women for life.

This Freudian reading becomes less convincing when the 'drame du coucher' is replaced in the context of the novel. For there is, to start with, no hint of any hostility between the Narrator and his father. The jealousy which later becomes so dominant a theme in the whole of *A la recherche du temps perdu* is completely different from the rivalry which Freudians see as existing between fathers and sons, and there is also the question of the Narrator's age. Although Proust's reluctance to mention dates or give his characters a precise age prevents us from telling how old the

Narrator is, the general impression is that he is between five and
seven. He is old enough to write a letter, though not yet to have
read what he calls 'real novels'. He is therefore well past the age of
three or four which Freudians see as critical in the development of
the Oedipus complex.

Proust would certainly not have been able to write about
Marcel's relationship with his mother in the way that he did if he
had read Freud. His knowledge of Freudian doctrine would
inevitably have coloured his presentation of a drama which has so
many apparently obvious Freudian overtones. Either he would
have strengthened these to emphasise the similarities; or he would
have toned them down to bring out the differences. There is no
evidence that he did this, and Proust's account of the causes and
the consequences of 'le drame du coucher' has a very different set of
implications from those which stem from a Freudian reading.
They represent an attitude which is comparable to that of Freud
in the importance which it gives to the impact of childhood
traumas on the emotional behaviour of adults. But these
implications differ very sharply from those of Freud in that
everything which happens takes place on the level of the conscious
and not of the unconscious mind.

Thus the Narrator in *Du côté de chez Swann* knows exactly why his
mother is behaving as she does. Together with her own mother, to
whom she is deeply attached, she is trying to make her son a little
more emotionally independent. She is trying to cure him of what
both she and his father think of as rather silly, unmanly conduct.
The Narrator understands and appreciates these motives, and
would like to make his mother and grandmother happier by
co-operating. But he cannot bring himself to do this – he is, after
all, only a child – and is as conscious as they are of his lack of
will-power. In this, as in other respects, there is a strong similarity
between the Marcel of *A la recherche du temps perdu* and Marcel
Proust himself. This is well brought out by George Painter in his
biography of Proust, especially in his treatment of the conviction
which both Proust and his Narrator had of being lacking in
will-power. Nobody, as Painter observed, could have struggled
against illness to complete a work as long and complex as *A la
recherche du temps perdu* without being quite exceptionally
determined, and both Proust and his Narrator are doing
themselves less than justice. But Proust did see himself as a
weak-willed person and there is ample evidence that the details of

'le drame du coucher' are based upon an incident or a series of incidents in his own life. The episode is described in comparable detail in *Jean Santeuil*, and Marcel's complete emotional dependence on his mother in *Du côté de chez Swann* is matched by Proust's feelings for his mother. When, at the age of thirteen or fourteen, he was asked to define his idea of misery, he replied that it was to be 'séparé de Maman' (separated from Mamma).[59]

The contribution of 'le drame du coucher' to the dominant themes and overall structure of *A la recherche du temps perdu* is nevertheless in no way dependent on the links it had with Proust's own experience. For it is on one of the evenings that Charles Swann comes to dine at Marcel's grandparents' house in Combray that the crisis occurs which the Narrator sees as determining his whole future emotional development, and *Du côté de chez Swann* is carefully constructed, as a work of art, to drive home an immediate dramatic and ironic parallel. Just as the Narrator cannot do without the constant reassurance of his mother's love, so Swann becomes increasingly dependent on the presence of Odette. Just as Marcel is intrigued by what he sees as the mysterious pleasures which his mother is about to enjoy with the other adults at dinner, so Swann becomes obsessed by the sensual delights which he suspects Odette of enjoying not only with other men but also with other women. The episode entitled *Un Amour de Swann* comes so soon after 'le drame du coucher' that there is no way in which the reader can avoid seeing this parallel. In both cases, the writing shows Proust at his most dramatic and effective. The reader can no more fail to identify with the small boy than he can prevent himself from sympathising with the grown man. The irony, of which the Narrator also intends the reader to be fully conscious, is that it is Charles Swann, the one person most able to understand the anguish of 'le drame du coucher', who is responsible for triggering it off.

Later in the novel, the Narrator is to develop an even greater dependency upon Albertine Simonet, and there is again a very conscious insistence on why this happens. It is, as Proust explains in *La Fugitive*, because even a love which we forget can 'determine the form of the love which is to follow it'.[60] This remark leads him to formulate the general law that the ways in which we habitually behave in our emotional life are like 'great uniform high-roads along which our love passes daily and which were forged long ago in the volcanic fire of an ardent emotion'. This generalisation does not come as a surprise to the reader of *La Prisonnière* and *La Fugitive*. It is not very long after he has begun to keep Albertine a prisoner in his apartment that the Narrator comments on how her kisses remind him of 'the night on which my father sent Mamma to sleep in the little bed next to mine'.[61] When, earlier in this relationship, the Narrator suspects that Albertine might be spending Christmas night in Trieste with the Lesbian friend of Mademoiselle Vinteuil, he makes an equally specific comparison:

> It was Trieste, it was that unknown world in which I could feel that Albertine took a delight, in which were her memories, her friendships, her childhood loves, that exhaled that hostile, inexplicable atmosphere, like the atmosphere which used to float up to my bedroom at Combray, from the dining room in which I could hear, laughing and talking with strangers amid the clatter of knives and forks, Mamma who would not be coming upstairs to say goodnight to me; like the atmosphere that, for Swann, had filled the houses to which Odette went at night in search of inconceivable joys.[62]

In one of the most famous attacks on Proust in English literature, Aldous Huxley makes the principal character in *Eyeless in Gaza*, Anthony Beavis, declare his hatred of Proust and evoke 'the vision of that asthmatic seeker of lost time squatting, horribly white and flabby, with breasts almost female but fledged with long black hairs, for ever squatting in the tepid bath of his remembered past'.[63] If, as Huxley had been shortly before the publication of *Eyeless in Gaza* in 1936, you are an ostentatiously exuberant humanist, this is fair comment. But the theme running through *Eyeless in Gaza*, and which increasingly preoccupies Anthony Beavis, is the more pessimistic one expressed by Ovid when he says, in words which, Huxley claims, 'sum up every biography': 'Video meliora proboque; deteriora sequor' (I see the best and approve of it; but I follow the worst),[64] and this, in his own eyes as well as in those of the reader, is what the Narrator does in *A la recherche du temps perdu*. When he is a child, he knows that he ought to be able to behave as his mother and grandmother would like him to, and stop what his father calls 'these absurd exhibitions'. But he cannot do so, and he is equally unable later on to put an end to what he recognises is the mutually unsatisfactory relationship which he has with Albertine. When there is no danger of his losing her, he is quite happy to bear the idea of her departure. It is only when she is about to leave that he realises how indispensable to him she really is. But the fact that he is totally aware of his predicament again suggests that Proust's psychology is not particularly Freudian. There is no question of the Narrator's coming to terms with his emotions by having them gradually extracted from his unconscious mind and placed where he can see them. He is already, as Sartre would say, totally transparent to himself. Everything that there is to know about himself, he knows. He has seen all the whys, and recognised all the wherefores. But there is nothing he can do about it. He cannot even attain what Freud thought of in psychoanalytical terms as a cure, and pass from neurotic obsessions to normal unhappiness.

Another similarity between Proust and Freud which is more apparent than real concerns the more general role of the unconscious, especially in the area of artistic creation. If you look at what Proust says about the 'petite madeleine' section, and at the importance which he gives in *Le Temps retrouvé* to the uneven paving stones and the starched napkin, you get the impression that the Narrator was able to write his novel only because of the physical accidents which brought back to life a set of memories which were buried deep in the 'vast, unfathomed and forbidding night'[65] of his unconscious mind. When you read 'le drame du coucher', this impression is less obvious. For there is no question, in the opening pages of *Du côté de chez Swann*, of the Narrator needing help of any kind in remembering the incident. He recalls every single detail: the unconscious ferocity with which his father suddenly decides to send him to bed early because he looks tired; the smell of varnish on the staircase as he goes upstairs; the suspicious glance which the servant Françoise casts at the letter which he asks her to take down to his mother and which contains details of an unbelievably important matter which he claims he has suddenly found it necessary to discuss with her; the way in which he decides, in spite of all the prohibition against such an unseemly display of affection, to wait on the landing until his mother comes upstairs to bed. He recalls how his father stood there 'like Abraham in the engraving after Benozzo Gozzoli which M. Swann had given me, telling Sarah how she must tear herself away from Isaac'.[66] And, most of all, he remembers the unexpected way in which the evening ends. For in a sudden access of either generosity or indifference – you cannot tell which – his father tells his mother to have the spare bed made up in Marcel's own room so that she can spend the night with him. For what is so dramatic about the incident is that it ends by the Narrator getting his own way. It is the bitter-sweet taste of this trumph which also enables him to remember the very colour of the binding on the books by George Sand which his mother then read to him in an attempt to calm his sobbing.

The tradition within which Proust is writing here is that of the 'poor monkey', the unhappy child in nineteenth-century fiction. But the fundamental change which Proust introduces into the tradition has nothing to do with either the incident of the 'petite madeleine' or with the tapping of the unconscious which this and other experiences provide. It is of more general, historical significance, and points to a change in our attitude towards childhood which Proust's own influence may well have helped to bring about. For when David Copperfield or the Pip of *Great Expectations* look back to their early years, what they immediately recall is the deliberate brutality or harsh indifference of the adults who made their childhood such a misery. The same is true of Daudet's *Le Petit Chose*, of the hero of Jules Vallès's *L'Enfant* and of the Kipling who recalled Auntie Rosa in *Baa, Baa, Black Sheep*, and the contrast with the world of Combray could scarcely be greater. Marcel is surrounded by kindly if slightly eccentric aunts, uncles and grandparents. Nobody frightens or ill-treats him, and any unhappiness which his mother causes him stems from a wholly genuine desire to help him. Both she and he know how important it is for him to free himself from his almost neurotic dependence upon her.

When she is suddenly and unexpectedly made to yield – by a husband who clearly has not read Freud either – Proust the novelist brings one of the most moving passages in French literature to a perfect ending. At the same time, *A la recherche du temps perdu* also becomes one of the most illuminating novels about the parent–child relationship in our own culture. For the efficiency of modern birth control methods – foreshadowed by the success with which Dr and Madame Proust limited their own family to two well-spaced boys – has now given virtually every child the overwhelming importance which it ought to have. Proust is thus able to highlight, in a suitably dramatic and exaggerated manner – his brother Robert, as usual, is not there – the dilemmas of all the well-meaning twentieth-century parents who agonise endlessly over what to do about their children before taking what invariably turns out to be the wrong decision. For the Narrator is not particularly grateful to his parents for the way they broke their own rules. On the contrary, he sees himself as marked for life by their failure to encourage him to develop more will-power. This, as George Painter points out, becomes one of the main themes in the book. It is not one which Proust's parents would have found very reassuring if they had survived to read *A la recherche du temps perdu*.

Proust thus needs no help either from his subconscious or from his unconscious mind in showing how a childhood crisis can determine adult behaviour. It is all there, seething away in his conscious mind, and it is the constant awareness which the Narrator has of himself that explains why Proust's psychology is ultimately so un-Freudian. The aesthetic theories which Proust builds up around the 'petite madeleine' experience also seem, in the context, to be little more than a necessary myth, the equivalent of the belief in the supposedly infallible doctrine of scientific determinism which provided Zola with the psychological support as well as the intellectual framework essential to the writing of *Les Rougon-Macquart*. You could even imagine an *A la recherche du temps perdu* in which the 'petite madeleine', the uneven paving stones and the sound of the spoon against the teacup were not there. It would be less poetic, and less interesting. But it would not be a wholly different book. It would still have Proust's great themes of love and jealousy; it would still have his account of the contrast between the worlds of Combray and of the Faubourg Saint-Germain; and it would still have his highly original demonstration of the prophet Jeremiah's saying that the heart is 'deceitful above all things'.[67]

For Proust does not ignore the possibility of unconscious motivation, and he does not suggest that every action we perform stems from motives of which we are totally aware. Early in *Le côté de Guermantes*, for example, the Narrator and his friend Saint-Loup are together in a theatre in Paris. A journalist standing close by them is smoking a cigar, which makes the Narrator start to cough. Saint-Loup very politely asks the journalist not to smoke, but the latter refuses.

At that moment [writes the Narrator], I saw Saint-Loup raise his arm vertically above his head as if he were making a sign to somebody I could not see, or like the conductor of an orchestra, and indeed – without any greater transition than when, at a simple stroke of a violin bow, in a symphony or a ballet, violent rhythms succeed a graceful andante – after the courteous words he had just uttered, he brought his hand down with a resounding smack upon the journalist's cheek.[68]

The passage is interesting stylistically. It is a conveniently short illustration of how Proust's description of events sometimes gives the impression of a film being played back in slow motion in order to show how something actually happened. It also has a social interest. This is how challenges to duels were frequently delivered, and the reader is not surprised when an ill-bred civilian does not wish to take matters further with an athletic-looking cavalry officer like Saint-Loup. It is one of several passages which show the protective attitude of Saint-Loup towards the Narrator, and which strengthen the impression that the often quite moving pages devoted to their relationship suffer from the slight disadvantage of reading rather like a wish fulfilment. But if you replace Saint-Loup's sudden violence in its immediate context, it is fairly obviously a reaction to the fact that his mistress Rachel has just humiliated him in public. In a way which he may not have consciously chosen, but which we can understand because we have acted like that ourselves, he takes out his anger on somebody else.

Proust's depiction of unconscious motivation is nevertheless more frequently reminiscent of the French seventeenth-century *moralistes* than of the twentieth-century psychoanalysts. At one point in *Un Amour de Swann*, the Verdurins have arranged an outing to the small town of Chatou, near Versailles, to which they have pointedly not invited Swann to accompany Odette. His exclusion stems from a double annoyance he has caused Madame Verdurin. First of all, he has refused to agree with her frequently expressed view that the aristocratic families whom she would like to know but does not are vulgar and ignorant. Secondly, with a reserve that would have been exactly right for the Guermantes but which merely makes him seem supercilious to the Verdurins, he has killed stone dead what promised to be a brilliant conversation on the nature of intelligence. Since he is by now totally dependent on Odette, and intensely jealous of what she might do when he is not there, he is furious at this exclusion and gives vent to his rage in a long denunciation of Odette's stupidity and the Verdurins' boorishness. Then, quite suddenly, he stops dead in his tracks, strikes his forehead and exclaims: 'I think I've found a way of getting invited to dinner at Chatou tomorrow'.[69]

At this point in the novel, you can almost hear the echos from the seventeenth century. La Rochefoucauld observed in number 115 of his *Réflexions morales* that it is 'as easy to deceive oneself without noticing it as it is hard to deceive others without their noticing it', and Swann's sudden switch of mood would have come as no surprise to an outside observer. Number 295 of the *Réflexions morales* – 'We are far from knowing all our desires' – also suggests that Freud had a perceptive ancestor in La Rochefoucauld as well as a potential rival in his near contemporary, Marcel Proust.

There are, of course, times when Proust seems to go a good deal further than his seventeenth-century ancestors, and to use a Freudian or even a semi-Freudian vocabulary. This even happens in the parts of his work which might at first sight offer little opportunity for an exploration of the subconscious. The social world which he describes, for example, is one in which virtually everybody fits the description given by Jeeves of the page-boy Harold in P. G. Wodehouse's *The Purity of the Turf*: 'somewhat acutely alive to the existence of class distinctions'. Normally this is a preoccupation which involves a keen awareness of what we are doing and why, and Proust is the great analyst of conscious snobbery in constant action. But in the case of an old family friend at Combray, Legrandin, this awareness is totally lacking. To the modern reader, his social ambitions might seem at first sight surprising. For he is highly qualified in the extremely rational discipline of engineering, and might therefore be expected to look for his prestige in the eyes of admiring outsiders or of his professional peers. He might also be considered, by the neophyte in social analysis, to have satisfied some of his ambition to rise in the world by having his sister married to the Marquis de Cambremer. But the Cambremers, as anyone will tell you, are very small beer indeed compared to the Guermantes, and Legrandin is more than just a snob. He is a frustrated and dishonest one. This is why he is made to express this frustration by a fierce denial of his desires. It is this which Proust analyses in a way which shows how clearly aware he was, as a novelist, of

certain forms of subconscious motivation, and how this awareness
can occur in a totally non-sexual context. For this old friend of the
Narrator's family has an *alter ego*,

> another Legrandin, whom he kept carefully hidden in his
> breast, whom he would never consciously exhibit, because this
> other could tell compromising stories about our own Legrandin
> and his snobbishness; and this other Legrandin had replied to
> me already in that wounded look, that twisted smile, the undue
> gravity of the tone of his reply, in the thousand arrows by which
> our own Legrandin had instantaneously been stabbed and
> prostrated like a St Sebastian of snobbery: 'Oh, how you hurt
> me! No, I don't know the Guermantes family. Do not remind
> me of the great sorrow of my life.'[70]

There is nevertheless a difference between the concepts and
technique in this passage and the intellectual atmosphere to be
found in a seventeenth-century writer. If, as seems highly
possible, Proust knew nothing of Freud, this difference seems to
point in the direction of some kind of *Zeitgeist*. Nobody was more
sensitive than Proust both to the way people behaved and to new
currents of thought. When Freud was working out his concept of
the unconscious, Proust was developing an alternative version. At
the same time, he was also anticipating a way of thinking about
the human condition which was not to become widespread in
France until some thirty years after his death. For although, in
Qu'est-ce que la littérature?, in 1947, Jean-Paul Sartre showed little
enthusiasm for Proust, criticising him in particular for
concentrating solely on the psychological problems of rich upper-
or middle-class males, the parallels between Sartre's view of
human beings and the ideas underlying Proust's vision of how and
why we behave as we do are often quite striking.

As Maurice Bardèche observes, Proust is one of the authors
whom Sartre quotes most frequently in *L'Etre et le Néant* in order to
illustrate his views on love and the desire for possession.[71] What is
even more important than this provision of examples for the
gloomier side of Existentialism is the similarity between Proust's
analysis of why all the love affairs in *A la recherche du temps perdu* fail
and Sartre's ideas on human freedom. In addition to offering an
intriguing and viable alternative to Freud's views on how
childhood traumas determine adult behaviour, *A la recherche du*

temps perdu is a novel which makes us totally conscious of what it is like to live in a world where our fellow human beings are free. The Marcel Proust who defined his principal characteristic as 'the need to be loved, and, to be more precise, the need to be caressed and spoilt rather than the need to be admired'[72] was peculiarly conscious of the dangers inseparable from this freedom. For it is only because they are free that those we love are constantly free to stop loving us. If we could bind them indissolubly to us, and if they could permanently surrender their freedom to those bonds, there would never be any reason for anyone to experience the jealousy which Proust sees as the central experience in love. The next chapter will, with some only apparently Proustian digressions – it was, Jean-François Revel said, his digressions which saved him from his obsessions[73] – try to explain in greater detail why jealousy plays so central a role in the fictional world which Proust constructed at least partly from these obsessions.

4

Love, Jealousy and Lesbianism

One of the main claims that Proust makes about his practice as a writer is that he is bringing out general laws. It is, he says, 'superfluous to make a study of sexual mores, since we can deduce them from psychological laws', and he repeats the idea in terms which obviously apply to himself when he declares in *Le Temps retrouvé* that it is the 'feeling for generality which, in the future writer, itself picks out what is general and what can for that reason one day enter into a work of art'. What he is concerned with is what he calls 'the general laws of love'.[74]

At first sight, and especially after you have read through *La Prisonnière* and *La Fugitive*, this is a difficult statement to accept. It is even harder to agree with George Painter when he argues that because Proust did know the love of woman, his 'picture of heterosexual love is valid and founded upon personal experience'.[75] *A la recherche du temps perdu* may well reflect Proust's own feelings and experiences. Jacques Rivière, who knew Proust quite well and gave one of the first public lectures on his work – at the Théâtre du Vieux Colombier, on 19 January 1924, on the role of the unconscious – said that one of the first things which struck you about him was 'an immense suspicion' of every emotion with which he came into contact. This led him, Rivière argued, to work away until he had 'unmasked love and brought it up for judgement in the court-room of the intelligence', and this was certainly what Proust saw himself as doing. But Rivière himself thought that Proust went a bit far and took the lid off too much, and it is instructive to see how early in the history of Proust criticism this particular objection is made.[76]

It is true that Proust makes Monsieur de Charlus show some appreciation of the role that one particular kind of love plays in

48

'les vertus de Combray'. A favourite book of the Narrator's grandmother is the Letters of Madame de Sévigné. She never travels without a volume either of these letters or those of the fictitious Madame de Beausergent. Her own relationship with her daughter, the Narrator's mother, is a greatly improved version of Madame de Sévigné's constantly disappointed love for her daughter, and Madame de Villeparisis is made to show the emotional limitations of the Guermantes family by the surprise which she expresses on learning that Marcel's mother and grandmother write to each other every day.[77] But Monsieur de Charlus is a cut above the rest of the aristocrats in *A la recherche du temps perdu* in many ways, and he puts Madame de Villeparisis right when she refuses to use the word 'love' to describe the non-sexual feelings. For when his aunt says that it wasn't 'love' in the case of Madame de Sévigné because it was her daughter, the baron replies, in a judicial, peremptory, almost cutting tone:

> What Mme de Sévigné felt for her daughter has a far better claim to rank with the passion that Racine described in *Andromaque* or *Phèdre* than the commonplace relations young Sévigné had with his mistresses. It's the same with a mystic's love for his God. The hard and fast lines with which we circumscribe love arise solely from our complete ignorance of life.[78]

This is an invaluable corrective to the tendency of most writers, including Proust himself, to limit the use of the word 'love' to the description of an intense sexual attraction between two people of roughly the same age and generally of different sexes. But even this kind of relationship is treated in so unusual a manner in *A la recherche du temps perdu* that you often wonder whether the description of what Proust calls 'cette maladie générale appelée amour' (the general malady called love)[79] has any general applicability at all. Only two love affairs are analysed in detail, and the similarity between the two suggests that Proust was basing his account of Swann's feelings for Odette, or of the Narrator's passion for Albertine, on nothing more than the obsessions which so visibly stem from the probably autobiographical 'drame du coucher'. This impression is confirmed by the fact that all the other love affairs are variations on the same theme, and there is something almost involuntarily comic in the way the Narrator explains to Albertine, in *La Prisonnière*, how 'the great men of letters have never created more than a single work, or rather have never done more than refract through various media an identical beauty which they bring into the world'.[80] Most readers will have noticed by this point in the novel that Proust has a tendency, especially in his passages of psychological analysis, to bear out the truth of the remark which Camus made in *Le Mythe de Sisyphe* about how monotonous the great creators can be. Indeed, Proust's tendency to repeat himself when discussing what he regarded as the inevitable link between love and jealousy reminds one at times of the slightly doubled-edged compliment which Janáček paid Beethoven when he wrote, of the Quartet in C sharp minor, that the latter had 'stopped caring whether he will appeal to the public or not and gives expression to his innermost self'.[81]

The first of these two love affairs, the one between Charles Swann and Odette de Crécy, is nevertheless over fairly quickly. Indeed, Proust's analysis of it provides the most traditional episode in the novel, and *Un Amour de Swann* may even have been given its present form in order to make the first two volumes of *A la recherche du temps perdu* more accessible to conventionally minded readers. The second takes place between the Narrator and Albertine Simonet, and is analysed in much greater detail. There is even a sense in which its presence in the novel explains why *A la recherche du temps perdu* is so long, since originally, as far as one can judge from the plan printed in the first volume, the book was to consist only of three parts: *Du côté de chez Swann*; *Le côté de Guermantes*; and *Le Temps retrouvé*. It would have occupied some eight hundred pages, and the section subtitled *A l'ombre des jeunes filles en fleurs* was scheduled to appear in the last volume. As it happened, however, the outbreak of the First World War in August 1914 prevented what was going to be part two from appearing. Proust consequently spent the war years revising his book, an activity which involved addition rather than subtraction. In particular, he incorporated into the Narrator's liaison with Albertine much of the anguish inspired by his relationship with Alfred Agostinelli and the latter's death on 30 May 1914.

It is the application of the view of love first developed in the Narrator's feelings for his mother in *Du côté de chez Swann* which gives those sections of *A la recherche du temps perdu* their intensely obsessive quality. The accident of Agostinelli's death, occurring as it did before the second part of the novel as originally planned had been published, gave Proust the opportunity to expand a concept which was already clearly established in his mind. It did nothing to alter his views on the matter of love; Jeffrey Meyers underlines this aspect of Proust's creative imagination when he writes in his *Homosexuality and Literature 1890–1930* that his novel 'demonstrates the truth of D. H. Lawrence's belief that "One sheds one's sickness in books – repeats and presents again one's emotions, to be master of them" '.[82] The only reservation one has about applying to Proust this remark of the English novelist who also wrote about the mother-fixation without reading Freud – for *Sons and Lovers* too appeared in 1913, and Lawrence does not seem to have read him before publishing his most autobiographical novel – is one to the effect that mastery of his emotions was possibly the last thing that Proust achieved.

This peculiarly Proustian concept of love, in which the lover is perpetually seeking to know everything about the beloved and possess her completely, is applied to other characters in *A la recherche du temps perdu*. The Duc de Guermantes, this 'Hercule en smoking' (that is, Hercules in a dinner jacket; in France, as Proust observes, 'we give to everything which is more or less British the name it happens not to bear in England'[83]) is originally presented as the embodiment of complete social self-confidence, robust good health, and a cheerfully promiscuous heterosexuality. It is only later that we discover how he resembles the Narrator in seeking to hide his mistresses from the eyes of the world by locking them away. Indeed, his pursuit of them is so eager at times that he sometimes sends them up to ten telegrams a day – a habit which 'slightly irritated the Duchess'.[84] But at the end of the novel, the Duke has become in his old age totally dependent upon Madame de Forcheville. This must have taken her back thirty years. It was exactly how Swann used to feel. Perhaps, though Proust does not say so, it explains how she manages to keep looking so extraordinarily young. It certainly reminds the reader of how the emotional patterns of *A la recherche du temps perdu*, like some of Proust's comparisons, reveal a mind which has only imperfectly mastered its obsessions. It would not occur to most of us to compare a doctor's reluctance to give us more details about our illness to the attitude of 'an adored mistress put to the question', or to speak quite as often as Proust does of how our mistresses constantly betray us.[85]

The Narrator's friend, the elegant and aristocratic Robert de Saint-Loup, is passionately in love with an actress-cum-prostitute to whom the Narrator gives the nickname of 'Rachel quand du Seigneur' (Rachel when of the Lord) because of her similarity to the heroine of Halévy's opera *La Juive*. Although the Narrator himself has been offered Rachel for twenty francs in a brothel to which he is taken by his friend Bloch, and although physically unattractive and often extremely disagreeable, she is everything in the world for Robert. The reason for this is a very simple one: once, when he was counting on seeing her, she proved unavailable. This, in Proust's view, is enough to set off what he calls the 'blessed bane' of love, and he writes in *Du côté de chez Swann* that it is not even necessary for us to have been physically fond of the person with whom we fall in love. All that is needed, he writes, is that:

> our predilection should become exclusive. And that condition is fulfilled when – in this moment of deprivation – the quest for the pleasures we enjoyed in his or her company is suddenly replaced by an anxious, torturing need, whose object is the person alone, an absurd, irrational need which the laws of this world make it impossible to satisfy and difficult to assuage – the insensate, agonising need to possess exclusively.[86]

This is what happens to Swann, and his love for Odette gradually becomes inseparable from an illness. His resemblance to his creator Marcel Proust is emphasised by the fact that he suffers from eczema, a disease rivalled only by asthma in its ability to be exacerbated by anxiety. Physically, Robert is much more robust. Emotionally, however, like all Proust's heroes, he is still very vulnerable. Oddly enough, the women, as I shall show when I discuss Odette, Oriane de Guermantes and Madame Cottard, never suffer in the same way. Any jealousy which they feel takes the form of envy at other women's social successes. Madame Proust probably knew that there was little danger of her ever losing Marcel; and when, in *La Prisonnière*, we learn that the Narrator's mother receives more than thirty visits in one afternoon, it is easy to appreciate that she had few anxieties on that score either.[87]

Proust nevertheless leaves no doubt in the reader's mind that Swann's feelings for Odette exactly reproduce Marcel's dependence upon his mother. This emphasises the personal nature of the Narrator's vision if not that of Proust himself; *A la recherche du temps perdu* is not one of those novels in which the reader is expected to work out for himself the emotional relationships between the characters. The strongly didactic tone to the various pronouncements on love leaves no need for him to do this, just as Proust's repeated demonstration of the all-importance of art even suggests, as Jean-François Revel points out, that the people Proust mixed with must have been a bit slow on the uptake.[88]

Proust's anxiety to persuade us of the truth about what he calls 'the general laws of love' also occasionally tempts his more fortunate readers to comment that they don't quite feel that way themselves. Indeed, it even prompted J. B. Priestley to make a much more forthright comment. For while describing Proust as 'unquestionably the greatest French novelist of this century and one of the masters of modern literature', he observed that 'no reader who has gone beyond infatuation, to love truly a member of the opposite sex, could be taken in for a moment by Proust's perverted notion of love, coming out of desire that has suffered a check; this is a mere mixture of sensuality and curiosity'.[89] The obviously obsessional nature of Proust's vision also tempts his less reverent admirers to comment on the unusual nature of his Jewish experience. For all his insistence that *A la recherche du temps perdu* was a carefully constructed work of art and not an autobiography, it does read at times like a great cry of complaint addressed to his mother for not having loved him enough. Readers acquainted with the Jewish mother in life as well as in legend cannot but be struck by an unlikeliness verging on the improbable.

There are also, when you stand back from Proust's hypnotic vision and from his all-absorbing prose, a number of other oddities in his presentation of sexual experience, which make his claim about establishing general laws rather difficult to accept. There is, for example, a total separation between sex and marriage. The Narrator's parents, like those of Jean Santeuil, are totally devoted to each other. When Monsieur de Norpois comes to dinner, there is nothing which the Narrator's mother will not do to make the evening enjoyable. The Marquis de Norpois is her husband's immediate superior at the Ministry, and she is clearly flattered by his obvious esteem for the man of whom she is so fond. Although the dinner for Monsieur de Norpois is given in Paris, the Narrator's home life is still imbued with 'les vertus de Combray', and mercifully free of any serious emotional conflicts among the adults. His father, it is true, suspects his mother-in-law's ability to organise a journey from Paris to Balbec without losing all the luggage; and events prove him right.[90] But this reminder of the tendency for all families to make jokes about the supposed incompetence of certain of their members merely adds to the atmosphere of emotional stability which characterises the Narrator's immediate family. Proust's general portrait of family life is fully consistent with his admiration for *The Mill on the Floss* and his enthusiasm for the almost idyllic realism of Chardin, and it may be for this reason that the relationships between the adults are so consistently asexual. But it does not strengthen the reader's ability to accept the account of human experience in *A la recherche du temps perdu* as having a universal validity.

The possibility that a husband and wife might experience anything more for each other than a general fondness is indeed totally absent from *A la recherche du temps perdu*. This strikes a slightly odd note in a book in which sex is otherwise so pervasive. By the time Swann marries Odette, his love for her has ended in the only way that either Proust or the Narrator find possible: by the slow growth of indifference and forgetfulness. She never gave much sign of being interested in him sexually anyway, and it is quite clear from the way she makes a little joke about it that she doesn't mind at all about the possibility of a liaison between her husband and the attractive young Renée de Cambremer. If, as the Baron de Charlus alleges, she did once try to shoot her husband with a revolver, it seems unlikely from what the Narrator tells us about their relationship that it was through sexual jealousy. Oriane de Guermantes is not over-enthusiastic about her husband Basin's perpetual philandering, but takes it in her stride. In her case – and quite possibly in Odette's as well – marriage has had a distinctly unerotic effect. During a discussion of a photograph of one of the Knights of Rhodes, the Duke says that there is little chance of his seeing it so long as it remains in his wife's bedroom.[91] But the accidental way in which he thus gives away the state of his relationship with his wife in her presence as well as in Swann's shows that the matter is not of any great concern to either of them. At a very different social level, we are told that Dr Cottard, a member of Madame Verdurin's little clan, is a very unfaithful husband. This has not prevented the young Madame Cottard from having what Odette refers to as her 'babies', and we are given no reason to think that she is worried by the failure of the sexual side of her marriage. The only married person in *A la recherche du temps perdu* who takes badly to being abandoned for someone else is Gilberte de Saint-Loup. In one of the few scenes in Proust in which you are made to feel sorry for a woman, this attractively fair-haired and freckled girl covers herself with make-up in an attempt to make her husband interested in her again.[92] But the reason for her failure is not that Robert has gone back to Rachel. It is that his inherited preference for men has become too strong for him.

The presentation of sexual relationships in *A la recherche du temps perdu* thus sometimes seems so far away from most adults' sexual experience as to preclude any possibility of the book ever offering the reader any kind of general law. The love affairs that matter take place in a curious twilight zone which may or may not precede marriage but which does not exclude sexual congress. Before meeting Rachel, Proust tells us, Saint-Loup had spent much of his time in 'le monde restreint de la noce', rather nicely translated as 'the restricted world of amorous adventure'.[93] Since he and Rachel are still very much part of this world, it is odd that he should expect total fidelity from her, just as it is peculiar for Swann to do the same for Odette. For when Swann first meets Odette, there is no doubt in his or anybody else's mind what she does for a living: she sleeps with men for money. She may do well enough to employ a servant and live in a house in la rue La Pérouse, in a very fashionable part of Paris. But her livelihood still depends upon her keeping enough lovers not to have to depend exclusively on any single one of them for her income. It is paradoxical therefore for Swann to require from her either the kind of fidelity which a husband might reasonably expect from a wife, or which the Armand in Dumas fils's *La Dame aux Camélias* succeeds in obtaining from Marguerite once the great Romantic passion has struck them both.

The same is true of Saint-Loup's relationship with Rachel. Although he is constantly causing great worry to his family by threatening to marry her, the couple are not officially engaged. Like Odette, she can therefore not really be blamed for keeping all her options open. I have argued in Chapter 2 that you do not need all that much sympathy with the women's movement to feel a certain admiration for Odette. In as blatantly unfair a society as the one depicted in *A la recherche du temps perdu*, where a man like

Swann regards it as perfectly normal to keep a string of mistresses, the ruthlessness with which she pursues her own interests is neither surprising nor reprehensible. Rachel also starts off with a weak hand in a harsh school, and there is a sense in which Swann and Robert de Saint-Loup have no one to blame but themselves. They are trying to enjoy the emotional security of monogamy in a section of society established by men and for men, and whose aim is to enable men to have as many mistresses as they want. They can therefore scarcely complain if the women they find in this *demi-monde* are reluctant to change the habits which a lifetime of male-encouraged promiscuity has imposed upon them.

Although Proust alters the Romantic myth of the grand passion in a number of important ways, he is still writing within the tradition which regards sexual love as the most important event to be experienced in most people's lives. He is also absolutely faithful to the belief that certain kinds of love are totally irrational, and in no way to be judged by common sense or rational standards. When the Princesse des Laumes comments how absurd it is for a man of Swann's intelligence to suffer for so common and stupid a creature as Odette, Proust observes, in one of his most famous medical comparisons, that it is 'rather like being astonished that anyone should condescend to die of cholera at the bidding of so insignificant a creature as the comma bacillus'.[94] But although Proust is still in the tradition which makes Catullus lament about the worthlessness of the girl with whom he is in love, he does move some distance from Romanticism by totally destroying the idea of reciprocity. Tristan and Isolde are a long way away, as also are Manon Lescaut and the Chevalier des Grieux. If Proust's women are unfaithful – and nobody at the time knows for certain whether they are or not – it is not because they are irresistibly attracted to another man. Unlike Hermione, Roxane or Phèdre, Proust's heroines love nobody except themselves, and have a lack of interest in physical relationships with men which points to the limitations of Proust's homosexual imagination. Neither are they unfaithful for the relatively unselfish reasons which inspire Manon Lescaut to take lovers in order to enable herself to enjoy with her one true love the life-style to which she sees both of them as entitled. There is never any question of Odette, Rachel or Albertine doing anything for their menfolk – apart, perhaps, from occasionally refraining from the activities which make them so unhappy.

Proust nevertheless does observe one of the conventions of established classics of romantic fiction such as *Manon Lescaut, Paul et Virginie* or *La Dame aux camélias* by making Albertine die young. Otherwise, as the Narrator observes, she would have become exactly like her aunt, Madame Bontemps, and the reader can appreciate how that would not have done at all.[95] She may, in so far as *A la recherche du temps perdu* is an account of Proust's own experience, have died because Agostinelli did. But her early death keeps her image alive in the way which is consistent both with this aspect of the myth and with the poetic terms in which she is most frequently presented, especially during the early stage of her relationship with the Narrator. She may indeed, as generally seems to be acknowledged, have had her starting point in the character of Agostinelli. But the extent to which she dominates so much of the central part of the book is the result of Proust's imaginative reworking of the emotions which a combination of his own obsessions and of his experience with Agostinelli inspired in him. If so many readers and critics have felt that the pages which Proust wrote about Albertine have had their starting point in his own private life, this is in fact one of the greatest tributes they can pay to his powers as a novelist. In spite of its inherent improbability, it all sounds terribly real.

In the very early stages of their relationship, Albertine is part of an almost undifferentiated group of young girls – the English title, *Within a Budding Grove*, apparently invented by Scott Moncrieff himself, exactly captures the atmosphere – who move along the sea front like a flock of seagulls or a luminous comet. It even takes Marcel some time to remember what she actually looks like, to situate her mole just beneath her nose and decide that her eyes are black and not blue. Later on, in one of Proust's most justly celebrated scenes, the Narrator watches her sleeping, until the moment comes when he can lie down beside her. Then, he writes,

> I would climb deliberately and noiselessly on to the bed, lie down by her side, clasp her waist in one arm, and place my lips upon her cheek and my free hand on her heart and then on every part of the body in turn, so that it too was raised, like the pearls, by the breathing of the sleeping girl; I myself was gently rocked by its regular motion: I had embarked upon the Tide of Albertine's sleep.[96]

But there is another Albertine apart from the innumerable different personalities she assumes in the Narrator's mind, and you do not have to indulge in a wildly Barthesian 'lecture plurielle' or make too much use of Michel Tournier's remark about the reader writing the other half of the novel to find out what she is like. Proust scatters enough clues in the text of *A la recherche du temps perdu* for us to piece together an Albertine with a fairly clear social identity, whose point of view on her relationship with Marcel is not unreasonable. She is relatively poor, and dependent upon an aunt, the not particularly inspiring Madame Bontemps.

Albertine actually comments that the only thing this aunt wanted to do was get rid of her, and it is doubtless her poverty which explains the 'charming quality of being always ready for anything, perhaps because she had been accustomed in the past to spend half of her time as guest of other people'.[97] Her family lost most of its money in the collapse of the Union générale bank in 1881, and Proust's contemporaries would not have needed to be especially alert to see why she is not allowed to play with Jewish children. It was the collapse of this bank, said to have been brought about by Jewish businessmen, which contributed to the anti-semitism that reached its climax in the Dreyfus case, and the account in *A la recherche du temps perdu* of the divisions which this produced in late-nineteenth-century French society is presented in a similarly indirect and intriguing fashion. One of the advantages of Proust's technique of narration, in which pieces of information which the traditional novelist would have highlighted in great detail are presented in an oblique and apparently accidental manner, is that the reader is given the freedom to work out a good deal of the plot for himself, as well as the satisfaction of doing so.

The sections of *A la recherche du temps perdu* devoted to Albertine have another advantage: they offer the reader privileged access to a mind which is both pathological in its obsessions and capable of the most minute analysis of how these obsessions work. At the same time, the reader is given the challenge and opportunity of also looking at the obsessional world in a broader and more general context. For if you once again step a little to one side, it is possible to feel even more sympathetic to Albertine than towards Odette. Once she accepts what one assumes must at some point have been a proposal of marriage – the Narrator tells his mother that he must marry her, and refers to her as his *fiancée* – she is kept as a virtual prisoner in his apartment. She is allowed out only under escort, and given the most marvellous Fortuny dresses. But she is refused the opportunity of ever meeting anyone apart from the Narrator who might appreciate how beautiful she looks in them. She is perpetually badgered by questions as to whether or not she has had Lesbian relationships with any of her friends, while being expected to indulge in sexual relationships with the Narrator which are of a very uncertain and unsatisfactory nature. She points out to him at one point that it isn't correct to describe her as his mistress since she isn't quite that,[98] so one assumes that anything they do stops short of the full sexual act. But the Narrator seems to be in no hurry either to satisfy her sexually or to marry her, and it is easy to understand why she finally decides to escape. Lorelei observed in *Gentlemen prefer Blondes* that 'kissing your hand may make you feel very very good but a diamond and safire bracelet lasts forever'. Albertine might well have felt that promises of yachts and Rolls-Royces don't really replace a gold or even a brass wedding ring.

Such a way of looking at one of the most tormented love affairs in world literature is a good deal less sympathetic to Proust's Narrator than the one to be found in most other studies so far published of *A la recherche du temps perdu*. By emphasising both the peculiarity of the Narrator's relationship with Albertine and his quite extraordinarily self-centred attitude, it seems to heighten even further the difficulty of seeing Proust's account of love as anything but an extrapolation from his own very peculiar temperament and experiences. But it does underline how Marcel is presented critically, as a character in a novel and not as an autobiographical and privileged version of Proust himself, and is thus wholly consistent with Proust's own insistence in *Contre Sainte-Beuve* on the need to separate not only the man who lives from the artist who creates but also the artist who creates from the characters in his books. This is Proust, the artist, writing about a character, Marcel. He is doing so by making Marcel talk about himself in the first person, and he is using the peculiarity of Marcel's experience to bring out by contrast the genuine universality of the vision of love underlying the whole of *A la recherche du temps perdu*. For what Marcel discovers in his relationship with Albertine is the same essential truth that Swann discovers in his affair with Odette and of which Saint-Loup becomes aware in his liaison with Rachel: that we can never

compel those whom we love to love us in return. We may, as
Marcel did with Albertine and as Swann would certainly have
liked to do with Odette, do everything in our power to keep the
person we love as a physical captive. But we have, when the chips
are down, no power over other people's minds. What is perhaps
even more important is that we have absolutely no reliable
knowledge of them.

This is why Marcel's failure to know what Albertine is really
like and what she has really done is so important. Even those
whom we need most intensely and love most passionately are
ultimately unknowable. They may return our love for a day, a
week or even a year. But there is no means whereby either they or
we can be absolutely certain that this will always be the case.
However much we love them, they always remain free to stop
loving us in return. This may be either through deliberate choice
or through a different, quite involuntary kind of change by which
their own personality is altered. 'Lord', as Ophelia remarked, 'we
know what we are, but we know not what we may be', and it is
even possible that Albertine would have liked to love Marcel in
the totally committed and exclusive way that he wanted. But there
is, in the experience which human beings have of themselves as
well as of other people, no way of ensuring that any emotion
remains permanent. This is an inevitable consequence of the
inescapable fact of human freedom, and there is more of a link
than either author would have suspected between Proust's great
theme of the changeability and impermanence of the self and
Sartre's vision of how we can prove the authenticity of our
emotions only by our acts. In a remarkable anticipation of this
aspect of Sartrian existentialism, a Protestant missionary in
André Malraux's *La Condition humaine* reminds his former pupil,
the terrorist Tchen, that the truly Christian life consists of a daily
reconversion to faith.[99] The same is true of human emotions. And
one day, as Proust tells us throughout *A la recherche du temps perdu*,
this reconversion may not take place.

In a society protected by 'les vertus de Combray', both this
general truth and people's awareness of it will remain hidden.
Seen in this context, the whole concept and practice of Christian
marriage is an attempt to protect people against the tendency to
emotional instability which is inseparable from their freedom.
There is no indication that the Narrator's parents have in fact
been married in Church, though Proust's own parents were. But

their behaviour towards one another shows what the Anglican ceremony for the Solemnisation of Matrimony calls the 'mutual society, help and comfort, that one might have of another', and which are so notably lacking in the 'monde de la noce' in which Saint-Loup loves Rachel or in the raffish world of the *demi-monde* where Swann pursues Odette. For there, all protective coverings are removed, and the truth about the potential effect of human liberty upon human emotions stands out in absolute and terrifying clarity.

There are a number of different ways in which the twentieth-century novelist Marcel Proust can be compared to the sixteenth-century essayist Michel de Montaigne. If the legend which credits Montaigne with a Jewish ancestry is true,[100] both writers combine the most attractive aspects of the Jewish and of the Christian tradition. Both, that is to say, bring together a passion for detailed analysis with an awareness of the importance of overall construction. Both are masters of introspection, with a fondness for recording the minutiae of daily life. Both of them bear out the truth of what Montaigne meant when he declared that 'chaque homme porte la forme entière de l'humaine condition' (Every man bears the complete impress of human nature).[101] For however odd Proust's analysis of sexual love at first sight might appear, his analysis of the effects of liberty on our human emotions does indeed apply to us all.

It is consequently fairly clear, if you follow Proust's own hints and establish the link between the 'drame du coucher' and the various love affairs described in *A la recherche du temps perdu*, why the quality of the sexual pleasure bestowed by the loved ones on their partners is not described in any detail or given any particular importance. What matters is the reassurance – or lack of it – which the lover derives from what he knows or thinks he knows about his mistress's behaviour and consequently about her emotional attitude towards him. We are told that Rachel, though very clumsy in everything else, is very good in bed, and is similar in this respect to the great passion in the life of the Baron de Charlus, Charles Morel. 'Charlie', as he is known to his many friends, is 'sufficiently fond of both men and women to satisfy either sex with the fruits of his experience with the other', and at one point in *La Prisonnière* is described as having had a highly satisfying tumble with the notorious Lesbian actress, Léa.[102] At least this would have solved the problem set out in the classic English limerick about who does what and with what and to whom, though it should be remembered that the sense of humour which serves Proust so well in his depiction of society, and even in certain homosexual scenes, totally deserts him in any discussion of the emotional side of Sapphic or of heterosexual behaviour. The only thing he tells us about the sexual side of Swann's relationship with Odette is that it increases his jealousy at the thought of her possibly doing something so delicious with somebody else. There is nothing in the book to justify the scene in the 1981 film in which Swann makes love to Odette in the Italian position, and this is not because there is any prudery in the presentation in *A la recherche du temps perdu* of either major or minor sexual deviations. In addition to the famous scene in *Le Temps retrouvé* in which Monsieur de Charlus has himself chained to a bed and whipped in a homosexual brothel, there is a reference to how two women 'became great friends, and used to go about together, one of them dressed as a man, picking up little girls and taking them home to the other to be initiated. One of them had a little boy with whom she would pretend to be displeased and would hand him over to her friend, who went to it with a will.'[103] But although Proust is not mealy-mouthed about sex, you never feel that it is the physical pleasure that matters.

This is especially noticeable in the area where Proust went further than Diderot, Laclos, Balzac and even Baudelaire in making Lesbianism into a main theme in a major literary work. Diderot had dealt with the topic in *La Religieuse*, and incorporated it into a characteristically eighteenth-century attack on the unnatural abuses which stem from the denial of nature in the monastic life. In *Les Liaisons dangereuses*, the interest which Madame de Merteuil takes in the sexual potentialities of the young Cécile de Volanges anticipates the way in which other more extreme supporters of the Women's Movement seek to show their superiority over men by a defiantly radical Lesbianism. In *La Fille aux yeux d'or* and *Femmes damnées*, Balzac and Baudelaire explore the religious as well as the moral overtones which they see as inseparable from Sapphic practices, and there is a reference in *Le Temps retrouvé* to Gilberte de Saint-Loup reading the Balzac short story. But no author before or since Proust has given quite so much importance to Lesbianism. And although he does link it with male homosexuality in his famous title of *Sodome et Gomorrhe* – appropriately translated as *Cities of the Plain* (cf. Genesis 19) – the role that Lesbianism plays in the overall structure and emotional atmosphere of *A la recherche du temps perdu* is quite different from that of homosexuality.

There is, it is true, at least one occasion when it gives rise to what is certainly unintended humour. When Odette has been badgered into telling him about an approach made to her one evening when she was dining in the Bois de Boulogne, Swann observes that 'vice is far more common than one has been led to believe'. This may well be true, but the imagination does rather tend to boggle when the Narrator tells us of a dinner party at Rivebelle at which the only characteristic common to the ten women guests was a preference for members of their own sex.[104] Lesbianism may, indeed, as Geneviève Dormann argues in her biography of Colette, have been particularly widespread 'in intellectual and fashionable circles in the France of President Fallières', and she may well be right to suggest that this was because 'many young women entered into marriages of convenience with unsuitable men, and then turned against men as a race and sought consolation from other women'.[105] George Painter quotes an illuminating remark made by one of the sisterhood to Robert de Montesquiou: 'People call it unnatural – all I can say is, it's always come naturally to *me*',[106] and there seems no reason to doubt that there were plenty of golden-eyed girls in the France in which Proust lived as a young man. But in this particular context, the Narrator's insistence that he is not interested in observation can and should be taken at face value. What is at stake is something much more interesting than the frequency or otherwise of a particular form of sexual deviance.

Both from a literary and an intellectual point of view, *La Prisonnière* and *La Fugitive* have aroused much less interest and discussion than the passages in *Le Temps retrouvé* in which Proust puts forward his ideas on art. The detailed account of Marcel's feelings for Albertine, and especially of his fruitless attempt to find out what she is really like and what she really did, has seemed to some critics rather tedious and lacking in the originality which is so visible elsewhere in Proust. These volumes nevertheless do bring out an important and even central theme in *A la recherche du temps perdu*, for as Malcolm Bowie has argued, both *La Prisonnière* and *La Fugitive* are essential to Proust's treatment of the spirit of scientific inquiry.[107] While this can be linked to Proust's family background, Marcel's interest in Albertine – and Swann's in

Odette – is closer to something slightly less laudable and which the medieval theologians would have called *libido sciendi*: the desire to know. Both Marcel and Swann want to discover everything there is to know about the women they love, and Proust is quite clear about the starting point for this desire. It is to be found in the comparison which I have already quoted between the unknowable pleasures to be tasted by Albertine if she visits Trieste and the mysterious delights savoured by the Narrator's mother as she dines with her adult guests after her son has been sent to bed. To the cold eye of common sense, this may seem very odd. But a glance at any textbook of morbid or even ordinary sexual psychology will show how the child is father to the man in these matters. It might even be, if biographical factors can be just temporarily used to link the man, the work and the obsessions, that it was Marcel Proust's anxiety about his mother which led to his decision to live his life upside down. By ensuring that he was awake all night, he could at least be on the watch to see what his mother was getting up to. In his poem describing how James James Morrison Morrison Weatherby George Dupree 'took great care of his Mother though he was only three', A. A. Milne treats the same phenomenon in a comic mode. With Proust, it wasn't funny. Come to think of it, it wasn't all that hilarious for J.J.M.M.W.G.DuP. She disappeared.[108]

It is in this context that the role which Lesbianism plays in this unhappy sexual drama becomes important, and that the sexual interest felt by one woman for another is explicable. We are concerned less with Proust's observation of what went on in the Paris of *La Belle Epoque* than with a kind of symbolism. For if you want to know everything there is to know about somebody, you will be particularly interested in what they feel like in the most intense and private moments of their life. These, by common consent, occur when people are making love, and one of Swann's torments is that of wondering whether Odette is having the same experiences with other men as she seems to be having with him. But if it is already difficult for a man to know what a woman is feeling when she is with another man, it is even harder if her partner is another woman. What both intrigues and tortures the Narrator Marcel in his relationship with Albertine is the desire to discover what he calls 'the palpitating specificity of feminine pleasure'.[109] It is this which constitutes the ultimate mystery, but which he is doomed never to discover. When, at the end of the novel, the Narrator turns to art as an activity more certain and satisfying in every respect than human relationships, it is because art offers the possibility of knowledge which the inquiry into other people's emotions and sensations can never provide.

It does not, in this respect, really matter whether Proust is talking about Lesbianism or not. What he has hit upon as a kind of symbol of the unknowability of other human beings could be any form of activity which is mysterious, exotic and impenetrable, and this is linked in the text of *A la recherche du temps perdu* to the frequency with which people's eyes do, or do not, reveal the way they are thinking and feeling. In the scenes of social comedy, this interest in how our eyes give us away is used primarily to make us laugh. In the passages of psychological analysis, and especially in this ambition to discover what the Narrator calls 'something unknown but conscious' ('de l'inconnu conscient'), the haunting question of what takes place behind a young girl's eyes becomes much more a source of anguish. When the Narrator first separates Albertine out from the group of young girls which he sees 'like a single warm shadow, a single atmosphere' moving along the sea front at Balbec, he notices the movement of her eyes and begins to reflect upon it. If we thought, he says, that the eyes of such a girl were merely 'two glittering sequins of mica', we should not be 'athirst to know her and to unite her life to ours'. But we sense, he continues, that there is more to it than that and that what there is, unknown to us, are

> the dark shadows of the ideas which that person cherishes about the people and places she knows . . . the shadows of the home to which she will presently return, of the plans she is forming, or that others have formed for her; and above all that it is she, with her desires, her sympathies, her revulsions, her obscure and incessant will.[110]

Even at this stage in their relationship, the Narrator realises that any idea of discovering such secrets is an impossible dream. He recognises that it is simply not possible to know people in this way, and there is no condemnation that even the sternest moralist might formulate of the ambitions and conduct of the Narrator which Proust has not already anticipated. Not only does he state unambiguously in *Le Temps retrouvé* that 'nothing is more limited than pleasure and vice'. He adds that 'one may say truly, altering slightly the meaning of the phrase, that we revolve always in the same vicious circle'.[111] He also makes the Narrator fully conscious of how self-defeating his desires are. When Marcel first looks at Albertine, and wants to 'tear off her dress to see her body', it is because he wants 'through her body to see and read the whole diary of her memories and her future passionate assignations'. But when he really does hold Albertine a prisoner, she is no longer interesting. He has changed her very essence, and made her into 'a dreary, docile captive'. She has ceased to be the 'fugitive, cautious, deceitful creature, whose presence was expanded by the thought of all those assignations she was skilful in concealing'. He has, he realises, 'clipped her wings'. She has ceased to be a 'winged Victory', and has become a burdensome slave of which he would like to rid himself.[112]

Once again, there is so close a parallel with the view of human relationships set out in *L'Etre et le néant* that you can easily understand why Sartre chose so many of his examples from Proust. For each one of us, according to Sartre, wants to possess other human beings completely, to fascinate them to the point where the intensity of their gaze sanctifies us in our own identity and provides us with the constant reassurance that we are who we are. This reassurance against the constant uncertainty and capacity for change which our freedom makes inevitable for us is, however, valid only if given by a free being. But fascinating someone to the point where they do what we want them to do takes their freedom away from them. The reassurance which they then give us is therefore totally valueless, and we remain caught up in a self-defeating circle which explains why Sartre calls man 'a useless passion'. We want to possess someone so that they will love us absolutely. But once this happens, their love is no longer worth having. 'Every person we love', writes Proust in a remark quoted from him in Philip Rieff's *Freud. The Mind of the Moralist*, 'and indeed, to a certain extent every person, is to us like Janus, presenting to us a face that pleases us if the person leaves us, a dreary face if we know him or her to be at our perpetual disposal.'[113]

When A. J. Ayer reviewed Sartre's *L'Etre et le néant* in 1946, he remarked that it was all very interesting but that it 'did not correspond empirically to the way people behaved'.[114] He was, fortunately, and as usual, quite right. Most of us, as Arthur Miller puts it in *A View from the Bridge*, 'settle for half'. The particular interest of Proust's analysis of love in *La Prisonnière* and *La Fugitive* is that he shows us somebody who does not agree to settle for half. Yet while the Marcel of *A la recherche du temps perdu* is, from this point of view, a potentially tragic figure in his quest for an impossible absolute, he is also afflicted by a characteristically Proustian contradiction. When there is no danger of his losing Albertine, he would be quite happy to let her go. But as soon as there is any danger of this happening, he is terrified at the possibility of what she might do when he is not there to keep an eye on her. It is, once again, fully in keeping with Proust's insistence that Marcel is not an autobiographical character to see the Albertine passages as a kind of cautionary tale. This, Proust is telling us, is what happens when people do not manage to shake off their childhood traumas. They remain unable to grow up and to enjoy ordinary relationships. They cannot achieve what Sartrean existentialism implicitly if unconsciously depicts as emotional maturity: the recognition that other people are free as well as ourselves.

It would nevertheless be a fundamental misreading of *A la recherche du temps perdu* to see Proust as setting out to teach you these very useful lessons in how not to make a mess of your sex life. It is true that he did, in March 1914, write to André Gide that he felt how, in writing *Un Amour de Swann*, he could have given him advice which would have made Odette love him.[115] If he does offer this kind of advice in *A la recherche du temps perdu*, it is by accident, just as the anonymous author of the Orpheus and Eurydice myth suggested by accident that we might well kill the thing we love by looking at it too early and at too close a range. Proust's fundamental and underlying conscious ambition was to show the superiority of art over life. This is why he writes, in a passage which should be read by the side of the Narrator's failure to find out about Albertine, that: 'As the spectrum makes visible to us the composition of light, so the harmony of a Wagner, the colour of an Elstir, enable us to know that essential quality of another person's sensations into which the love for another person does not allow us to penetrate.'[116] If your experience of human relationships is like the one which Proust attributes to Marcel, it is inevitable for you to seek in art what life has so resolutely refused to give you. This applies just as much to knowledge as it does to happiness.

5

Heredity, Homosexuality and Science

Proust himself would have been surprised to read that *A la recherche du temps perdu* would be analysed as an exploration of the consequences of human liberty. For he was very much a nineteenth-century thinker in his insistence that human beings are totally determined by what has happened in the past. Not only does the link between 'le drame du coucher' and the failure of Marcel's relationship with Albertine show how impossible it is for a man to escape from the impact of his early emotional conditioning. Proust's treatment of the other major sexual theme in *A la recherche du temps perdu*, the nature and problems of homosexuality, is dominated by two essential presuppositions: that a preference for members of our own sex is something that we can do nothing about; and that both female and male homosexuality are in-born. They both stem in Proust's view from a cruel, physiological joke whereby the feelings of a man are emprisoned in a woman's body, or those of a woman in a man.

Proust's belief in physiological determinism is not limited to sexual matters. When the Narrator meets Swann again after a long absence in *Le côté de Guermantes*, he is struck by how much he has changed. The reason, he realises, is that Swann is not only very ill but has also reached the exact age at which his mother died. This leads him to comment that our lives are 'as full of cabbalistic cyphers, of horoscopic castings as if sorcerers really existed'.[117] This idea comes as no surprise to the reader who can recall the frequency with which Swann is described in the first volume of the novel as having the same gesture as his father of rubbing his eyes, or who can remember being struck by a peremptory statement in *A l'ombre des jeunes filles en fleur*. There, the Narrator is made to declare that 'even mentally, we depend a great deal more than we think upon natural laws', since our minds possess in advance 'like some cryptogamous plant, the characteristic that we imagine ourselves to be selecting'. It thus follows, he continues, that we take from our biological family, 'as the papilionaceae take the form of their seed, as well the ideas by which we live as the malady from which we shall die'.[118] The term 'genetic code' did not become part of our day-to-day vocabulary until forty years after Proust's death. But neither the term nor the idea it stands for would have come as any surprise to him.

There is thus no question of Proust sharing Sartre's view that we choose a particular form of sexual behaviour because this fits in with our own idea of the kind of person we would like to be. Neither is there anywhere in *A la recherche du temps perdu* any suggestion that some people may have been fortunate enough in their inheritance or early conditioning to be able to grow up into moderately happy heterosexuals. Whether we acquire it as a result of a childhood accident or inherit it from our ancestors, the inbuilt tendency to behave in one way sexually rather than another is bound to make us unhappy. The pessimism which is such a marked feature of French nineteenth-century scientific thought, and which is at its most intense in the world of Zola, informs the whole of Proust's vision of what we are and why we behave as we do. It provides yet another reason for his acceptance of the religion of art, and in this respect his work looks forward to the argument in André Malraux's *Les Voix du silence* and *La Métamorphose des Dieux*. Just as Malraux sees art as the means whereby man triumphs over the built-in tendency of all civilisations to decay and disappear, so Proust's vision of the artist presupposes the creation of an autonomous world which defies our inability to do anything to change our physiological destiny.

The famous clerihew which said that 'People thought with horror / Of Sodom and Gomorrah / Till they were given a boost / By Proust' is thus true only in a literary sense. He was no apostle for the Gay Liberation Movement, and no prophet for the general delights of the permissive society. He told André Gide, a brother officer in the Middlesex Irregulars, that 'you can say anything at all, so long as you don't use the first person singular',[119] and the two most famous homosexuals in the history of French literature seem to have discussed matters quite fully. But Proust apparently told his housekeeper, Céleste Albaret, that Gide was 'the author who had done most harm to French youth',[120] and you can see what he meant. If you think, as he did, that homosexuality is a curse laid upon the unfortunate inhabitants of the Cities of the Plain, you are bound to disapprove of the attempt which Gide made by the open publication of *Corydon*, in 1924, to argue that it was so natural as to be virtually desirable.

Proust was one of the first authors to give homosexuality pride of place as a major theme in literature. Balzac, who is the novelist most frequently mentioned in *A la recherche du temps perdu*, had raised the question only indirectly. You do not, it is true, need much imagination to realise why Vautrin is so interested in Rastignac in *Le Père Goriot*, and why this interest is transferred to Lucien de Rubempré in *Splendeurs et misères des courtisanes*. But the precise nature of the interest is never openly acknowledged, and even the Michel of Gide's *L'Immoraliste* is recognisably homosexual only to the relatively initiated. The same even used to be true of Gide's long novel, *Les Faux-Monnayeurs*. For although this was published in 1926 as a kind of fictional accompaniment to *Corydon*, I remember hearing lectures on it in the 1950s which cast no light at all on why one of the main characters, l'oncle Edouard, is so interested in Bernard and Olivier, and even less on the reasons which, at the end of the book, lead him to transfer this interest to young Caloub. Until the publication of *Sodome et Gomorrhe* in 1922, no major novelist had treated the theme in such immense detail and with such apparent frankness as Proust, and a major part of the contribution which he made to the development of the novel was in the way he showed how serious fiction could be openly used for the discussion of unconventional sex. But as far as the attitude expressed towards homosexuality itself in *A la recherche du temps perdu* is concerned, he was as stern and uncompromising a moralist as any supporter of the moral majority could wish.

For it is not possible to decode *A la recherche du temps perdu* as a kind of allegory for 'the love that dare not speak its name'. There is, it is true, an implied reference to Oscar Wilde in the remark about the poet who was 'one day fêted in every drawing-room and applauded in every theatre in London, and the next day driven from every lodging, unable to find a pillow upon which to lay his head'.[121] But nowhere is there any suggestion that Proust shared Wilde's view, put forward at his second trial, in April 1895, that homosexuality, the 'love that dare not speak its name', is 'such a great affection of an elder for a younger man as there was between

David and Jonathan, such as Plato made the very basis of his philosophy, and such as you find in the sonnets of Michelangelo and Shakespeare'.[122] If André Gide's account of the second conversation which the two men had in 1921 is to be believed, Proust confessed to having transferred any 'gracious, tender or charming' memories which he may have had of his homosexual experiences to the idyllic presentation of young girls in the 'budding grove' section of the book. This rings true in the sense that the rather brutal play-acting of Albertine and her friends at Balbec occasionally evokes memories of how the Baron Kuno von Pregnitz liked his young men to behave in Christopher Isherwood's *Mr Norris changes trains*, and Maurice Bardèche suggests that the scene in which the young Marcel dominates the tea-time conversation at Gilberte Swann's becomes more convincing if you change the sex of everybody there but the Narrator. But both male and female critics of Proust have commented on how very feminine both Gilberte Swann and Albertine Simonet are – to say nothing of Odette de Crécy – and *A la recherche du temps perdu* loses rather than gains by being decoded into an account of Proust's adventures with his various young men. It is also true, if you look in more detail at what he says about homosexuality, and how he makes his homosexuals behave, that Proust's attitude is at the furthest possible distance from Oscar Wilde's vision of 'a deep, spiritual affection that is as pure as it is perfect', which has 'nothing unnatural about it', which is beautiful, fine and 'the noblest form of affection'. If you judge Proust in the only way he deserves to be judged, as the author of *A la recherche du temps perdu*, he had no liking whatsoever for the sexual tastes with which he saw himself afflicted.

One of the principal reasons why the overall architecture of *A la recherche du temps perdu* does not, as André Gide observed in 1938, 'leap immediately to the eye',[123] is the inclusion in the novel of long passages which could without much difficulty have been published in essay form. This does, for Proust's fellow insomniacs, have considerable advantages. You can read what he has to say about Normandy place-names or learn why old silverware is so scarce in France – after the treaty of Utrecht, in 1715, Louis XIV gave his own plate to be melted down to meet the cost of the war he had just lost, and was imitated by the aristocracy – and then go back to sleep again without feeling that you are missing out on the story. The twenty or so pages of *Sodome et Gomorhe* which deal

with what Proust calls 'the race of men-women' also fall into this
category. For they do not throw any particular light on why any of
the characters in the novel behave as they do, and are most
interesting when read as a kind of detachable essay in
autobiographical guilt. For this, indubitably, is how Proust felt
about his own homosexuality. He belonged, he was convinced, to
what he calls in this essay:

> A race upon which a curse is laid and which must live in
> falsehood and perjury because it knows that its desire, that
> which constitutes life's dearest pleasure, is held to be
> punishable, shameful, an inadmissible thing; which must deny
> its God, since its members, even when Christians, when at the
> bar of justice they appear and are arraigned, must before Christ
> and in his name refute as a calumny what is their very life; sons
> without a mother, to whom they are obliged to lie all her life
> long and even in the hour when they close her dying eyes;
> friends without friendships, despite all those which their
> frequently acknowledged charm inspires and their often
> generous hearts would gladly feel. . . .[124]

But although Proust feels intensely sorry for homosexuals and is
putting in a plea for tolerance, he does not see any way in which
they might find sexual happiness or fulfilment. For, as he explains
further on in the essay, 'they are enamoured of precisely the type
of man who has nothing feminine about him, who is not an invert
and consequently cannot love them in return', and Proust's
analysis of homosexuality is exactly the same in this respect as
that of Jean Genet. For in spite of the lyrical passages about Divers
in *Notre-Dame-des-Fleurs*, Genet thinks that homosexuals are
doomed to frustration by the very nature of their desires. The real
men by whom they would most like to be loved are precisely
characterised by an exclusive and virile preference for women. If
such men were to respond to the homosexual's overtures, they
would therefore cease to be desirable. Admittedly, Proust differs
from Genet in insisting on how the attitude of society towards
homosexuality has changed with the replacement of the easy-
going approach of the Greeks by the intolerance of the Judeo-
Christian tradition. But he does not go on from this to argue that
society is to blame. Since the broad-minded attitude of classical
times has disappeared, the men who might in earlier times have

enjoyed sex with men or women alike now stick exclusively to women. The only homosexuality which now remains, he argues, is the one which is physiologically determined. Those who practise it would like to give it up but they can't. They consequently live in a permanent state of guilt, and any attempts to deny their own nature merely have the effect of making other people unhappy as well as themselves.

This is what happens when Robert de Saint-Loup marries Gilberte Swann. He does so partly for her money – she is said to be worth a hundred million[125] – and partly because his family is anxious to get him away from Rachel. However, although he is quite fond of her in a way, the marriage is not a success. It does produce children – something relatively rare in Proust's world since neither Oriane nor Marie Gilbert have any, and the Guermantes line seems therefore to be dying out as far as direct descent is concerned – and the Narrator meets one of them at the *matinée chez la Princesse de Guermantes* in *Le Temps retrouvé*. This is a highly significant encounter, since it brings together the two sides of the countryside round Combray, the middle-class *côté de chez Swann*, with its splendid view over the plain, and the aristocratic well-watered *côté de Guermantes*, which Marcel had always, in his childhood, considered as so different as to remain permanently separated. But Mlle de Saint-Loup is the child of a marriage which failed because of the influence of one of the 'general rules' which Proust claims on a number of occasions to be using his novel to illustrate. 'Homosexuals', he writes in *La Fugitive*, 'would be the best husbands in the world if they did not put on an act of loving other women',[126] and Robert is being unfaithful to Gilberte in a kind of desperate attempt to prove his heterosexuality. This is, however, doomed to failure. After all, he is the Baron de Charlus's nephew, and his other uncle on his mother's side, Gilbert, Prince de Guermantes, pays Morel fifty francs to spend the night with him in the brothel at Maineville.

Proust's account of homosexuality is nevertheless not always so unremittingly gloomy as the essay in *Sodome et Gomorrhe* on 'the men-women' might suggest. He makes the point, echoed in the *British Medical Journal* for January 1955, that homosexuals are equipped with a kind of 'divine discernment'[127] which enables them to detect potential partners in people on whom the average heterosexual would not bestow a second glance. At the beginning of *Sodome et Gomorrhe*, this enables the Baron de Charlus immediately to recognise Jupien, the ex-tailor whose shop opens onto the courtyard of the town house of the Duke and Duchess de Guermantes, as one of those who are 'predestined to exist in order that they may have their share of sensual pleasure on this earth: the man who cares only for elderly gentlemen'.[128] The suggestion of a sexually providential universe which this phrase rather ironically implies is nevertheless confirmed by the long and rather splendid comparison which precedes the encounter between Charlus and Jupien. This comparison is based on the fact that certain female orchids can be fertilised only by an insect which has just, against all the apparently enormous laws of statistical improbability, happened to visit a male flower of the same species. One of the many pleasures to be derived from the slow and attentive reading which *A la recherche du temps perdu* both requires and deserves is afforded by a study of the almost uncountable variety of Proust's comparisons and images. They are taken from so extraordinary a range of activities – anthropology, art, astronomy, botany, chemistry, cooking, diplomacy, electricity, entomology, finance, genetics, medicine, music, religion, sculpture and the theatre – that you quite rightly feel you are in contact with a mind in which a great and complex civilisation had reached its culminating point in the experience of one man. Proust's use of an extended botanical comparison to introduce the theme of Charlus's homosexuality also has another effect. It reminds us that whatever disapproval society may feel for certain sexual practices, nature is neutral.

There is, in this respect, an attractive inconsistency in Proust's attitude to homosexuality. In spite of the obviously personal anguish which informs the famous passage on the 'hommes-femmes', his description of their behaviour in society brings out the best of his own occasionally slightly bitchy humour. In one of the most famous set pieces in *Sodome et Gomorrhe*, Proust compares the way in which all the members of one particular diplomatic delegation are hand-picked because of the similarity of their sexual tastes to those of the Ambassador to the care which Mardochée, in Racine's *Esther*, has taken to choose only Jewish children to form the choirs which escort the Queen. Monsieur de Vaugoubert, who has spent his life sacrificing his sexual tastes to what he sees as the need for the professional diplomat to avoid damaging his reputation, and has followed what Proust sees as the universal law whereby homosexuals marry rather heavily masculine women, can scarcely believe his eyes at the wonder of the spectacle he beholds.[129]

There is nothing in Proust's treatment of Lesbianism to compare with the exuberance with which he uses his portrait of Charlus to bestow upon Robert de Montesquiou the literary immortality which the Count so signally failed to achieve through his own works. Towards the end of his life, the man who had patronised Proust and admitted him only slowly into the higher circles of the Faubourg Saint-Germain was reduced to referring to himself as MontesProust, and Charlus stands out among the ranks of splendidly completed characters whose presence in *A la recherche du temps perdu* places Proust on the same level as Dickens. Perhaps because Lesbians do not, at least in legend, behave in the attractively flamboyant way which so often characterises male homosexuals, there are few Sapphists to rival either Palamède de Charlus, or the Anthony Blanch of *Brideshead Revisited*, or 'l'oncle Alexandre' in Michel Tournier's *Les Météores*, or the Mr Deakin of *A Dance to the Music of Time*. Neither, so far at any rate, has any declared Lesbian used her difference from the sexual norm to attain the notoriety of the real-life figure of Quentin Crisp. To judge from the best-known novel which it has so far inspired, Radclyffe Hall's *The Well of Loneliness*, Lesbianism is even more guilt-ridden than homosexuality, and Proust's account of it insists upon slyness, secrecy and deceit. This may, of course, be linked to the symbolic role which it plays in Proust's depiction of the ultimate unknowability of other people. Alternatively, the more complex portrayal of male homosexuality may be linked to the possibility that the Baron de Charlus is also something of a self-portrait. Proust, too, on occasion, had the same tendency to shriek and to declaim. He also had the same sado-masochistic tendencies which the Narrator discovers, through a not uncharacteristic indulgence in voyeurism, in the character of Monsieur de Charlus.

The parallels here are interesting enough to justify once again going against the injunction in *Contre Sainte-Beuve* and breaking down the watertight compartment which Proust would like to see separating the man who lived and the author who wrote. For what we are told about the fictional Charlus and what has been discovered about the real Marcel Proust shows them both displaying the same kind of apparent contradiction in their behaviour. Thus Charlus, throughout the first volumes of the novel, has an almost exaggerated cult of virility and it is only as he progressively reveals what the Narrator calls the 'graces inherited from some grandmother whom I had not known' and shows the constant 'desire to appear a great lady' that we understand why this should be so. It is that Charlus is constantly seeking to deny the tender, feminine characteristics which Proust regards as creating the essence of his homosexuality. Freud would have been interested in this as confirming the validity of his thesis about the nature of repression and compensation, as would the Horace who wrote 'naturam expellas furca; tamen usque recurret' (You can throw nature out with a pitchfork; it comes back in through the window). For whatever Charlus does, he cannot prevent himself from being like 'an affected old woman . . . who, as a result of seeing in his mind's eye only a handsome young man, thinks he himself has become the handsome young man, and betrays more and more effeminacy in his risible affectations of virility'.

This behaviour gives rise to what Proust calls in the same passage one of his 'general laws', one so generalised, he claims, 'that not even love exhausts it entirely'. It is that 'we do not see our bodies, though others do, and we "follow" our thoughts, the object that is in front of us, invisible to others'.[130] To the modern reader, this comment on how we reveal our 'being for others' without realising what we are doing again has a very Sartrian ring, and can certainly be confirmed by the way in which we ourselves see other people behaving. But when, in *Le Temps retrouvé*, Charlus goes to Jupien's brothel to have himself whipped in the most brutal way possible, he is living yet another 'general psychological law' not mentioned by Proust but confirmed by the way in which he himself behaved. For Proust also had a strongly sado-masochistic side to his personality, which came out in the perversions in which he indulged in the homosexual brothel run by Albert le Cuziat. As George Painter explains in the second volume of his biography, Proust too would indulge in sadistic rituals, and of a kind which makes Monsieur de Charlus's peccadilloes seem relatively mild. For Charlus, after all, hurt nobody but himself. Proust used to have live rats brought to him in order that he might 'watch while the wretched creatures were pierced with hatpins or beaten with sticks'.[131]

This incident, like the scene of the Baron de Charlus's chosen humiliation, took place in the later years of the First World War. Within the novel, the scene in Jupien's brothel matches in violence and absurdity the way Western civilisation was tearing itself to pieces, and helps to justify the claims made for *A la recherche du temps perdu* as a great piece of historical fiction. The general account which *Le Temps retrouvé* gives of wartime Paris also fits very well into the satirical side of Proust's comic genius, but it has a fundamental psychological truth to it as well. For the young men whom Jupien has managed to recruit in order to play the brutal role in this curious ritual are the most harmless and inoffensive specimens imaginable. Precisely because of this, they cannot ultimately give the Baron the kind of satisfaction he is seeking, and the imaginative accuracy of Proust's treatment of sexual perversion can be confirmed by a brief glance at the life of Sacher-Masoch. However hard he persevered, he could not find women prepared to treat him with the cruelty he desired. There is also an illuminating if unintended comment on Proust in Jean Genet's 1956 play, *Le Balcon*. What both Proust and Genet show is that the practitioners of this kind of unorthodox sex are not really looking for physical satisfaction at all. What interests them is what also interests Swann, Marcel and Saint-Loup, and in this respect the difference between these characters and the Baron de Charlus is a fairly superficial one. They are all alike in wanting to live out a psychological relationship of a particular kind, and in wanting to exist in a particular emotional mode. Marcel wants to feel himself entirely and exclusively the object of Albertine's unwavering attention, just as he did with his mother when he was a child. Charlus wishes to attain a particular mode of being, one in which his dream of total virility is achieved in the only way in which it is ultimately possible: by the giving and receiving of intense physical pain, and the participation in an act of unbounded if imaginary authority.

There is perhaps no imaginative author in French literature apart from Jean Genet who seizes the essentially mental nature of sexual perversion quite so well as Proust does, and American and English fiction offers only a slightly wider range. Vladimir Nabokov does it marvellously in the opening section of *Lolita*, and Anthony Powell in a characteristically more restrained and English way in the characters of Sir Alfred Donners and Kenneth Widmerpool in *A Dance to the Music of Time*. The first, it will be remembered from the scene at Stourwater in *A Buyer's Market*, has quite a Charlus-like interest in dungeons and dog leashes, while the second is credited with an intriguing variant of the compulsion which led King Candaules to exhibit his wife to his best friend.[132] Simon Raven's more baroque treatment of Somerset Lloyd-James in the *Alms for Oblivion* series offers comparable entertainment, but in order to come closer to the Proustian vision you have to turn – appropriately enough – to a more scientifically conceived and presented treatment. Indeed, in so far as such a subject can be treated scientifically, the similarity between Proust's diagnosis and that of Gillian Freeman in her *The Undergrowth of Literature*[133] is quite uncanny. For what characterises the sado-masochistic and other fantasies which are depicted in the openly pornographic books which she studies is their extreme physical improbability. Like the Baron de Charlus, the readers – and perhaps even the authors – of this kind of fiction are striving after a state of psychological being which is virtually impossible to achieve. In some of the perversions studied, it is a state in which, while still remaining men, they become like women by dressing up as them. In others, it is one in which they are back, with adult sexual appetites, in what Baudelaire called 'le vert paradis des amours enfantines'. In others, they are entirely at the mercy of another human being, whose interest is exclusively in them. Alternatively, they may exercise comparably unlimited power over somebody else. In his perception of how the Baron de Charlus tries to live his dreams instead of just reading about them, Proust was writing with infinitely great perception about the nature of unorthodox sexual behaviour than he was when he cast his account of homosexuality into the old-fashioned nineteenth-century mould of physiological determinism. He was, once again, anticipating the peculiarly Sartrian notion of how we are all striving, in one way or another, to be a particular kind of person.

It is possible, as Phyllis Grosskurth suggested in a review of a number of books dealing with the medical background to Proust's life and work, that he borrowed the theoretical aspect of his account of homosexuality from a German scientist called Ulrich, whose theory of 'congenital androgyny' was widely current at the time.[134] The insistence elsewhere in *A la recherche du temps perdu* on the overwhelming part played by heredity suggests that this might not be the case. He is so taken up with its general importance that he even describes how Andrée's hair ripples in the same way as her mother's, 'forming here a swelling, there a depression like a snowdrift that rises or sinks according to the irregularities of the land'.[135] The only Ulrich mentioned in Proust's letters is Robert

Ulrich, the nephew of Félicie Fitau, the Proust family cook who served as a model for some of Françoise's characteristics. Proust is, in any case, much more interesting when he relies on his imaginative perception as a novelist and makes Charlus try to realise his own homosexuality through his extraordinary quest for virility through cruelty. Neither does the interest of Proust's apparently less scientific account of homosexuality stop there. For the similarity between Charlus and Proust himself in this respect brings out another tendency which is so frequent a phenomenon as almost to qualify as a scientific law. It is indeed possible, as George Painter argues, that Proust's behaviour with the rats can be explained in terms of a repressed aggression towards his parents. If you look as closely into the links between Proust's personal life and the events of *A la recherche du temps perdu* as George Painter does, it can certainly be seen as directed against the mother who had refused the bedtime kiss so many years ago. But it can also be explained in another way.

In 1973, a remarkable book was published about Proust. It was the memoirs of Céleste Albaret, who had entered his service some sixty years earlier, and looked after both him and the manuscript of *A la recherche du temps perdu* in the nine years between 1913 and his death in November 1922. It is a fascinating account of what he was like during the time that he lived in virtual isolation from the world in order to complete his novel, and an indication that at least one person could disprove the proverb about no man being a hero to his valet. For Céleste certainly did see Proust as a hero – or, as she herself puts it, as 'a prince among men and prince among minds'. Any suggestion that he might possibly have indulged in any unusual sexual practices, especially those involving rats, are dismissed as idiotic ('des stupidités'), as also is any idea that he might have sequestered young men in his flat as the Narrator sequesters Albertine. Céleste will allow that Proust might have had close relationships with members of his own sex – and why not? she adds, he was a free agent – but will not accept that he was anything but an adorable domestic tyrant and a kind of secular saint in the kingdom of the mind.[136]

This discrepancy between the facts which do seem to be established and the portrait of Proust by the person who undoubtedly saw the most of him during the last years of his life is less surprising than one might think. Indeed, one might even rewrite Proust's own statement in *Du côté de chez Swann* that 'our social personality is a creation of the thoughts of other people' and assert two other truths: that our sexual personality is the creation of other people as well; and they generally get it wrong. It is true that you are not especially surprised at Somerset Lloyd-James in Simon Raven's *Alms for Oblivion*. He is, after all, already 'bald and spotty' at the age of twenty-seven; and what else can you expect from a man who uses his position as umpire in a cricket match in order to enable his house to win?[137] But the reader is almost as taken aback as William Bradshaw by the discovery of Arthur Norris's 'singular pleasures', and it comes as something of a surprise to the admirer of *In an English Country Garden* to learn that Percy Grainger was a vigorous sado-masochist. It is almost as though certain people created a public persona for themselves which was deliberately designed to hide as well as to compensate for their private proclivities. In this analysis, a man as civilised, cultivated, gentle and sensitive as Marcel Proust could scarcely avoid giving expression to the Hyde part of his personality in the way that he apparently did, and it is within the same context that the Baron de Charlus's insane pride and obsessional cult of virility find their inevitable counterpart in the humiliations he chooses to undergo in Jupien's brothel. Neither he nor Proust would have been surprised at the behaviour of T. E. Lawrence. For the man whom King Fahood described as being 'of manhood the man, of courage the brave, of freedom the free' took his pleasures in a way that was strikingly similar to those of the man who so haughtily described himself to Gustave Verdurin as 'Duke of Brabant, Squire of Montergis, Prince of Oléron, of Carency, of Viareggio and the Dunes'. While serving with the Tank Corps under the assumed name of Shaw, Lawrence 'persuaded a young Scotsman, John Bruce, to flog him at regular intervals'.[138]

It is nevertheless not only in the Pompeian-like world of wartime Paris that the reader of *A la recherche du temps perdu* shares with the Narrator the slightly suspect excitement of acting as a voyeur at a scene of sado-masochism. Such practices are not unknown in the lost paradise of Combray, and the fact that the Narrator witnesses one of them has a crucial impact upon his subsequent relationship with Albertine. For when he is still a child – the scene takes place well before his early adolescent passion for Gilberte Swann, at a time when he seems to be only ten or eleven – Marcel sees the daughter of the musician Vinteuil behaving in a very odd way. Together with an older woman, she is engaged in a sado-masochistic ritual which reminds the modern theatre- and cinemagoer both of Genet's *Les Bonnes* and of Robert Aldrich's 1969 film, *The Killing of Sister George*. This ritual involves Mademoiselle Vinteuil in proving her friend's ascendancy over her by spitting upon her dead father's portrait.[139] It is not, except for the two people involved, an especially hurtful activity, but it is another episode in *A la recherche du temps perdu* which recalls an incident in Proust's own life. For he too, according to the information discovered by George Painter, performed comparable ceremonies with photographs of his parents in Le Cuziat's 'house of illusions', and perhaps for reasons comparable to those which inspired Mlle Vinteuil: a desire to profane that which was most dear to him in an attempt to punish himself for those aspects of his personality of which he most disapproved. Mlle Vinteuil, in keeping with Proust's general theory about the nature of homosexuality, is also a somewhat hoydenish girl, of so boyish and robust an appearance 'that it was hard to restrain a smile when one saw the precautions which her father used to take for her health, with spare shawls always in readiness to wrap round her shoulders'.[140] But this counterpart to Proust's theory about the origin of a taste for members of one's own sex stemming from an inherited biological mix-up is not taken very far. Albertine, in spite of the rather coarsely grained skin on her thickish neck, is a very feminine creature, as is also Odette. In the case of Mlle Vinteuil, Proust is more interested in exploring other, perhaps more interesting ideas.

The first of these is the challenge which the mystery of Lesbianism offers to the Narrator's obsessive desire to discover 'the specific palpitation of feminine desire'.[141] For the critical moment in Marcel's life occurs when he discovers, by a chance remark of Albertine's, that she had been brought up at one stage in her childhood by this same older woman with whom he had seen Mlle Vinteuil disporting herself. It is this knowledge which suddenly makes it imperative, at the end of *Sodome et Gomorrhe*, for him to decide to marry Albertine and take her off to Paris. From the moment he does this, what Samuel Beckett calls 'the central catastrophe'[142] in *A la recherche du temps perdu* – the relationship between Albertine and Marcel – takes a further turn for the worse. The fact that there is some doubt, later on in the novel, as to whether Albertine had really been brought up by Mlle Vinteuil's friend or whether she merely said it to make herself more interesting adds both to the reader's perplexity and to his admiration for what he hopes is Proust's conscious skill as a novelist. For Albertine remains a mystery to the very end of the book and the interplay between the various themes of the novel is perhaps more interesting here than anywhere else in *A la recherche du temps perdu.*

Proust had as keen an eye as Gide or even Dostoevski for the complexities and oddities of human behaviour and motivation. Monsieur de Charlus, who is so arrogant and unpleasant in his dealings with Madame de Saint-Euverte or Madame Verdurin, is impeccably generous in his relationship with the young violinist, Morel. However cruelly the Verdurins may humiliate one of their more timid guests, the archivist Saniette, they nevertheless save him from a poverty-stricken old age by arranging, in total secret, for him to receive a small income which they make him believe has been left to him by the Princesse Sherbatoff, and there is a comparably unexpected twist in the story of Mlle Vinteuil and her Lesbian friend. For Vinteuil left behind him a mass of apparently indecipherable musical scores which nobody had ever thought could be made to serve as a basis for actual performance until his daughter's friend devoted untold effort and patience to the task of making them readable. This enables Vinteuil's true greatness as a musician to be finally revealed, and it is the discovery of the originality of his genius which helps to confirm the Narrator in his artistic vocation. But the revelation of how this genius comes to be revealed is more than a reminder of how unexpectedly people can sometimes behave. It also recalls a major theme in the love affair between Swann and Odette, and brings the reader's mind back to a crucial difference between Swann and the Narrator.

Before the true range of Vinteuil's genius is revealed by the deciphering and discovery of his septet, he had been known principally for his sonata. This is now discovered to have been only a prelude to his greatest work, and Proust comments on the illustration which this provides for the common phenomenon whereby the enthusiastic applause attracted by the early work of the greatest artists comes to seem curiously misplaced when we discover the full extent of their originality. Taking, as he so often does, Wagner as his example, he writes what is in fact a short essay on the theme of what he calls 'our surprise that for years past, pieces as trivial as the *Song to the Evening Star* or *Elizabeth's Prayer* can have assured in the concert-hall fanatical worshippers who wore themselves out applauding and shouting *encore* at the end of what after all seems poor and trite to those of us who know *Tristan*, the *Rhinegold* and the *Mastersingers*'.[143]

Within the overall structure of *A la recherche du temps perdu*, Vinteuil also plays an exemplary role as an artist whose work enables him to triumph over what Proust sees as the inevitable disappointments of our private, emotional life. Early in their relationship, at one of the parties at which Madame Verdurin shows that readiness to encourage relatively unknown artists which is her one redeeming feature, Swann and Odette listen together to a performance of his sonata, and a little phrase from it becomes a kind of National Anthem for their love. Later on, when Swann has begun to realise that this love is dead – and, perhaps, when Vinteuil has begun to penetrate to more elegant circles – he hears it again, at the soirée Saint-Euverte, and it brings back to life for him, as the 'petite madeleine' does for the Narrator, 'the specific, volatile essence of his lost happiness'. It recalls in particular 'the showers which fell so often that spring, the ice-cold homeward drive in his victoria, by moonlight; all the network of mental habits, of seasonal impressions, of sensory reactions, which had extended over a series of weeks its uniform meshes in which his body found itself inextricably caught'.[144] The description of how a piece of music can spark off involuntary memories in this way is one of Proust's most sustained pieces of writing on the link between aesthetics and memory, and one that can be fully understood only in the context of what happens in *A la recherche du temps perdu*. It can, of course, like so much of Proust, be detached from the novel and read as a separate essay, and its two closing sentences have been quoted with justifiable frequency as a summary of the most positive side of Proust's religion of art.

> We shall perish, but we shall have as hostages these divine captives who will follow and share our fate. And death in their company is somehow less bitter, less inglorious, perhaps even less probable.[145]

But what gives particular force to the incident in which Swann listens to the Vinteuil sonata at Madame de Saint-Euverte's is the way it anticipates what happens in the rest of *A la recherche du temps perdu*. For the whole pattern of themes and incidents in which Vinteuil is involved brings home to us how even an activity as unattractive as Lesbianism can somehow form part of a providential network: it is only through the intervention of Mlle Vinteuil's friend that the even greater works which Vinteuil himself left behind him come to be known to the public.

This pattern also provides an essential contrast between, on the one hand, characters such as Swann or the Baron de Charlus, and, on the other, creators such as Vinteuil, Elstir and the Narrator himself. For Swann is not only an *alter ego* of the Narrator in that his liaison with Odette prefigures Marcel's love affair with Albertine. He is also a contrast to Marcel, in that he is a dilettante who achieves nothing of ultimate value. All the suffering which he undergoes as a result of his love for Odette merely gives him what Proust considers as the unimportant virtues of an indulgent father and a paternalistically protective husband. The Narrator's existence, in contrast, is going to be justified by the writing of *A la recherche du temps perdu*. The same gap separates Charlus from the Narrator, and the difference between the two echoes and amplifies the contrast between Robert de Montesquiou and Marcel Proust. The former wrote some verses and sketches which would be forgotten if he had not known Proust and served, together with the Baron Doasan, as one of the starting points for the Baron de Charlus. The second wrote *A la recherche du temps perdu*.

In this respect, both Proust's own life and the text of *A la recherche du temps perdu* have a kind of 'Brighton rock' quality. Whenever you look at either of them, they tell you about the importance of art. Indeed, for Proust himself, as for the Narrator, this importance is so great that there is a sense in which a number of issues I have discussed so far and a number of qualities which I have admired in *A la recherche du temps perdu* are not really to be considered as all that important. They are, to use the image in *Le Temps retrouvé*, part of the cement which holds together other really important, lyrical passages revealed and rediscovered by involuntary memory and cast into eternal beauty through art. One of the principal originalities of *A la recherche du temps perdu* is that of being a book about literature and about the act of writing. It is time to look in more detail at this aspect of Proust's work.

6
Literature in Theory and in Practice

When you finish reading the last volume of *A la recherche du temps perdu* and follow the implicit invitation to turn back to the first page in order to start reading it all again, there should be no doubt in your mind about what Proust intends you to expect. The long passage in *Le Temps retrouvé* in which the Narrator describes the final discovery of his vocation contains a detailed account of what he intends to put into his book, and of the qualities which he hopes the reader will find there.

If you then take this passage in *Le Temps retrouvé* as a kind of introduction to the book as a whole, it suggests that Proust – clearly identified on this occasion with the Narrator himself – is pursuing five principal aims. The first is the essentially personal one of giving meaning to the whole of his past by incorporating it into a work of art. This aim is clearly linked to the fact that the words 'le temps perdu' are a kind of pun. They mean time wasted as well as time lost, and evoke the idea that the years apparently wasted on social activity and unhappy love affairs can be redeemed by being made the substance of the book which the Narrator finally decides to write. This in turn is associated with the idea that 'the true paradises are the paradises that we have lost',[146] and emphasises the intensely Romantic nature of Proust's vision. Like Wordsworth, Baudelaire and Rimbaud – and like the Alain-Fournier whose *Le Grand Meaulnes*, published in the same year as *Du côté de chez Swann*, helped to make 1913 an *annus mirabilis* in French literature – Proust carries to its ultimate conclusion the idea encapsulated in Baudelaire's definition of genius as 'childhood clearly formulated, and now able to express itself with powerful and manly organs' ('l'enfance nettement formulée, douée maintenant pour s'exprimer d'organes virils et puissants').[147] His childhood will always be available because he has incorporated it in a work of art.

Proust's second aim is to show us new ways of looking at our experience. His third is to present us with a work of art which has its own organic unity. His fourth is to enable us, by means of what he calls 'a three-dimensional psychology', to appreciate more fully the impact of time on society and individuals.[148] His fifth is to convince us that only art offers true values.

These aims are clearly interrelated, and they are accompanied by a further claim about the function of metaphor. This makes us more conscious of the quality common to two otherwise different sensations by linking them together in the same phrase and thus liberating them from the contingencies of time. The unity of *A la recherche du temps perdu* is thus very much the product of the kind of language which Proust is using, and he is one of the writers who would most enthusiastically endorse Mallarmé's dictum that literature is made of words.[149] Perhaps because of this endorsement, Proust omits from his statement of aims in *Le Temps retrouvé* all reference to one of the major themes and one of the principal qualities of *A la recherche du temps perdu*. He does not mention homosexuality; and he gives no indication of the fact that his novel is a very funny book. He refers to the unhappy love affairs which take up so much of the novel only to assert his belief in the neo-Romantic notion that an artist has to suffer if he is to create. You can almost, he writes, say that 'a writer's works, like the water in an artesian well, mount to a height which is in proportion to the depths which suffering has penetrated his heart'.[150]

Not all of Proust's five stated aims seems to me to be equally achieved. The first, for example, is both very far-reaching and very dependent upon one man's personal experience. There is certainly no reason to doubt Proust's own inner conviction that he had redeemed the time which he had lost by incorporating it into a work of art. But we can accept this as a way of making sense of our own lives only if we accept the view that experience in its raw, immediate and undigested form is always disappointing. If the concept of paradise is meaningful, it may well be that the state it designates exists only in the past. But that does not mean that it is impossible for some human beings to attain some degree of happiness here and now. Proust's own childhood is marvellously recaptured in *Combray*. But not everybody's childhood was so blissfully poetic, or so full of pleasures that adult experience is constantly doomed to be a series of frustrations. The incident in *Du côté de chez Swann* in which the Narrator is finally allowed to go to the theatre and see his favourite actress, La Berma, in the role of Phèdre, is marvellously presented. He does not, it will be recalled, enjoy her performance as much as he had hoped to. He has built up his expectations to the point where it would indeed be impossible for anything to satisfy them, and it is only when he thinks about her performance in retrospect, and is told by Monsieur de Norpois how good it is, that he finally realises that he has really enjoyed it. This combination of initial disappointment and retrospective pleasure is a kind of microcosm of Proust's concept of art. He sees art as supremely important because it alone enables us to bridge the gap between expectations and reality. We are able, at one and the same time, to have the experience and to savour the fact that we are having it. But this view of human beings as unable to enjoy climbing Helvellyn when they are actually doing it is, when you think about it, simply not true.

When you are actually reading *A la recherche du temps perdu*, the same quality in the writing which makes 'le drame du coucher' such a vivid and moving episode in the life of a small boy also makes his disappointment on first hearing La Berma, or his disillusionment on first arriving at Balbec, totally convincing as events which happen to his Narrator. The problem only arises when you stop reading, think about what Proust is saying, and compare it with what happens to you. One of Proust's many achievements is to have used the novel to present essentially philosophical considerations. As John Cocking observed, he was one of the first novelists to 'describe with a clear mind' how the novel can do something else apart from telling a story.[151] In this respect, there is a parallel between Proust and the Dostoevski about whom the Narrator lectured Albertine at such length in *La Prisonnière*, and he also looks forward to philosophically-minded mid twentieth-century French novelists such as Sartre, Malraux and Camus. But the problem about the philosophical novel is that the first reaction of most readers to the presentation of ideas, especially when they take the peremptory form which Proust so often gives them, is to question their validity. Proust himself seemed almost to recognise this when he wrote in *Le Temps retrouvé* that a work of art with theories in it is like an object which still has the price tag on it.

The idea of art recapturing experience, and thus giving it a validity which it originally lacked, also raises the problem of the status which the reader is expected to give to Proust's long analyses of social behaviour. I have already suggested, in Chapter 1, that it is misleading to take him at his word and regard such sections merely as cement holding together the interesting, poetic passages. I shall also, in Chapter 7, try to show this aspect of *A la recherche du temps perdu* is not without interest or value as a guide to how we might conduct ourselves in late twentieth-century English society. But if these passages of social analysis are, as many readers have found them to be, among the most amusing, interesting and satisfying parts of *A la recherche du temps perdu*, their presence in a work which aims to redeem time by presenting it through art is rather strange. For what art then does is to give philosophical as well as literary value to a set of social activities which, on Proust's own submission, are essentially worthless.

One of the reasons why Proust's work has aroused so much critical discussion is that his views on the relationship between time, art and experience raise so very many intriguing and unanswerable questions. The area for disagreement about the answers is smaller when one looks at his second claim, that of the way in which the artist shows us how we look at our own experience. For Proust's statement in *Le Temps retrouvé* that his book is going to be 'a sort of magnifying glass like those which the optician at Combray used to offer his customers'[152] is closely linked to a number of scenes in the novel itself.

For all his insistence that he is not interested in observing how people behave, Proust does have a very marked tendency to comment on the ways our eyes show what we are or are not thinking, and this is not limited to people like Legrandin and Norpois. When the Narrator tells the Duchesse de Guermantes that the Baron de Charlus has been very kind to him in Balbec and in Paris, the knowledge which Oriane has of why her brother-in-law might have shown this kindness to a young man comes out in the way she 'appeared surprised' and allowed her eyes to 'turn, as though for a verification of this statement, to some much earlier page of her internal register'.[153] On at least two occasions,

Monsieur de Charlus's eyes are described as shifting uneasily from side to side like those of an illicit street trader afraid of a sudden visit by the police,[154] and it is also through her eyes that the Princesse de Parme unwittingly reveals the truth about the slightly embarrassing situation in which she finds herself. However energetically she gesticulates to show how much she admires Gustave Moreau's *Le Jeune Homme et la Mort*, the intensity of her mimicry cannot 'fill the place of that light which is absent from our eyes so long as we do not understand what people are talking to us about'.[155]

But Proust is not only interested in how our eyes enable other people to see what we are feeling or thinking. He is even more intrigued by the relationship between what we see and what we know. As is so often the case, it is the Narrator's relationship with his grandmother which provides one of the best examples of how this relationship works in practice. For on his return to Paris from a stay with Saint-Loup in the garrison town of Doncières, the Narrator comes into a room in his parents' apartment and suddenly catches sight of his grandmother when he is not expecting to do so. All that he then sees, when the eye of love has ceased to complement the force of habit is, 'sitting on the sofa beneath the lamp, red-faced, heavy and vulgar, sick, vacant, letting her slightly crazed eyes wander over a book, a dejected old woman whom I did not know'.[156]

In this scene, Proust is behaving exactly like Elstir, his ideal imaginary painter. For what Elstir does is to show us reality 'not as he knows it to be but according to the optical illusions of which our first sight of them is composed'.[157] Madame de Sévigné, the favourite author of the Narrator's grandmother, is also mentioned as having the same ability to present things to us 'in the order of our perception of them, instead of explaining them in relation to their several causes', and there is here a clear and convincing connection between what happens to the characters in *A la recherche du temps perdu* and the more general ideas which Proust uses his novel to express. Since the Narrator, as will be remembered, first sees Rachel in a brothel to which he is taken by his friend Bloch and where he is offered her services for twenty francs, the vision which he has of her will always be different from that of Saint-Loup, who does not start with this knowledge and sees her only through the distorting mirror of the desperate need which he has of her love. When the Narrator first sees the

Princesse Sherbatoff, he mistakes her for the madam of a large brothel, 'a procuress on holiday'.[158] It is only later that he discovers her to be the most respectable if poverty-stricken of ladies, the ideal member of Madame Verdurin's 'Faithful'.

Intellectually, Proust is not telling us anything we did not know before. Under the effect of a love potion, Titania saw Bottom the Weaver in an ass's head as the embodiment of absolute perfection. What we are given in *A la recherche du temps perdu* is a more detailed and leisurely explanation of this idea, and one which is perhaps most important for the light which it casts upon Proust's own concept of himself as a writer communicating a totally new and entirely inner vision. He is so obsessed with the idea that all great artists bring us a vision which is so new that they are doomed to be ignored and misunderstood at the beginning of their career, that he even interrupts his account of the Narrator's grandmother's death to remind us how Bergotte is only now just beginning to be recognised by the general public. When he points out in *A l'ombre des jeunes filles en fleurs* that Beethoven's late quartets took fifty years to produce the public capable of appreciating them, he is certainly thinking of himself and of how difficult people will find *A la recherche du temps perdu*. There is perhaps no French author who more clearly illustrates Wordsworth's view that 'Every author as far as he is *great* and at the same time *original*, has had the task of *creating* the taste by which he is to be enjoyed'. But although Proust's novel is certainly not as easy a read as Galsworthy or Trollope, its excellence does not always lie in its total novelty or in its ability to make us look at our experience in an entirely new way. It may indeed be true, as Proust wrote in December 1920 in a letter to Emile Henriot, that 'the great innovators are the only true classical artists, and form a virtually uninterrupted succession'.[159] *A la recherche du temps perdu* often gives us the more reassuring awareness that another person has had the same experience as we have.

This is especially true when Proust talks about sleep. For when I first read his description of how we know that we are finally dropping off to sleep by the increasingly disordered and improbable nature of our thoughts, I knew that here was a man who was writing about what happens to me. I also felt that Proust had actually been watching inside my head when he described how Madame Cottard, the devoted but deceived wife of the boorish physician adopted by the Verdurins, is afflicted with the tendency to fall asleep after a meal. In company, she gives way to what Proust calls a 'mal implacable et délicieux' (this implacable and delicious malady), and the experience of how we fall into the 'vast and gentle slumbers' which overpower us after a good meal has never been better described. It is perhaps true that only an insomniac like Proust could have compared taking a new kind of sleeping pill with setting out for a first rendezvous with a new mistress. But once the 'delicious expectancy of the unknown' which is common to both experiences has been brought to your attention, you can never think of soporifics in quite the same light again. The same is true of Proust's other comments about sleep, such as the observation that a short, very deep sleep is as refreshing as a long one if it is accompanied by violently improbable dreams, or the phrase about the way in which 'to a man accustomed to sleeping only with the aid of drugs, an unexpected hour of natural sleep will reveal the vast, matutinal expanse of a landscape as mysterious and more refreshing'.[160] It may not quite correspond to Proust's claim in *Le Temps retrouvé* of how truth will be attained by the writer 'only when he takes two different objects, states the connexion between them – a connexion analogous in the world of art to the unique connexion which in the world of science is provided by the laws of causality – and encloses them within the links of a well-wrought style'. It may not be an adequate illustration of the idea that 'truth – and life too – can be attained by us only when, by comparing a quality common to both sensations, we succeed in extracting their common essence and in reuniting them to each other, liberated from the contingencies of time, in a metaphor'.[161] But the glass which Proust holds up for you to examine your own experience makes you realise what Pascal meant when he said that you sometimes expect to meet an author but find yourself face to face with a man. Proust is, above all, the novelist of our inner life, of how we experience ourselves. It is essentially in this respect that he behaves like the ideal painter in Browning's 'Fra Lippo Lippi', the one who makes us see 'First when we see them painted, things we have passed / Perhaps a hundred times nor cared to see'.

The unity of *A la recherche du temps perdu*, the third subject of Proust's stated intention in *Le Temps retrouvé*, is primarily one of style. There is the characteristic Proustian sentence, full of apparently digressive surbordinate clauses, enriched by a choice of original, vivid and poetic adjectives, themselves often arranged in trios whose ascending order of importance is underlined by the fact that Proust's self-conscious attempt to satirise his own style involves the detailed discussion of the Dowager Duchess of Cambremer's own habit of presenting her adjectives in a diminishing order of intensity – which leads her to tell the Narrator that she was delighted to meet Robert de Saint-Loup because of his 'unique – rare – and real' qualities – and whose complex meanderings remain, unlike some English sentences, under perfect control until their final resolution in a phrase whose construction is so deliberately planned to heighten the emphasis accorded to a particular character's name by revealing it only at the end that the reader is less surprised than the Narrator by the fact that the figure in Jupien's 'Temple de l'Impudeur', 'chained to a bed like Prometheus to his rock, receiving the blows that Maurice rained down upon him with a whip which was in fact studded with nails'[162] is none other than that of the arrogant, virile but basically feminine Monsieur de Charlus.

Proust himself said that style was a matter of vision rather than of technique. There is therefore a close link between these complex sentences and Proust's insistence that his novel gives us a new way of looking at experience. He is telling us that our thoughts do not move in the short, straight sentences of Hemingway or Voltaire. They follow a more devious, sinuous and irrational path, whose syntax needs only the slightest dislocation to produce the interior monologues of Joyce or Faulkner. In this respect, the revelation provided by the Proustian sentence changes the way we see the world more fully than any other aspect of his work. As the Narrator observes, 'it is difficult, when one's mind is troubled by the ideas of Kant and the yearnings of Baudelaire, to write the exquisite French of Henri IV',[163] and Proust's view of language looks forward in this respect to the more successful attempt made from the 1960s onwards by thinkers such as Roland Barthes, Jacques Lacan or Jacques Derrida totally to destroy the classical concept of French as a language of limpid communication.

Proust's third claim, the one concerning the unity of his book, is thus closely linked to his style. But although this unity is highly satisfying in so far as it is inseparable from an attitude and a vision, it is hard to accept that *A la recherche du temps perdu* also has the kind of structural unity suggested by two of Proust's comparisons. Admittedly, the Narrator evokes the idea of a cathedral only by the slightly ambiguous phrase 'combien de grandes cathédrales restent inachevées' (How many great cathedrals remain unfinished).[164] He is not seriously suggesting a sustained parallel, and this is perhaps fortunate. There can be few readers who have not felt that *La Prisonnière* and *La Fugitive* are too long and rather repetitive. A cathedral constructed on the model of *A la recherche du temps perdu* would have a disproportionately large south transept – or perhaps a very long nave – and the Narrator's more modest comparison between his book and a dress made by his servant Françoise invites similar comment. The left-hand sleeve would almost reach the floor.

Such comments are naturally subjective. Other readers might well find that there was too much about the Baron de Charlus, and could point to the fact that Proust's original plan did not indicate that Palamède – Mémé (= Grandma) to his friends – would become quite so important. This plan did not even mention Albertine, and consisted, as I mentioned in Chapter 4, of a fairly simple structure in three parts. *Du côté de chez Swann* was to have been followed by *Le côté de Guermantes*, and the two volumes rounded off by *Le Temps retrouvé*. We should still, if he had stuck to this plan, have had Marcel's description of high society, the account of his grandmother's death, the conflicts between Monsieur de Charlus and the Verdurins, and the bringing together of the two ways of Méséglise and Guermantes in Robert de Saint-Loup's marriage to Gilberte Swann. This would all have been rounded off by the Narrator's discovery of his artistic vocation, and the theme of how the time wasted in society and in love affairs could be redeemed by art. The eight hundred or so pages could well have had the architectural unity suggested by Proust's mention of the cathedral, and a dress made to this pattern could well have fitted a normally shaped human being.

The outbreak of the First World War in August 1914 prevented Proust from following out this original plan. He revised the text of *A l'ombre des jeunes filles en fleurs* to the point where Jacques Copeau exclaimed in May 1919 that this was a whole new book,[165] and this was even truer for the later volumes. The growth of the original eight hundred or so pages to over three thousand certainly makes the structure of *A la recherche du temps perdu* difficult to identify at times, but did not affect the fundamental unity which it derived from Proust's vision. In a mention of Françoise, the Narrator compares his book to one of her most suc-cessful dishes, the *bœuf mode* which Monsieur de Norpois 'had found so delicious, just because she had enriched the jelly with so many carefully chosen pieces of meat' ('apprécié par M. de Norpois et dont tant de morceaux de viande ajoutés et choisis enrichissaient la gelée').[166] It is true that some of the more detailed speculations about Albertine are a bit indigestible, and that some of Professor Brichot's disquisitions on the place names of Normandy are as little to everyone's taste as the adjunction of a dumpling would be to a dish of *bœuf bourguignon*. But Proust is not alone among great novelists in riding some of his hobby-horses very close to death. There can be few readers who have enjoyed every repetition in *War and Peace* of Tolstoy's conviction that individuals play no role in history, or who have not skipped Melville's assimilation of whales in Chapter 23 of *Moby-Dick* to the differently sized volumes in a library.

It should also be remembered that the circumstances in which Proust wrote the last two-thirds of *A la recherche du temps perdu* did not lend themselves to the process of trial and error, of elimination and rejection, of the abandonment of certain chapters and their replacement by others, and of the constant process of rewriting and revising by which writers with less confidence in the originality of their vision try to give order, balance and readability to their work. If Céleste Albaret's account is accurate, Proust would copy out his first draft from one set of exercise books to another, and then proceed to make additions. These would start by filling the margins, and then extend themselves onto a series of separate sheets, which Proust rightly feared might easily get lost at the printer's. Céleste solved this problem by suggesting that he left sufficient space at the top and bottom of each sheet to enable them to be stuck together, and Proust showed the characteristically ecstatic gratitude with which the person who has no practical ability greets any useful suggestion, however simple. One set of sheets formed a thick ribbon some five feet long.

It would be interesting to know whether Proust was making a joke about himself when he penned one of his most characteristic generalisations about the nature of prestige: 'Like a book, like a house, the quality of a "salon", Mme de Guermantes rightly thought, is based on the corner stone of sacrifice'.[167] There are certainly times when you feel that he must have been casting an ironical eye at his own performance when he made Saint-Loup include in his thoughts on the conduct of operations in the First World War the statement that: 'A general is like a writer who sets out to write a certain play, a certain book, and then the book itself, with the unexpected potentialities which it reveals here, the impassable obstacles which it presents here, makes him deviate to an enormous extent from his preconceived plan.'[168] There is no reason to doubt what Proust said in December 1919 in a letter to the critic Paul Souday: that the passage in *Le Temps retrouvé* describing the Narrator's discovery of his Vocation was written immediately after the account of the 'petite madeleine' incident in *Combray*.[169] The letter which he wrote in February 1914 to Jacques Rivière, congratulating him on seeing that *Du côté de chez Swann* did form part of a carefully constructed work in which all the incidents would fit together, is an invaluable guide as to how to approach *A la recherche du temps perdu*. It still remains true that *A la recherche du temps perdu* has an organic and essential unity rather than a structural and architectural one.

This unity stems from Proust's style, from his personal vision and from the intensity of his beliefs, and stands out especially well in the link between his interest in how we see things and his concept of the role of the artist. Since Proust believed that only art was capable of making life meaningful, it is understandable that he should have set about illustrating the fourth of the principal proclaimed aims of *A la recherche du temps perdu*, that of the superiority of art to life, by making three of the major characters into artists. They are the writer Bergotte, the painter Elstir and the musician Vinteuil, and from an anecdotal point of view they all have something in common: each is unlike the idea of him which you might get from his work. For when the Narrator finally meets Bergotte, he finds him totally different from the 'gentle bard with snowy locks' of his imagination. He is a 'youngish, uncouth, thickset and myopic little man, with a red nose curled like a snail-shell and a goatee beard'.[170] It also takes the Narrator some time to realise that Elstir, whose style of painting succeeds so admirably in depicting things just as they are, and not as the intelligence reconstructs them, has quite a different social personality from the one suggested by the delicacy and sensitivity of his art. For he is also the rather ridiculous little man with the absurd name of Biche, the butt of some of the less tasteful jokes in the salon of the pretentious Madame Verdurin. Vinteuil, the composer whose music has so unique an accent that it is a proof of the individual existence of the soul, looks like a drearily respectable member of the lower middle class ('un petit bourgeois bienséant'), and has a private life which is made miserable by the scandalous behaviour of his daughter.

It is thus only when we know what they have achieved that we can see Bergotte, Vinteuil and Elstir as they really are. There is an obvious link here with Proust's insistence in *Contre Sainte-Beuve* on the gap between the man who lives and the writer who creates, and you sometimes feel that Proust is so preoccupied with the idea of how wrong Sainte-Beuve was that he cannot leave it alone. It is not long after the Narrator has met Madame de Villeparisis that she is made to deliver a long speech in which she disparages his enthusiasm for Chateaubriand, Balzac and Hugo because they had been so lacking, in their lifetime, in the qualities of self-effacement which the Faubourg Saint-Germain had taught her to regard as so desirable. 'I think I have the right to speak about them', she concludes, 'since they used to come to my father's house; and as M. Sainte-Beuve, who was a most intelligent man, used to say, in forming an estimate you must take the word of people who saw them close to and were able to judge them exactly at their real worth.'[171]

One of the advantages of looking at Proust as a novelist is that it encourages you to see how funny this literary in-fighting can become by being placed in context. The Marquise de Villeparisis is one of Proust's most successful middle-ranking characters, and the way that both she and her lover, Monsieur de Norpois, speak about literature shows Proust at his best as an intellectual as well as a social satirist. Indeed, once you have listened to Madame de Villeparisis, you do not need to read *Contre Sainte-Beuve*, and the Narrator makes a neat if slightly complicated joke at his own expense which again shows Proust using the novel in order to express ideas which other writers would have cast in essay form. For the Narrator has just discovered a new author whose originality of style and vision are even more interesting than those of the now ageing Bergotte, when he comes up against a rather surprising fact: that this new writer is none other than his old friend Bloch. And Bloch, as we remember, is not only the son of a Jewish family whose pretentious stupidity surpasses even that of the undoubtedly Gentile Verdurins. He is also a pompous oaf whose physical clumsiness makes him the laughing-stock of everybody in polite society. The Narrator reacts exactly as Madame de Villeparisis would have done. He no longer feels that he need make the effort to understand this writer who a moment ago seemed so admirable to him.[172]

It is not only knowledge which changes the way we see people. Time plays its part as well, and does not always do so in a way that owes a great deal to what Proust calls 'the purely mental character of reality'.[173] One of Tante Léonie's friends at Combray is a certain Madame Sazerat, who lives in very straitened circumstances as a result of her father having been ruined by a certain unnamed but very beautiful Duchess. It is only towards the end of the novel that this exotic temptress is revealed to have been none other than Madame de Villeparisis. Up to then, the reader has been made to see her mainly as the first person to receive the Narrator into polite society, the holder of some unfortunate views about literature, and the now white-haired mistress of the Marquis de Norpois. Indeed, the suggestion has always been that the absence from Madame de Villeparisis's drawing-room of the really smart ladies of the Faubourg Saint-Germain is a direct consequence of her liaison with the Marquis, and it is an interesting surprise to discover that she had also kicked over the traces during her first marriage to the Duc d'Havré. For it was then that she had been the scarlet woman who ruined poor Monsieur Sazerat. But the reader's surprise at the interesting past which this respectable old lady is gradually revealed to have had is as nothing to the astonishment of Madame Sazerat when she finally sees her dining in a restaurant in Venice. Instead of the painted Jezebel of her imagination, she sees only the tiny, hunchbacked, red-faced, hideous figure into which Madame de Villeparisis has been changed by the passage of time.[174]

It is an anticipation of the great scene of 'la matinée chez la Princesse de Guermantes' in the last chapter of *Le Temps retrouvé*. For it is there that the reader becomes conscious of another aspect of the unity of *A la recherche du temps perdu*, and the twin themes of perception and the passage of time come together in the moment when the Narrator fails to recognise the slender and graceful Gilberte whom he had loved so painfully in his youth – when she would 'slip away from him like a water-sprite' – in the fat, middle-aged woman she has grown into with age. As she points out to him, he has mistaken her for her mother.[175]

It is indeed at the 'matinée chez la Princesse de Guermantes' that we see Proust's views on the impact of time on society working out in practice. Madame Verdurin's 'nombreux millions' have enabled her to become the new Princesse de Guermantes, while the advent of old age has led the Baron de Charlus to make heroic efforts to greet Madame de Saint-Euverte, a woman he referred to in his prime only in terms of the most scatological contempt. Proust himself, if we infringe the interdicts of *Contre Sainte-Beuve*, and identify the author with his Narrator, has ceased to be the rather precious young man with a camellia in his buttonhole who sat in 1892 for his portrait by Jacques-Emile Blanche. In his place, dangling his puppets before us like Thackeray at the end of *Vanity Fair*, there is the bearded Hebrew prophet denouncing the sins and illusions of his people, though with a very different message of salvation. For *A la recherche du temps perdu* is not only the story of how a little boy grew up to be a writer. It is also a book which sets out to show that the supreme truth of life is in art. It is more than a book which bites its own tail, in that it expects the reader to start again at the first page as soon as he has read the last one. It is a novel which bases the idea of the supremacy of art on what Proust calls our 'inherent powerlessness to realise ourselves in material enjoyment or in effective action'.[176]

There are obvious and easily statable objections to some of the ideas surrounding Proust's concept of the supremacy and all-importance of art, especially in the form given to them in *A la recherche du temps perdu*. In spite of the devotion shown to him by Robert de Saint-Loup, the Narrator frequently insists on the incompatibility between art and friendship. He may not put it quite so brutally as Samuel Beckett does when he writes that, for Proust, 'friendship is a social expedient, like upholstery or the distribution of garbage buckets',[177] but the thought is there. The conversations which we have with our friends, Proust argues, distract us from that absolute attention to the inner life which is the sole source of literary creation. The price is a high one, and not all great creative writers have found it necessary to pay it. As I have already suggested in Chapter 3, the sexual life of Proust's characters is also rather unusual. The possibility that married people might be quite fond of each other sexually as well as in other ways is never even mentioned, and 'les vertus de Combray' seem able to flourish only in a totally non-sexual world. If this divorce between affection and sexuality is another precondition of access to the artistic life, the price is again rather a high one, and there is no mention of anybody who is not an artist finding value in the world of work. It is only if one of Proust's aristocrats is already 'extremely rich' that he might condescend to take on the chairmanship of one of the larger companies, and the only character in *A la recherche du temps perdu* who ever does anything practical is the servant Françoise. But her cooking, as the comparison between the care she showed in choosing the right cuts of meat and the precautions of Michelangelo in selecting the right kind of marble makes clear, is really on the same level as art. It is not to be admired primarily for its usefulness, and Proust also makes a significant change from his own family experience in the profession which he gives to the Narrator's father. Adrien Proust devoted his life to preventing the spread of infectious disease. It is an activity immune to the criticism of even the most determined nihilist. The Narrator's father also works very hard, but in the much less obviously useful world of the higher civil service. His immediate superior is Monsieur de Norpois, whose speech and behaviour do not encourage you to believe that anything useful was ever achieved.

Although Proust was brought up as a Catholic, he had no formal religious beliefs. His mother kept her own Jewish faith, but made no attempt to transmit it to her children. Proust retained enough enthusiasm for the artistic achievements of Christianity to become one of the most fervent defenders of the cathedrals of France against the anti-clericalism which led in 1905 to the separation in France between Church and State, but had little time for other aspects of Christianity. It would, for example, be impossible to imagine anything more opposed to the Christian vision of love set out in I Corinthians 13 than the analysis of what Proust calls love in *A la recherche du temps perdu*. Indeed, the more one looks at how he goes about achieving the fifth of his declared aims in *A la recherche du temps perdu*, the demonstration that 'real life, life at last laid bare and illuminated – the only life in consequence which can be said to be really lived – is literature', the more open to objections does it become. Not only is this belief in the all-importance of art a substitute for the Narrator's own inability, which he quite gratuitously attributes to other people, to derive any satisfaction from either work or human relationships. It is also associated, at least at first sight, with a concept of salvation which makes the most austere Calvinist sect seem quite absurdly generous in the number of those it sees as predestined to glory. For if the Elect are to be made up only of the great creative artists, there is not much chance for the rest of us.

Proust nevertheless does produce a corrective to this view in the way he talks about what art can do for other people. Just as St Paul explained in I Corinthians 12:4 that there are 'diversities of gifts, but the same spirit', so Proust says that the real life which is revealed by literature 'is in a sense all the time immanent in ordinary men as well as in the artist'. It is thus not a question of limiting the Elect to the practising artist alone. For art is first and foremost a means of communication. It is 'the revelation, which by direct and conscious methods would be impossible, of the qualitative difference, the uniqueness of fashion in which the world appears to each one of us, a difference which, if there were no art, would remain for ever the secret of each individual'.[178] This more catholic vision of art is put before the reader on a number of occasions as one of the articles of the creed expounded in *A la recherche du temps perdu*. The world, the Narrator tells us in *La Prisonnière*, is 'real for us all and dissimilar to each one of us', and we have, as the Narrator puts it in *Le Temps retrouvé*, 'as many different worlds at our disposal as there are original artists, worlds more different one from the other than those which revolve in infinite space, worlds which, centuries after the extinction of the fire from which their light first emanated, whether it is called Rembrandt or Vermeer, send us still each one its special radiance'.[179] Proust himself can be seen as offering us a world which we can use to enrich our own without necessarily having to accept his opinion on the illusory nature of love and the pointless-ness of ordinary life, or his dismissal of friendship as a waste of time.

The fact nevertheless remains that Proust's statement of ambition and intent in the second volume of *Le Temps retrouvé* is a mixed blessing both for him and for the reader. He does, it is true, avoid the objection most commonly levelled against authors who expect to be judged in accordance with their intention. Since such intentions are generally set out in prefaces, letters, interviews or essays, they can be discounted on the grounds that they represent ideas or attitudes which do not form part of the work itself. They tend to represent, it is argued, either hopes which occurred to the writer only after he had finished the book or ambitions which he insists on restating mainly because he now sees that they have been imperfectly realised.

At first sight, Proust does seem to have made himself immune to this particular objection. For he makes the statement of his intentions into an integral part of the text of *A la recherche du temps perdu*. These cannot therefore be dismissed as *post facto* generalisations, especially when the whole thrust of the main story line has been to direct the reader's attention to the way in which the Narrator solves his problems by writing the book described in *Le Temps retrouvé*. It is of course true that Proust supplemented the description of his novel in *Le Temps retrouvé* by letters, interviews, and remarks he made in conversation. The comparison with a cathedral, for example, occurred quite frequently in his discussions with Céleste, amplified by the hope that his book would also stand for a long time. A number of the central ideas set out in *Le Temps retrouvé* had already been drawn to the attention of the French reading public in 1913, when Proust gave a long interview to Elie-Joseph Bois in order to explain what he was doing in *Du côté de chez Swann*. He spoke then of his concept of time, and illustrated it by the same distinction between a two- and a three-dimensional psychology which recurs at the very end of *Le Temps retrouvé*.[180] He also talked about his concept of style and vision, and in January 1920, in a long article entitled 'A propos du "style" de Flaubert', he drew his readers' attention to the 'rigorous if veiled composition of his work'.[181]

It is indeed fascinating, for anyone interested in how works of literature are written, to look at the ideas which Proust incorporated into the text of *A la recherche du temps perdu*. But any creative writer who talks about his intentions cannot avoid giving hostages to fortune. Proust's five declared aims of writing a book which recaptures lost time, teaches new ways of seeing, has an internal and an architectural unity, shows the effect of time on people and societies and convinces the reader that only literature makes life worth living make up a fascinating statement of intent. But they also constitute a tall order for anyone, even the greatest genius. If Proust had not made his Narrator talk in such detail about his literary ideal, it might not have occurred to readers or critics to evoke quite such testing criteria when discussing the various qualities of *A la recherche du temps perdu*. Neither would there have been so great a temptation to point out how many important features of Proust's novel are not mentioned in *Le Temps retrouvé*. For not only does Proust's *ars poetica* omit all reference to his humour and to his treatment of homosexuality. It does not mention one of the most interesting aspects of his analysis of society, the link between exclusion and prestige.

7

Exclusion, Society and Advice

When Marcel is sent to bed early because his parents are having guests for dinner, it is from his exclusion from the mysterious pleasures about to be savoured by his mother that he suffers most acutely. It is when Odette is suddenly inaccessible to Swann that she becomes most indispensable to his peace of mind, and the experience of exclusion is an essential element in Proust's analysis of love. The transfer of this theme of exclusion and inaccessibility from his psychological analysis of Swann and Marcel to his sociological account of how society works also provides one of the most interesting strands in the unity of *A la recherche du temps perdu*. For it is not only his interest in childhood, his enthusiasm for the countryside and his fondness for digressions which make Proust the most English of French novelists. It is also his preoccupation with class. Like his Narrator, in whom Monsieur de Crécy is delighted to recognise a kindred spirit, he is someone for whom the social universe exists. One of the greatest misfortunes to have befallen the Comte de Verjus as a result of the poverty to which he has been reduced by Odette de Crécy is that of mixing with people who cannot tell the difference between a Guermantes and a Cambremer.[182] The Narrator can and does. What is even more important, he knows that it is not only birth which distinguishes the first from the second.

Even at the humble level of Combray, the valetudinarian Tante Léonie acquires immense prestige in the eyes of her servant Françoise because of the large number of people whom she refuses to welcome as visitors. The fact that she turns them away because of her terror that they will either tell her that she is so ill that she is about to die, or will try to make her break her comfortable routine by going out for a good brisk walk, makes not the slightest

difference. The fact is that she is very choosy about whom she does
and whom she does not let in, and this criterion for social prestige
is a constant in Proust's world. Swann, we are told in *La Fugitive*,
once knew 'une princesse de la Maison de France' (a princess of
the House of France) whose drawing-room lost all claims to
elegance because 'anyone at all was welcome there'.[183]
 Nothing else could really have been expected of the Bourbons,
of course. As Madame de Villeparisis observes, they lost all claim
to genuine breeding by their misalliance with the Medicis in the
sixteenth century. Similarly, one hardly needs to comment on how
non-U the Bonaparte family was. Napoleon quite ruined the
natural balance of the classes by creating an aristocracy into
which it was possible to rise by merit alone. It is therefore fully
understandable that Robert de Saint-Loup, undoubtedly the
smartest of Proust's heroes, should 'combine a democratic love of
humanity with a contempt for the nobility of the Empire'.[184]
Nobody could possibly accuse the young nobles with whom
Saint-Loup is serving at Doncières of being snobs. They are
perfectly prepared to mix with their brother officers from the
middle class, even if these young men do have Republican
sympathies, so long as they wash their hands and go to Mass. But
these noblemen understandably have a much higher regard for
Saint-Loup than for their Captain, the very capable Prince de
Borodino. For the Prince descends from one of the upstart families
ennobled by Napoleon I, and the attitude of Saint-Loup's young
companions in arms echoes that of Oriane de Guermantes, again
the most elegant of the great ladies in *A la recherche du temps perdu*.
When her husband Basin goes to pay a call on the Princesse
d'Iéna – 'as in the bridge, you know, and a battle as well, I think,'
– she stays at home. She is, as the Narrator observes, not only
'difficult to get but liked people to know as much'.[185]
 There is every hope that Proust intends this to be funny. For
when she is first struck down by the heart attack which will
eventually lead to her death, the Narrator's grandmother seeks
refuge in the lavatory of the Champs-Elysées. There, she
overhears the attendant – nicknamed 'la Marquise' – describing
in great detail to one of the keepers the principles on which she
decides who will – and, more importantly, who will not – be
allowed to use any of the closets which happen to be free. ' "I
heard the whole of the 'Marquise's' conversation with the
keeper", she told me. "Could anything have been more typical of

the Guermantes, or the Verdurins and their little clan?" '[186] she comments to the Narrator, and it is once again 'les vertus de Combray' which provide the moral standard by which to judge what happens elsewhere.

When Proust talks about society – 'le monde' – he gives the word the same immediate meaning which it had in late nineteenth-century England when Lady Bracknell reproves Algernon Moncrieff for speaking disrespectfully of it. 'Only people who can't get into it do that', she tells him, and her remark has a doubly Proustian ring. It emphasises the idea of exclusion; and it underlines the fact that society, in this context, meant first and foremost people rich enough not to have to work for a living. This means that prestige, in the analysis of it in *A la recherche du temps perdu*, is totally divorced from any idea of anyone's earning power or of their contribution to society. Nobody in Proust's world derives prestige from what they do, and even the reputation of an Elstir, a Bergotte or a Vinteuil is largely a matter of fashion. Madame de Villeparisis paints flowers beautifully, and the Baron de Charlus is an excellent pianist. But the lack of prestige of the first, like the superiority of the second, is no way linked to their talents. It is connected solely to their ability to decide who is socially acceptable and who is not. The Marquise de Villeparisis is so badly off for guests that she has to take more or less anyone who comes, and the people the Narrator meets in her salon are a very mixed crowd. Monsieur de Charlus ends up by finding nobody really acceptable apart from a few members of his own immediate family.

The higher you go in the world of *A la recherche du temps perdu*, the wider the gap becomes between social elegance and intellectual achievement. Madame Leroi, whose immense prestige is quite rightly never explained, lets the famous artists and writers who frequent her salon play poker.[187] So, too, does Oriane de Guermantes, until she finally abandons all attempts to keep up her position and mixes with artists and intellectuals. It is only the upstart Madame Verdurin, who positively chases after people to make sure that they will not abandon her at Christmas or at Easter, who makes her guests listen to Wagner.

Neither, in Proust's world, is social prestige linked to wealth. You have to be rich, and the authenticity of Monsieur de Crécy's title is of no real use to him once Odette has relieved him of all his money. Both mothers and sons are very interested in the fortune of any prospective bride, and Robert de Saint-Loup's mother, the saintly Madame de Marsantes, is anxious to find 'an immensely rich' wife for her son. She is consequently quite happy for him to marry Gilberte de Forcheville, and seems unperturbed by her future daughter-in-law's Jewish ancestry . But money alone is not enough. The Duc de Guermantes, one is pleased to learn, is a multimillionaire, 'formidably rich in a world where people were becoming steadily less so'.[188] But the man whom the Narrator's grandfather calls 'young Verdurin' has kept firm hold of his millions as well, and yet belongs to a totally different social world. An important minor theme in Swann's love affair with Odette is the immense distance which he has to descend in order to meet her at the Verdurin salon, and Madame Verdurin's dislike of him has its origin in the fact that he is always 'ensconced with La Trémoilles, the Laumes and all that lot'. These are people whom Madame Verdurin would very much like to get to know, but whom she recognises – in the 1880s, at any rate; after the First World War, matters will change – as belonging to a social world from which she will for ever remain excluded.

In the section of *Le Temps retrouvé* in which Proust outlines his ideas on what the novel ought to be, he writes that 'there is a feeling for generality which, in the future writer, itself picks out what is general and can for that reason enter into a work of art'.[189] In this respect, *A la recherche du temps perdu* can usefully be read by the side of more empirically based studies such as Vance Packard's *The Status Seekers*, or Paul Fussell's *Caste Marks*. For like them, it deals with a society – in the general as well as in the Wildean sense – which is rich enough to look for something other than money as a source of prestige. At the same time, it also carries these studies a stage further by suggesting a more general principle on which prestige and hierarchy can be based. It is true that there is an important initial difference. Unlike the citizens of the affluent and officially egalitarian twentieth-century America, the members of Proust's world can look for prestige in birth. When Monsieur Verdurin suggests that Monsieur de Cambremer, who is a Marquis, might be superior to a mere Baron, Charlus not only reminds us of the immense gap which separates two families which appear to be the same because they both happen to include the particle 'de'. He somewhat haughtily points out that he is also 'duc de Brabant, damoiseau de Montargis, prince d'Oléron, de Carency, de Viareggio et des Dunes' (Duke of

Brabant, Squire of Montargis, Prince of Oléron, of Carency, of Viareggio and of the Dunes).[190]

But birth is not everything. Madam Leroi, whose failure to invite Madame de Villeparisis to dinner is the most painful thorn in the Marquise's side, has no formal titles of nobility at all. Yet she is clearly at the very top of the social tree, in contrast to the unfortunate Princess of the Blood, referred to by Swann, who fell right to the bottom by letting every Tom, Dick and Harry – or, one should say, every Jane, Margaret and Sue – into her drawing room. For just as it is a disadvantage for Odette Swann to have a drawing room frequented mainly by men, it is a mark of Oriane de Guermantes's prestige that she is able to exclude the women whom Odette would like to attract. She even entrusts her husband Basin with the mission of explaining to the Princesse de Parme just why the strain which her existing social obligations place upon her health will continue to prevent her from receiving the Marquise de Souvré.

If you read *A la recherche du temps perdu* even partly as an autobiography, it is easy to see why Proust finds the essence of prestige in exclusion. The experience leading up to 'le drame du coucher' made him particularly sensitive to what it meant to be missed out, and it could even be argued that the portrait which he gives of French society is a distorted one precisely as a result of his private obsessions. For he did, after all, live through the period which saw the final defeat of the old, monarchical, aristocratic France and its replacement by the parliamentary democracy of the Third Republic. But the Republicans come even lower in the social pecking order than the members of the Imperial aristocracy. Françoise, who passes into the service of the Narrator and his family after the death of Tante Léonie, can scarcely believe that a Marquis like Saint-Loup can have Republican sympathies in politics. It is true that this is because she is a Royalist, but the Narrator himself comments that in the days of his early childhood 'everything that pertained to conservative society was worldly – *mondain*, fashionable – and no respectable salon would ever have opened its doors to a Republican'.[191] Since the inner chronology of *A la recherche du temps perdu* gives the year of the Narrator's birth at about 1880, this means that the social acceptability of the Republicans was ten to twenty years behind their assumption of political power, and Proust's world is one where any political or financial power exercised by classes or individuals is as irrelevant to their prestige as their wealth, intelligence or artistic achievements. Proust's social world is certainly a very odd one. Just as everyone at Combray knows enough about Lesbianism to be aware of what Mademoiselle Vinteuil is up to, the snobbery about titles of which Proust himself was so often accused in his lifetime seems to recur at every level in French society. The obscure provincial lawyers whom the Narrator and his grandmother meet in their hotel at Balbec are obsessed by aristocratic titles, just like the young officers serving with Robert de Saint-Loup at Doncières. But what most counts for these lawyers – and their wives – is the fact that while some of them will be invited to visit Madame de Cambremer, others will certainly not. Going somewhere may not in fact be all that exciting. It might even be rather a bore. Not being invited is a tragedy.

Whether the experience described in 'le drame du coucher' was Proust's own or not, it is certainly depicted in the text of *A la recherche du temps perdu* as having imprinted itself in the mind of the Narrator in two quite indelible ways. In the first place, it made him aware that his mother might stop loving him. This awareness was, one hopes, if it was Proust's own, based upon an illusion. But the feelings to which it gave rise were no less real. They lie behind the terrifying consciousness of other people's freedom which inspired his analysis of jealousy. As I have argued in Chapters 3 and 4, it is the frustrated desire for possession which is the driving force behind Swann's feelings for Odette or Marcel's need for Albertine, and this frustration stems from the knowledge of the power which other people's freedom gives them to stop loving us in return. At the same time, the knowledge that he might be shut out of his mother's love – again, one hopes, based upon an illusion – gave Proust the equally terrifying awareness of what it was not to be needed. For it is through their ability to do without us that other people acquire most prestige in our eyes; and it is this equation of prestige with the power to exclude which makes *A la recherche du temps perdu* more than the portrait of an absurdly restricted section of what Thorstein Veblen called 'higher barbarian culture'. Indeed, it is this equation which enables Proust to fulfil his ambition of presenting a general law. If you reduce social prestige to its chemical essence, it does indeed lie in the power to tell other people that you can do without them. Everything else apart from this particular manifestation of human freedom can be remedied. You can always make yourself richer, more powerful, more cultured or more knowledgeable. You cannot make somebody else need you if they don't want to, and Tom Sawyer derives considerable benefit from his understanding of how dearly some people will pay to overcome the stigma of exclusion. By his initial refusal to allow any of his friends to help him whitewash Miss Polly's fence, he ends up by making them pay for the privilege of being included in what might otherwise have seemed an unattractive task.

So much would be obvious from the novel even if we knew nothing of Proust's life or were able to believe absolutely in the doctrine enunciated in *Contre Sainte-Beuve* of the separation between the man who lives and the author who writes. The unity of *A la recherche du temps perdu* is not only one of style and vision. It is a unity given to it by its emotional climate, a climate which pervades the analysis of prestige just as it does the equation between love and jealousy. Quite how conscious Proust was of this climate is perhaps open to question. What is equally intriguing is whether or not Proust was aware of how useful certain passages of *A la recherche du temps perdu* might be as a guide to how we, his late-twentieth-century readers, might conduct ourselves in our own society. For it is surprising to see how much advice Proust's novel has to offer to anyone living in an environment where the natural tendency of human beings to think primarily of themselves is masked by an elaborate code of formal politeness.

The crucially instructive scene occurs in *Le côté des Guermantes* and is prefaced by a remark about the gap between the behaviour of the Guermantes family and their real feelings. ' "But you are our equal, if not our superior", the Guermantes seemed, in all their actions, to be saying; and they said it in the nicest way imaginable, in order to be loved and admired, but not to be believed.'[192] Anyone who did believe them might make a serious mistake, just as you might make a serious mistake at your first meeting with a British senior civil servant. For if you accepted at face value the repeated insistence on your intellectual superiority, or actually took up the invitation to 'drop in and have lunch next time you are in Whitehall', you might well find your name suddenly disappearing from the waiting list of the Great and the Good.

The incident which brings out these dangers and emphasises how important it is to understand the real function of good manners occurs when the Narrator is at a reception for the King and Queen of England during their visit to Paris. The Duc de Guermantes is escorting the Queen to the buffet, and espies the Narrator from afar off. He makes the most energetic signs of welcome, so much so that anyone uninitiated in what Proust calls 'the exact value of the language, spoken or mute, of aristocratic affability' might have felt fully justified in accepting the invitation to join the royal party. But the Narrator restricts himself to making a deep bow before proceeding on his way, and the appreciation which the Guermantes subsequently show for his discretion attains previously untold heights of enthusiasm. Oriane mentions it in the most flattering terms to the Narrator's mother, and is most careful not to suggest that he should have come forward in response to such apparently insistent beckoning. 'Had I written a masterpiece', comments the Narrator, 'the Guermantes would have given me less credit for it than I earned by that bow'.[193]

The Narrator's ability to read the social signs correctly thus enables him to profit from the advantage which he also acquires by happening, on the first few occasions when he is invited to dinner, to be already committed elsewhere. But it is not enough to be able thus to accede, by a happy accident, immediately but temporarily to the first rank of the Elect. You still have to step very carefully if you are to avoid relegation. When the Marquis de Vaugoubert and his wife are invited to a reception held to celebrate the alliance between France and Theodosia which Monsieur de Vaugoubert has been instrumental in arranging, she lets him down very badly. She could easily have used her influence with the King and Queen of that country, whom she had known for years, to ensure that they spent their whole time talking to the wife of the President of the Republic and to the wives of the other social nonentities and unfashionable Republican politicians who happened to be there. Had she done this discreetly, 'using all her influence in order to appear to have none',[194] her husband would have advanced even further in the career for which he has already made so many sacrifices. But she misses the opportunity and keeps the royal couple to herself. Neither she nor her husband can explain the rapidity of his premature and involuntary retirement.

Proust's pessimism about human nature thus gives him an acute awareness of the advantages of *realpolitik*, so much so that he anticipates de Gaulle's description of great powers as 'cold-blooded monsters' ('des monstres froids'). Nation states, writes Proust, are 'creatures of selfishness and cunning, which can be tamed only by force, by consideration of their material interests which may drive them to murder',[195] and there is a sense in which it can be misleading to take Proust's official lack of enthusiasm for realism too literally. For *A la recherche du temps perdu* is not only realistic in its minutely detailed account of how memory, vision and perception actually work. It is realistic in the sense of presenting us with a world which is remarkably similar to that of Racine or Laclos. It is one where quarter is neither asked nor given in the quest for personal satisfaction, but in which the struggle is governed by a complex set of very clear formal rules.

These come out very plainly in the long description in *Sodome et Gomorrhe* of how Prince von Faffenheim-Munsterburg-Weinigin – generally known, for obvious reasons, simply as 'le Prince Von' – goes about ensuring his election to the Académie des Sciences Morales. He knows that Monsieur de Norpois commands enough votes to make this election a certainty. But he is equally well aware that neither a straightforward request nor the proposal of a direct bargain will do any good. He tries a number of different tactics, and it is some time before he hits on the right one. This is to request that the Marquise de Villeparisis – Monsieur de Norpois's mistress – be asked to accept an invitation to attend the smallest and most insignificant supper party which is to be held to celebrate the visit to Paris of the King and Queen of England. The measured readiness with which Monsieur de Norpois greets this suggestion fills the Prince Von with delight at the realisation that he has at last hit upon the right key with which to make the lock yield, and there are obvious parallels for the English reader with the practice of Squaring as set out in F. M. Cornford's *Microcosmographia Academica*:

After walking five paces in the opposite direction you should call me back, and begin with the words, 'Oh, by the way, if you should happen . . .' The nature of Your Job must then be vaguely indicated, without mentioning names; and it should be treated by both parties as a matter of very small importance. You should hint that I am a very influential person, and that the whole thing is a secret between us. Then we shall part as before, and I shall call you back and introduce the subject of My Job, in the same formula. By observing this procedure we shall emphasise the fact that there is *no connection whatever* between my supporting your Job and your supporting mine. This absence of connection is the essential feature of Squaring.[196]

It is, once again, all some distance from the 'petite madeleine', though perhaps less so from 'le drame du coucher'. If you are afraid of being shut out, you become peculiarly sensitive to the ways in which you might annoy the people on whose good will your acceptability depends. In *A la recherche du temps perdu*, this awareness comes out in the frequent notation of how annoying we can all be in minor as well as in major ways, and in a number of epigrams which remind you of yet another French writer of the seventeenth century. For when the Narrator observes that the really difficult problem in being on a diet is to avoid imposing it on other people,[197] you once again think that La Rochefoucauld has come back to life. Neither is it difficult, once you have absorbed the pessimism common to Proust and La Rochefoucauld, to invent comparable epigrams to sum up the lessons presented in *A la recherche du temps perdu*. Just as the Narrator comments that 'there is no one we appreciate more than a person who combines with other great virtues that of placing those virtues wholeheartedly at the service of our vices',[198] one could well imagine him using the unfortunate end of Monsieur de Vaugoubert's career to drive home the maxim that we nowhere show ourselves better qualified to exercise influence than in our ability to do so in total secret.

Proust recognises that the constant tendency of human beings to think primarily of themselves makes them touchy and easily offended. This is a good principle on which to base one's social behaviour, for good occasions as well as bad. For when the Narrator's grandmother makes a present to Saint-Loup of her Proudhon letters, he cannot prevent himself from blushing violently. If you are unaccustomed to such acts of kindness, you will make a really excellent impression by the spontaneity of your pleasure when something like this does happen. When Saint-Loup makes his famous run along the benches of the restaurant, in *Le côté de Guermantes*, in order to place a cloak around the Narrator's shoulders, his athletic generosity stands out all the more clearly because of its contrast with the rudeness previously extended to the Narrator. Before his prestige rose so markedly with the arrival of his aristocratic friend, the Narrator had been ignored by everyone and placed in a draught.

While Proust would obviously like everybody to behave with the spontaneous generosity of Saint-Loup, or in accordance with the more settled kindness of 'les vertus de Combray', he accepts that they generally won't. He does not therefore disapprove of the way good manners can mask the fact that such behaviour is relatively rare. He is not writing as Jean-Jacques Rousseau, and does not share the desire of Alceste in *Le Misanthrope* to denounce social hypocrisy. The ability to interpret what other people really mean, which enables the Narrator to make such an excellent impression on the Guermantes, is a necessary part of the lubricating oil which enables the wheels of society to keep turning smoothly over. It is not Jesuitical – in the bad sense of the word – to take precautions in order to ensure that you do not annoy people. With a little more thought for their feelings you might make them happier and you yourself more popular.

There are indeed plenty of hints in *A la recherche du temps perdu* as to how we might improve our own conduct. We should, for example, avoid the deplorable habit of the Marquis d'Argencourt of indulging in 'that peculiar form of insolence which consists in ascribing to the other person an opinion which one plainly knows he does not share'.[199] It is a piece of advice which might prevent eminent Professors of Civil Engineering from telling their colleagues in Arts Faculties how much 'you cultivated people despise those of us who get our hands dirty when we go to work'. Only fools, Proust reminds us, keep trying to obtain a reply to a letter which they ought never to have sent in the first place. If somebody doesn't reply the first time, it is sensible to assume that you are being a bore. If you decline an invitation to dinner because you know that your presence will be annoying to one of the guests, it is self-defeating to let anyone else know why you are not going to be there. When Proust writes of how much more annoying it is for a clever man to bear the contempt of a fool than of someone whose intelligence equals his own,[200] you know you should watch out. You will meet a lot of people who do not think you are very bright. You should avoid giving them the impression that you do not think highly of them.

It is easy to take advice of this kind from Proust. Nobody, you feel, has either a better grasp of how annoying we can all be in minor as well as in major ways or a greater ability to understand what we find annoying in other people. There would, for example, be no need to explain to him the disappointment you feel

when the person to whom you have sent a copy of your latest book
limits his reply to the observation that there is a misprint on page
213. But it would be a mistake to imagine that his advice will
enable you to obtain anything you really want. The Narrator
becomes the guest without whom no dinner party at the
Guermantes' is a success only after he has ceased to worship
Oriane de Guermantes from afar. In his childhood, he had seen
the Guermantes residence as the incarnation of all the poetry and
magic of the French nobility, the sacred dwelling-place of their
medieval splendours. He had longed to be admitted there, and the
force of his desire had been enough to ensure his exclusion.

It is also fortunate, in this respect, that he behaves on the first
time he dines at the Guermantes' in a most peculiar way. He has
heard that they have a magnificent collection of Elstir's paintings,
and asks permission, immediately on arrival, to go and look at
them. The Duke is delighted to be of service and the Narrator is so
enraptured by the new world that the paintings reveal to him that
he completely forgets the passage of time. But far from making
himself unpopular with his host and hostess by keeping them and
their guests waiting three-quarters of an hour for dinner, he finds
himself treated with even greater respect than before. The Duke
insists on asking him for his views on Elstir. The opportunity to
display his excellent manners by extending this additional
courtesy to his guest does not displease him. What is important is
that the Narrator has not tried to ingratiate himself with his new
friends by an undue display of enthusiasm to meet their
aristocratic guests. He has not alienated them by an excess of zeal
in the way that he terrified Gilberte Swann by his desire to know
everything about her. For when, at the end of the novel, they
become close friends and look back at the events of the past, she
explains to him just why the love which he felt for her in his teens
was doomed to come to nothing: 'You were too fond of me', she
says. 'I felt you were prying into everything I did.'[201]

If you take Proust as your guide through the thickets of the
social world, you will not go far wrong. You will anticipate the
precise way in which other people want you to fit into their plans,
and take particular care never to be there when you are not
wanted. But in your private, emotional life, you will always find
yourself in the paradoxical situation where you can get what you
want only when you no longer want it. If Marcel had been able to
tell his mother to stop coming up to fuss over him after he had gone

to bed, his childhood would have been pure bliss. If Swann had been able to treat Odette with the slight gruffness of manner which she seemed to find quite attractive in l'oncle Adolphe, or with the touch of brutality which one suspects was occasionally her lot with de Forcheville, he would have had no problems. But Proust is also sufficient of a realist to know that nobody who is really involved emotionally with another person can behave like that. There is no question, for him, of human beings being able to take control of their own lives, and it is probably for this reason that *A la recherche du temps perdu* contains so few references to the writers of the eighteenth century.

8
Humour, Observation and Realism

With the possible exception of Marcel's mother, almost everybody in *A la recherche du temps perdu* is seen at some time or other as funny. When she accompanies him to Balbec, for example, Marcel's grandmother – a faithful disciple of Rousseau – cannot bear the idea that the great bay window in the dining room of the hotel should be preventing the healthy sea air from coming in. So she surreptitiously opens one of the panes, with the result that she sets flying, together with the menus, 'the newspapers, veils and hats of all the people at the other tables, while she herself, fortified by the celestial draught, remained calm and smiling like Saint Blandina amid the torrent of invective which, increasing my sense of isolation and misery, those contemptuous, dishevelled, furious visitors combined to pour on us'.[202]

The humour here is essentially kindly, and addressed to one of the most attractive characters in the book. In 1891, Proust said in reply to one of the questionnaires which it was fashionable to complete in polite society that the greatest tragedy of his life would have been not to have known his mother and grandmother,[203] and this autobiographical detail comes out very clearly in almost every aspect of the novel. But even in the most tragic scene in *A la recherche du temps perdu*, when Marcel's grandmother eventually dies, Proust cannot resist a joke at the expense of one of his favourite targets, the medical profession. The situation has become so desperate that the family finally agrees to call in the eminent specialist Professor X. He arrives with his bag, 'packed with all the colds and coughs of his other patients, like Aeolus's goatskin', and insists on inspecting everybody's nose. Grandma refuses point blank, and is shown to have been quite right to do so. The rest of the family finally if reluctantly agree to allow the eminent Professor to verify his theory that every illness stems from some kind of nasal infection, and he proves to be mistaken only on a matter of timing. The following day, everyone is suffering from catarrh, and, 'when, in the street, he ran into my father doubled up with a cough, he smiled to think that an ignorant layman might suppose the attack to be due to his intervention. He had examined us when we were already ill.'[204]

As a lifelong invalid, and a member of a distinguished medical family, it was perhaps natural that Proust should follow the tradition so well established by Molière and make fun of the medical profession. *A la recherche du temps perdu* deals with very much the same moment in medical history as the one satirised by Shaw in *The Doctor's Dilemma* in 1906, and Professor X is a worthy contemporary of Cutler Walpole and his conviction that every illness could be cured by the removal of the nuciform sac, or even of Sir Ralph Bloomfield Bonnington, with his enviable ability to effect a cure 'by the mere incompatibility of disease or anxiety with his welcome presence'. But as his portrait of Dr Cottard shows, Proust's humour is more complex than that of Shaw, and is used to reinforce his very realistic awareness of how complex and many-sided human beings are. For when we first meet him, in Madame Verdurin's drawing room, Cottard is rather a fool. He suffers from an intense provincial nervousness which makes him wear a perpetual half-smile in case the remarks made to him in Parisian society turn out to be jokes, and makes himself ridiculous by religiously following his mother's advice and pouncing on every unfamiliar expression in order to demand a definition. But neither this nor his habit of making idiotic puns prevents him from curing Marcel of a very serious illness by putting him on a milk diet, and his success makes the whole family realise that 'this imbecile was a great physician'. Yet Proust is also aware of how professional success can spoil as well as improve talent. When, in the later volumes, Cottard reaches the top of his profession, he becomes as incompetent as any Harley Street knight. A Grand Duke, on holiday near Balbec, is suffering from an inflamed eye. Cottard, who has become a famous specialist in blood-poisoning, decides to treat him in accordance with his speciality. He comes to see him in return for a wad of hundred franc notes – 'the Professor never saw anyone for less', the Narrator adds – and puts the inflammation down to a toxic condition. He 'prescribes a disintoxicant treatment', but the inflammation disappears only when the local doctor removes a speck of dust from the Grand Duke's eye.[205]

It is thus professions as well as individuals who serve as targets for Proust's humour in *A la recherche du temps perdu*, and the representative of the Diplomatic Service, Monsieur de Norpois, is so splendid an example of what Proust diagnoses as 'l'esprit du gouvernement' (the governmental mind) that he has become, in the world of the French novel, almost the equivalent of Polonius in that of the English theatre. But since thoughts on the nature of literature are never far from Proust's mind in any section of *A la recherche du temps perdu*, Monsieur de Norpois is also made to encourage the Narrator's literary ambitions in a way which shows how his total lack of originality in political matters works just as well in other contexts. He mentions the son of one of his colleagues who, having decided to leave the Quai d'Orsay 'où la voie lui était pourtant toute tracée par son père' (although the way had been paved for him by his father), decided to write. 'Two years ago', de Norpois observes, adding that he is, of course, considerably older than Marcel, 'this young man produced "a book about the Sense of the Infinite on the western shore of Lake Victoria Nyanza", and added to it this year "a short treatise, less weighty but written with a lively, not to say a cutting pen, on the Repeating Rifle in the Bulgarian Army" '.[206]

Monsieur de Norpois is undoubtedly one of Proust's great creations, the equivalent for his profession and social class of what the servant Françoise is for hers. He does in fact greatly appreciate Françoise's cooking, and comments to the Narrator's parents, on the memorable evening when he comes to dinner, how rare it is to find 'a spiced beef in which the aspic doesn't taste of glue and the beef has caught the flavour of the carrots'. He is – perhaps understandably – less enthusiastic about the pineapple and truffle salad, and rather disappoints his hostess by fastening on it 'the penetrating gaze of a trained observer' and eating it 'with the inscrutable discretion of a diplomat, without disclosing his opinion'.[207] You need a moment's reflection on what such a dish must have tasted like to see why this scene is funny.

If, like the publisher to whom Proust first sent the typescript of *Du côté de chez Swann*, and like a number of readers since, you have some initial difficulty in getting into Proust's world, it is not a bad idea to use the excellent index which concludes the Pléiade edition, or the synopsis at the end of the most recent English translation, simply in order to read through the various scenes in which Monsieur de Norpois appears. This will not only enable you to familiarise yourself with some of the other characters, especially the Narrator's family and the Marquise de Villeparisis; it will make you aware of the flavour of the variety of linguistic humour running through the whole of *A la recherche du temps perdu*. For even the portrait of Albertine, at least when the Narrator first meets her, gives Proust an opportunity of practising one of his favourite stylistic devices, that of leaving the last and most telling word until the end. Her way of speaking, we are told, produces 'a drawling, nasal sound, into the composition of which there entered perhaps a provincial heredity, a juvenile affectation of British phlegm, the teaching of a foreign governess and a congestive hypertrophy of the mucus of the nose'.[208]

It is, not surprisingly, more difficult to find conveniently compact quotations to illustrate the verbal humour associated with Monsieur de Norpois. For not only does he personally tend to make fairly long speeches. He is also the cause of even longer speeches in others, as when Monsieur de Charlus, in *Le Temps retrouvé*, devotes some two thousand words to an analysis of how the need to present a permanently optimistic view of events during the First World War has led Monsieur de Norpois to constantly replace the future tense by the verb 'to know'. As Charlus observes, this makes him write sentences such as 'the region of the Lakes would not know how to fail to fall speedily into the hands of the allies' when he means that he hopes the allies will soon capture them, and Proust's anticipation of Orwell's analysis of the misuse of language for political ends gives these sections of *A la recherche du temps perdu* a disconcertingly mid-twentieth-century flavour. The same is true of the more throwaway humour whereby the Narrator comments on how alarmed he is, in August and September 1914, by the speed at which the French military victories are drawing closer to Paris.[209]

The presentation of French society in *A la recherche du temps perdu* becomes even more critical in the pages dealing with the First World War than it is in *Le côté de Guermantes*. Even Gilberte de Saint Loup is used to illustrate its hypocrisy and self-deception, and Proust's anxiety to underline these characteristics even leads him to change the geographical location of Combray. This moves from South-West of Chartres, the position of Illiers itself, to a point in the East of France, somewhere between Laon and

Rheims. It thus becomes part of the battlefield between the French and German armies, and a place of such strategic importance that the Germans lose more than six hundred thousand men in what Gilberte describes in a letter to Marcel as an unsuccessful attempt to take it. She goes there in September 1914, initially in order to escape with her daughter from the first German air raids on Paris. A little later on, however, she writes a second letter to the Narrator in which this prudent precaution is presented as inspired by her sense of duty towards her tenants at Tansonville. This amusing but very human inconsistency also has the advantage of being more in keeping with the rather sly and deceitful personality which Gilberte had revealed in *A l'ombre des jeunes filles en fleurs* – doubtless something she had inherited from her mother – and what Jean-François Revel called 'le bourrage de crâne et l'émulation chauvine' (wartime propaganda and chauvinistic rivalry).[210] This swept over France during the 1914–18 war and certainly seems to have confirmed Proust in his disillusioned view of human nature. For Madame Verdurin, never one of his more attractive characters, is used to even more critically comic effect than Gilberte is in her flight to Combray in the way she reacts to the sinking of the *Lusitania* in May 1917.

Since she would otherwise suffer unbearable migraines, Madame Verdurin has a special prescription made for her by Cottard – something which, as the Narrator observes, is more difficult to obtain than the appointment of a General – so that she can still have her morning croissant made with butter.

The first of these special croissants arrived on the morning on which the newspapers reported the sinking of the *Lusitania*. As she dipped it in her coffee and gave a series of little flicks to her newspaper with one hand so as to make it stay open without her having to remove her other hand from the cup, 'How horrible!' she said. 'This is something more horrible than the most terrible stage tragedy.' But the death of all these drowned people must have been reduced a thousand million times before it impinged upon her, for even as, with her mouth full, she made these distressful observations, the expression which spread over her face, brought there (one must suppose) by the savour of that so precious remedy against headaches, the croissant, was in fact one of satisfaction and pleasure.[211]

Madame Verdurin is someone who is always presented as a figure of fun, and the slightly bitchy tone noticeable in Proust's presentation of his society hostesses may be linked to his homosexuality. The famous passage at the beginning of *Sodome et Gomorrhe* makes an unaccustomed use of four adjectives to describe homosexuals as forming 'une colonie orientale, cultivée, musicienne, médisante' – an oriental, cultivated, musical and sharp-tongued colony – and this final adjective is certainly consistent with the portrait of how Oriane de Guermantes 'languished whenever people spoke of the beauty of any woman other than herself' and leaned back 'delighted by this analysis of her character' as her husband Basin explains just how deeply her sensitive nature was hurt by Swann's inconsiderate marriage to the socially impossible Odette de Crécy.[212] The laughter to which Sidonie Verdurin is made to give rise is often of a cruder and more direct type. On one occasion, we are told, she herself laughed so heartily at a joke made by one of the guests in her little coterie that she gave an unexpected reality to the expression 'rire à se décrocher la mâchoire' and actually dislocated her jaw in her mirth. As a result, she took to adopting a silent mimicry of laughter in which she would:

> utter a shrill cry, shut tight her little bird-like eyes, which were beginning to be clouded over by a cataract, and quickly, as though she had only just time to avoid some indecent sight or to parry a mortal blow, burying her face in her hands, which completely engulfed it and hid it from view, would appear to be struggling to suppress, to annihilate, a laugh which, had she succumbed to it, must inevitably have left her inanimate. So, stupified with the gaiety of the 'faithful', drunk with good-fellowship, scandal and asseveration, Mme Verdurin, perched on her high seat like a cage-bird whose biscuit has been steeped in mulled wine, would sit aloft and sob with affability.[213]

Madame Verdurin's supposed sensitivity to artistic emotion is also so great that it is in perpetual danger of moving her to tears, and these would infallibly lead, if certain precautions were not taken, to her being afflicted with a severe head cold. But one of the late Professor Cottard's pupils – 'Ah yes, there we are, he died, he was carried off very quickly, poor fellow. He'd killed enough people for it to be his turn to have a bit of his own medicine'[214] –

advises her, before a concert, to grease her nose with rhino-gomenol. The 'far from pleasant odour' of this specific thus announces to the whole world the possible extent of the suffering she is prepared to undergo for the sake of Art. As in the gentler and more Dickensian portrait of Tante Léonie, Marcel's aunt at Combray, there is again a possible autobiographical link with Proust himself. Admittedly, the illness which obliged Tante Léonie to spend the whole of her life in bed is never clearly defined. Since her principal terror is that her husband might suddenly come back to life and force her to go out for a healthy walk, the presupposition is that those of her visitors who earn her displeasure by suggesting that there is nothing very much wrong with her are probably right. But although Proust had quite genuine medical as well as artistic reasons for spending the last eleven years of his life in bed, there is an element of self-satire in his description of Tante Léonie, as well as perhaps yet another nod in the direction of his views on the inescapable nature of heredity. The sensitivity of Madame Verdurin to colds and bronchitis also gives her an interesting similarity to Proust himself, and one which takes on further connotations when you read the passage in *Jean Santeuil* about how enjoyable it is to be in bed reading a freshly printed copy of *Le Figaro* with an equally freshly made croissant conveniently to hand.[215]

There is nevertheless no need to bring in the private life of the man who wrote *A la recherche du temps perdu* to see the Narrator Marcel cast in a comic role. Proust does this quite deliberately on a number of occasions, and it is a pity that there are not more of them. For if you change your angle of vision very slightly, the spectacle of a young man keeping his girl friend as a prisoner in his apartment and worrying incessantly about whether or not she is a Lesbian is not without its funny side. Neither is it always possible to suppress a wry smile at the frequency with which the Narrator comes back to the theme of the impermanent and fleeting nature of the self. From a philosophical point of view, this is one of the central ideas in *A la recherche du temps perdu*, and it places Proust in the same tradition as the David Hume who said that all he found when he looked into his mind was a 'bundle of sensations'. Within the overall framework of the novel, it also adds another reason why the episode of the 'petite madeleine' is so important: it tells the Narrator that he is still basically the same person that he was when a child, and that the various changes which he has undergone since then are to some extent illusory. It is almost, he suggests, a proof of the immortality of the soul. It is nevertheless rather strange that a book which speaks so often about the impermanent nature of the self should present, in the hero-Narrator Marcel, a person who shows such a remarkable sameness of personality at every stage in his life's history.

There are, it is true, a number of episodes in *A la recherche du temps perdu* in which you feel that Proust is rather more deliberately showing his Narrator in a comic light. Marcel carries his adolescent worship of Gilberte to the point where he wants to be as bald as her father and rubs his eyes in an attempt to make them as weary and bloodshot as those of Swann. When his father comments on how idiotic this makes him, we laugh at the familiar spectacle of the awkward age and the parental reactions it evokes. Later on, we share Oriane's impatience at this young man's persistence in being there to greet her every time she goes out, and Marcel's occasional recourse to alcohol also gives rise to a scene in which he makes us laugh because we suddenly see him from the outside. He drinks so much that he goes into a positive mystical ecstasy at the blueness of the blind in the railway carriage in which he is travelling and the kindliness of the guard collecting the tickets. It is only as he begins to sober up that he and the reader become aware of the fact that he has been sitting there with his mouth hanging half open.[216]

But you can laugh at people, emotions and events only if you can stand aside and look at what is happening with a certain emotional detachment. Proust is able to do this with the female characters in his novel only so long as the Marcel to whom he attributes so many of his characteristics is not in love with them. Sex, in *A la recherche du temps perdu*, is too heavy with potential anguish to allow more than the occasional joke about it, and one regrets at times the absence of even the involuntary humour which occurs in Ian Fleming's *Goldfinger* when James Bond shows Pussy Galore the error of her ways and gives Marcel a retrospective lesson in how he ought to have behaved towards Albertine. For most of the time, Marcel is also too bound up with his own artistic and emotional problems to introduce any humour into his account of his own sexual behaviour. *La Prisonnière* and *La Fugitive* have none of the slightly mocking tone in which he writes about his early relationship with Gilberte.

There are, indeed, a number of occasions in *A la recherche du temps perdu* where Proust's decision to tell the story in the first person singular rather lets him down, and these are not limited to the inconsistencies which I have mentioned in Chapter 1. For while it is possible to accept that the older members of the Guermantes family might treasure the Narrator's company for qualities which, as he modestly observes, he does not know he possesses – the only real explanation seems to be that he was unavailable on the occasion when they first decided to invite him – it is much harder to see why the athletic, elegant and aristocratic Robert de Saint-Loup should find him so irreplaceable a companion. For he has such a high esteem for his friend Marcel's intelligence that he insists, during the latter's visit to him in barracks at Doncières, that his brother officers remain absolutely silent in order to listen to this civilian oracle's pronouncements.[217] This does not provide an account of service life which rings immediately true.

Part of the problem, of course, is that the dominant tradition in English comic literature is one of the first person narrator whose self-deprecation is part of his charm. The English reader who comes to Proust with the memories of his own literature still very much in his mind thus has some difficulty in adjusting to a first person narrative in which the 'I' is so self-absorbed and so given to self-congratulation. The Pip of *Great Expectations* is totally aware of how much of a snob he has become when he moves to London and can no longer look upon Joe Gargery as anything but a vulgar blacksmith, and there is a moral note to his comic self-criticism which could profitably have found its way into *A la recherche du temps perdu*. We should find Bertie Wooster much less attractive and very much less amusing if he did not recognise how mentally negligible he really is, and it is a rather embarrassing contrast to be told by Proust's Narrator how he has inherited from his grandmother a total incapacity to bear a grudge. Neither does he make himself all that attractive when he reminds us that the friendship which others bear him is really rather tiresome because of the way it distracts him from his vocation as an artist.

It is also hard to feel an overwhelming sympathy with the Narrator Marcel when he tells us how he has 'always trusted the common people'. For this particular piece of self-congratulation does rather jar when placed side by side with his earlier comment on how the violinist, Charles Morel, though the son of his great-uncle Adolphe's valet, was so well dressed that he 'did not look like a servant'.[218] The Narrator's claim to 'trust the common people' is even harder to reconcile with his obvious resentment that this young man should have 'affected to speak to me as to an equal'. And when the Narrator insists for a second time on telling us about his lack of *amour-propre* (self-importance) you are not only tempted to use one of Odette de Crécy's favourite English expressions and say that he is 'fishing for compliments'. You are also reminded of how Josephine, in Gilbert and Sullivan's *H.M.S. Pinafore*, knew that Sir Joseph Porter, K.G.B. was a great and good man because he had told her so himself.

Neither is this the only passage in *A la recherche du temps perdu* in which the Narrator makes us smile in a way that Proust never intended. What makes revolutions so unjust, we are told in *Le Temps retrouvé*, is the fact that only the nobility respects 'clever men who are not of good family' – or, as the French version puts it, has 'ce respect des hommes intelligents pas nés (qui ne fleurit vraiment que dans la noblesse et rend les révolutions si injustes)'.[219] This remark is on the same level as the assertion in *La Prisonnière* to the effect that the revolutionary spirit stems 'from an embittered love for the nobility', and rather reminds you of the description of Madame Bontemps arriving in the Faubourg Saint-Germain like a newly hatched chicken still shaking off the fragments of the unfashionable shell from which she has recently hatched.[220] For Proust the novelist occasionally bespatters his disillusioned account of what the aristocracy is really like with fragments from his earlier incarnation as Proust the upwardly mobile man about town. The result is a little disconcerting.

For most of the time, of course, and especially when he is deliberately setting out to be funny, Proust much more obviously knows what he is doing. There are marvellous scenes of sustained comedy, as when Marcel and his grandmother meet the Princesse de Luxembourg on the promenade at Balbec. In her anxiety not to appear 'enthroned in a higher sphere than ours', the Princess looks at them with eyes that are so infused with benevolence that the Narrator foresees the moment when she might 'put out her hand and stroke us like lovable beasts who had poked our heads out at her through the bars of our cage at the Zoo'.[221] An itinerant vendor comes along, selling cakes, sweets and biscuits. The Princess buys the only article he has left, a loaf of rye bread, and holds it out to the Narrator, telling him it is for his grandmother. Doubtless, he comments, she 'thought my pleasure would be more complete if there were no intermediary between me and the animals', and this prolonged study of aristocratic amiability and condescension is one of the best examples of the comic detachment with which Proust can and generally does present his aristocrats. There is a comparable study of what the Narrator calls in *La Fugitive* 'cette morgue qu'on croyait réparer par une scrupuleuse amabilité' (that haughtiness for which they thought to atone by a scrupulous affability)[222] in the behaviour of a lady to whom Marcel is introduced on the first occasion when he dines with the Guermantes, and whom he eventually discovers to be the Princesse de Parme. Even before Marcel has been officially introduced to her by the Duke, the lady in question has started to smile at him in the most agreeable way possible, and once the Duke has told her who he is, she begins to speak to him in terms of the greatest affection. Unfortunately, the inefficiency of the Duke's introduction has prevented Marcel from discovering who the lady actually is, and he is initially quite baffled by her insistence on talking to him about his supposed friendship with her son Albert – whom he has no recollection of ever having met – but with whom he is obviously supposed to be on terms of the greatest intimacy. But suddenly, from the tone in which the Duke has spoken of the lady and the similarity of her speech with that of the Princesse de Luxembourg, he 'discerns the nature of the beast'. She is 'a royal personage'. Although she had never previously heard either of him or his family she is nevertheless 'a scion of the noblest race and endowed with the greatest fortune in the world' and consequently seeks 'in gratitude to her Creator, to testify to her neighbour, however poor or lowly he might be, that she did not look down upon him'.[223]

One of the minor and highly attractive stylistic features of *A la recherche du temps perdu* is the frequency with which Proust introduces us to a character by means of a pen-portrait in the style of La Bruyère. This is particularly noticeable in the description of the Princesse de Parme which follows this incident, and which describes in some detail how her mother's training had instilled in her 'the arrogantly humble precepts of an evangelical snobbery'. For after the enumeration of the indisputable facts about her which might justify her pride – her ancient lineage and immense wealth – there comes the characteristically Proustian summary of these precepts:

Therefore never seem in your speech to be recalling these great privileges, not that they are precarious (for nothing can alter the antiquity of blood, while the world will always need oil), but because it is unnecessary to point out that you are better born than other people or that your investments are all gilt-edged, since everyone knows these facts already. Be helpful to the needy. Give to all those whom the bounty of heaven has been graciously pleased to put beneath you as much as you can give them without forfeiting your rank, that is to say help in the form of money, even your personal service by their sickbeds, but of course never any invitations to your soirées, which would do them no possible good and, by diminishing your prestige, would reduce the efficacy of your benevolent activities.[224]

Much of the underlying humour of *A la recherche du temps perdu* comes from the permanent and recurring contrast between the Narrator Marcel's early, romantic vision of the aristocracy and the reality which he comes up against when he eventually penetrates the fastness of the Faubourg Saint-Germain. His awareness of this reality informs his whole presentation of the Guermantes as he discovers them to be – idle, selfish, cowardly and hypocritical – and takes on an interesting variant in the portrait of the Princesse de Parme. For in his childhood, when he believed that names were the incarnation of the mysterious and poetic qualities characterising the spirit of the place which they designated, he had thought of the word 'Parme' as being 'compact, smooth, violet-tinted and soft', and of everything associated with it as endowed with the same qualities. But all these associations are shown to be an illusion when he meets the Princesse de Parme and discovers her to be this 'little dark woman taken up with good works and so humbly amiable that one felt at once in how exalted a pride that amiability had its roots'.[225] One of the great qualities of Proust as a novelist lies precisely in his ability to evoke both the poetic illusion and the less intoxicating but more entertaining reality. He is, on occasions like this, totally in command of his material, just as he is when he makes Robert de Saint-Loup speak in obviously unfeigned admiration of how one of his cousins 'does a tremendous lot for her old governesses; she's given orders that they're never to be sent in by the servants' staircase when they come to the house'. It is reassuring to see that Saint-Loup can be presented as just a comical prisoner of the presuppositions of his class as his aunt Oriane, and Proust's wit and timing are as certain and satisfying here as they are when the Narrator speaks of 'the tone in which a Catholic lady might tell a Jewish lady that her parish priest denounced the pogroms in Russia and admired the generosity of certain Jews'.[226]

When you look at the text of *A la recherche du temps perdu*, and reflect on how Proust's aristocrats behave, it is very difficult to accept George Painter's view that they 'fashioned in miniature the last social culture that our world has seen, a beautiful, fugitive and irreplaceable thing that history produced and history has destroyed'. For the drawing rooms that Proust describes do not contain what Mr Painter calls in the same lyrical passage 'a gay elegance, a fantastic individuality, a chivalrous freedom, a living interplay of minds, morals and emotions'.[227] It is made very clear, in *Le côté de Guermantes*, that Oriane's drawing room is a graveyard of talents and it is the vulgar and pushing Madame Verdurin rather than any elegant Guermantes lady who protects and encourages Vinteuil. The enthusiasm of Proust's aristocrats for art can be seen in the fact that the Elstir paintings in the possession of the Duc de Guermantes are kept carefully hidden away where nobody can see them, and are brought down only when Elstir becomes fashionable. When it comes to helping their friends or serving their country, only Robert de Saint-Loup provides any justification for George Painter's description of us as 'twentieth-century barbarians' whose 'duty' it is to 'salute the nineteenth-century civilization which we have overwhelmed'. Compared to the Guermantes, we really do rather well, and you don't need to go to the National Theatre or Opera North to see why. Attendance at a meeting of the Barnsley Literary Society will do, and this is not a joke: the standard of discussion there makes the conversation in the salons of *A la recherche du temps perdu* seem what it is: ignorant and pretentious.

It is not only Swann who measures the extent of the selfishness and hypocrisy which characterise the way the Guermantes behave in society. Oriane's legendary ability to defy social conventions does indeed disappear completely when it is a question of giving the man who is supposed to be her greatest friend the happiness of seeing his daughter received into the Guermantes drawing room, but there is also no sign of Basin de Guermantes having inherited any social, moral or physical courage from his feudal ancestors. When Marcel receives an invitation to attend an evening party at the house of the Duke's sister-in-law, the Princesse de Guermantes, he is afraid lest it be a hoax, and has an understandable reluctance to be ejected as a gate-crasher. But both Oriane and her husband are curiously evasive when he asks them to check up with their nearest relatives to see whether the invitation is genuine or not, and it is only after Marcel has taken his courage in both hands and turned up at the party that the Duke gives him the bluff reassurance that 'one's always invited'.[228] For the English reader, brought up on the depiction in the novels of P. G. Wodehouse of an equally idle upper class, the comparison with the Faubourg Saint-Germain is entirely to the advantage of the members of the Drones club or the inhabitants of Blandings Castle. The Code of the Woosters requires Bertie to do anything to help a pal, while Clarence, ninth Earl of Emsworth, defies not only his sister Constance but also the head gardener, Angus McAllister, in order to bring a little happiness to his girl friend Gladys.

Not all Proust's humour, of course, has the note of social criticism which runs through the portraits of his aristocrats. The wife of the Turkish Ambassador in Paris, for example, whose catholic curiosity and powers of intellectual assimilation enable her to be equally well informed on Xenophon's *Persian Expedition*, political economy, sexual perversion in birds, forms of masturbation or the philosophy of Epicurus, invites the same kind of disinterested hilarity as that aroused by the 'unnecessary detail' which Orwell found so characteristic of Dickens. The same is true of the way in which Great-uncle Adolphe's manservant would come to ask what time the carriage should be brought round:

> My uncle would then become lost in meditation, while his servant stood agape, not daring to disturb him by the least movement, curiously awaiting his answer, which never varied. For in the end, after a supreme crisis of hesitation, my uncle would utter, infallibly, the words: 'A quarter past two', which the servant would echo with amazement, but without disputing them: 'A quarter past two! Very good, sir . . . I'll go and tell him. . . .'[229]

This is one of the few episodes in *A la recherche du temps perdu* in which there is an undoubted similarity between the world of Proust and the ideas of the philosopher with whom he so often used to be compared, his cousin Henri Bergson. Proust's habit of

disparaging the abstract intelligence seemed to his early critics to
be a natural counterpart to Bergson's exaltation of man's intuitive
faculties, while the virtually complete omission of dates from *A la
recherche du temps perdu* corresponded, it was thought, to Bergson's
preference for what he called *la durée* – felt time – over scientifically
measured temporality. Proust himself played down these
apparent similarities,[230] and it is true that a knowledge of them
adds little to one's enjoyment of his novel. But the behaviour of
Uncle Adolphe's manservant is a very apt example of Bergson's
description of how laughter is caused when living things suddenly
take on the attributes of machines, and the only disadvantage of
using it as an example to illustrate the Bergsonian nature of
Proust's humour is that it is almost the only example of its kind in
the whole of *A la recherche du temps perdu*.

What it does nevertheless illustrate is a quality of Proust's
humour, as well as of his work as a whole, which immediately
strikes you when you read his novel for the first time: the
impression which it so often gives of being the direct and accurate
transcription of what he has actually seen. It seems, at first sight,
almost impossible to believe that there was not a particular
manservant who behaved in just this way, just as it is initially hard
to credit that Proust did not at some time see somebody who, like
the Duchesse de Guermantes, revealed her feelings on being
introduced to two nonentities by 'performing certain movements
of her nostrils with a precision that testified to the absolute inertia
of her unoccupied attention'. Similarly, when Albertine betrays
her potentialities for deceit by answering a question 'only with a
"no" of which the "n" would have been too hesitant and the "o"
too emphatic', your first thought is that Proust was writing after
and not before the invention of the tape recorder.[231]

Yet time and again in *A la recherche du temps perdu* the Narrator
tells us that he has no ability for observation and no interest in it.
At one point, he goes so far as to say that the observer who sees
things from outside 'sees nothing at all', and there is a long
passage in *Le Temps retrouvé* in which Proust seems to go out of his
way to attack what he calls 'une littérature de notations' (a
literature of description). It may well be, of course, that Proust
was talking about one of the fashionable literary theories of his
day. This is certainly how Emile Zola was popularly supposed to
have worked, and the second paragraph of Christopher
Isherwood's *A Berlin Diary* opens with the most famous claim for

this kind of literature when he writes: 'I am a camera with its shutter open, quite passive, recording, not thinking'. It is certainly easy to agree with Proust when he rejects this simplistic notion and contrasts it with the idea that 'in the state of mind in which we "observe", we are a long way below the level to which we rise when we create'.[232] But although you can see what he means, it does initially seem very strange for Proust to denigrate the role of observation in the way that he does. For it leads him to give the impression, as John Cocking puts it, that he was 'ashamed of the mastery of reality which is one of his greatest assets'.[233]

Proust's dismissal of the role of observation can naturally be explained as a necessary comment on how he saw his creative process working. He knew how his own mind worked, so what he tells us must be true. But any acceptance of the accompanying view that the essential criterion for aesthetic excellence is the intensity of the inner experience on which it is based does create problems. This is a theme which runs through the whole of the essays in *Contre Sainte-Beuve* and recurs as a dominant idea in *Le Temps retrouvé*, and it certainly corresponds to Proust's own ideal vision of himself as a writer. But any serious acceptance of it has two disadvantages: it seriously limits our enjoyment of *A la recherche du temps perdu* as one of the most interestingly realistic novels in the whole of French literature; it neglects the fact that most people who talk or write with complete sincerity about themselves are very boring. Proust did in fact ensure that his novel would remain interesting to those with limited enthusiasm for the details of one person's feelings by keeping copious notes about what he saw. It was doubtless these which enabled him to offer such details as the fact that it was regarded as non-U in Alençon to eat hard-boiled eggs with salad, or that it was the custom in France for the husband and not the wife to rise from the table as a sign that the meal was over.[234]

This objective and more anecdotal realism of *A la recherche du temps perdu* is not equally apparent on every page. Marcel's childhood is curiously devoid both of boredom and of the presence of other children, and it is very hard for any parent to believe in the existence of a child whose time is so completely taken up – except for the occasional experiment in auto-eroticism – with admiring churches and hawthorn blossom, going for walks with adults, and reading books. One also feels that there must have been some people in late nineteenth- and early twentieth-century France who were not either snobs or homosexuals, or both, and Proust is immediately out of his depth when he tries, in *Le Temps retrouvé*, to reproduce the speech habits of the working class. Apart from one or two complimentary remarks about electricians – nowadays, the Narrator tells us, they 'must be included in our truest order of Chivalry'[235] – the genuinely new class of skilled technicians is absent from *A la recherche du temps perdu*. It is only when he follows out his concern for general laws and writes almost as a sociologist that Proust's description of the role that classes play in society is realistic in the sense of probable or convincing. His portrayal of the family servant Françoise is brilliant. But she is, as she would be the first to tell you, the only one of her kind.

The description in *A la recherche du temps perdu* of the French nobility as a caste which has ceased to perform any useful function in society nevertheless has a remarkably convincing ring of social and historical accuracy. This comes out particularly clearly in the scene which takes place when, as the Narrator puts it, Monsieur de Guermantes 'required some information upon a matter of which my father had professional knowledge'. For the Duke would then 'come up to him in the courtyard, straighten the collar of his greatcoat with the obliging deftness inherited from a line of royal body-servants, take him by the hand, and, holding it in his own, stroking it even, to prove to him, with the shamelessness of a courtesan, that he did not begrudge him the privilege of contact with his ducal flesh, would steer him, extremely irked and thinking only of how he might escape, through the carriage entrance out into the street'.[236] You do not need much knowledge of French history to see where this particular form of aristocratic behaviour originated. There are some very obvious clues in the passage itself which point the reader's attention towards the policy which Louis XIV pursued with some success when he required the French nobility to leave their estates in the country and come to Versailles. There, deprived of all political power, they danced attendance on his person with exactly the anxiety which the Duke shows when he straightens the collar of the greatcoat, and proceeded from that point onwards to play an increasingly episodic and ineffective role in their country's history. Proust caught them precisely at the moment when their last bid for political power had failed. This was, curiously enough, at the time of one of the few precise historical events mentioned in

A la recherche du temps perdu: the resignation of Maréchal Mac-Mahon on 30 January 1879, the day when the newspaper boys crying out the news so disturbed Odette de Crécy and her unnamed lover that they had to get out of bed to see what was happening. For although Mac-Mahon's own loyalty to the Republic had prevented him from collaborating with the royalists who wanted to use him as a kind of General Monk in order to bring back the Bourbon monarchy, any success of his attempt to be a President who exercised genuine political authority would have certainly left the door open to an eventual restoration. Once he had failed, the French nobility became more and more like a chicken running round with its head cut off. No aristocracy can long survive as a meaningful class unless it has a king, even one who denies it political power.

You nevertheless do not need to know what the social and political situation of the French aristocracy was at the period depicted in *A la recherche du temps perdu* in order to appreciate the attitude which the Narrator Marcel adopts toward Oriane de Guermantes. Although the glimpse which he has of her in the church at Combray, when he is still a child, endows the woman who is then still only the Princesse des Laumes with all the magical qualities of her distant ancestor, Geneviève de Brabant, the reader knows that this is not how she really is. She may, in Marcel's childish imagination, belong to 'la race mystérieuse aux yeux perçants, au bec d'oiseau; la race rose, dorée, inapprochable' (that mysterious race with the piercing eyes and the beak of a bird, the unapproachable rose-coloured golden race) and her eyes may have all the beauty of the sky on a summer's afternoon in the Ile de France.[237] But as he comes to know her as a person in the society in which she actually lives, she is entirely different. She has, indeed, kept the family name intact by marrying her cousin, Basin. But he starts being unfaithful to her almost immediately after they are married. The only way in which he helps her is in preparing the ground for her supposedly witty remarks, but when she eventually produces one of these, it is almost embarrassingly unfunny to anyone except the members of her own immediate circle. They repeat it to one another, serving it up cold at luncheon on the following day, and it is perhaps significant that the only one of the jokes which is remotely funny when compared to the way Saki makes his society ladies talk is one which emphasises the unhappiness of her married life. The duke does, she says, like her to go and make 'une petite visite de digestion' on each of his new mistresses 'une fois qu'il avait consommé' (a 'digestive visit' once he had been 'entertained').[238]

The mature Proust's refusal to perpetuate Marcel's idealised vision of the aristocracy beyond the first volumes of *A la recherche du temps perdu* nevertheless provides an important link between his humour and his realism. The reader is quite deliberately invited to laugh both at Marcel's early illusions and at the reality which he subsequently discovers, and there are other incidents apart from the transformation of Oriane de Guermantes from a fairytale princess to a bored society hostess and not especially reliable friend which show how Proust exploits the comic gap between the aristocratic ideal and the social fact. It is not only the Princesse de Parme who illustrates the difference between the dreams which can be inspired by a name and the more prosaic reality of the person who bears it. The first Duc d'Arrachepel, we are told, owed his social eminence to his ability to go forward and pull out the stakes planted in the ground to impede the advance of the cavalry during a siege. It was, as one can imagine, a difficult as well as a dangerous job, whose successful execution (the etymology is 'arracher', to pull, and 'pieu', stake) might well justify both wealth and prestige. But the man who has inherited not only d'Arrachepel's house but also his coat of arms is the Marquis de Cambremer, who spends the First World War rather quietly as a colonel in the War Ministry in Paris. We do indeed, in *A la recherche du temps perdu*, meet some of the great names of the French aristocracy. But although Comte Louis de Turenne is presumably the direct descendant of the man who invaded Bavaria in 1647 before going on to conquer the Palatinate in 1674, he has inherited few of his ancestor's warlike attributes. His role in society is to hand round the orangeade and *petits fours* in Madame Swann's drawing room.[239] He is helped in this exalted task by the Duc d'Estrées, presumably the descendant of the man who, in the sixteenth century, was Master of the Royal Artillery. The presence of these and other aristocrats does, it is true, lead the Princesse d'Epinoy to effect an upward revision of her ideas about the current social standing of the former Odette de Crécy. But this is not how the infant Marcel saw the aristocracy as incarnating the whole spirit of French history. Neither does the reminder it offers of the kind of role to which Louis XIV had reduced the aristocrats of his time give much support to the elegiac tones in which George

Painter claimed that they 'gave their last young blood in the war, then perished because they had served art instead of power'.[240]

This particular incident nevertheless helps us to see what Proust had in mind when he dismissed the idea that any of the scenes in *A la recherche du temps perdu* were based upon observation. For the real Comte de Turenne d'Aynac, whom Proust knew, had behaved in exact accordance with the ideal of a warrior aristocracy when he conducted himself with considerable gallantry during the Franco-Prussian war of 1870, and there certainly have been many individual French aristocrats who have served France with courage, devotion and efficiency. A number of these figured among Proust's many acquaintances – Bertrand de Fénelon, a possible 'model' for Saint-Loup, became a distinguished diplomat before being killed in action in 1914 – and Proust the man had an understandably high regard for them. But Proust the creative writer would have underwritten the very Marxist comment which Alexis de Tocqueville made when he prefaced *De l'ancien régime et de la révolution* with his famous: 'On peut m'opposer des individus. Je parle des classes. Elles seules doivent occuper l'historien.' (There may be individuals who do not bear this out. I am talking about classes. They alone should occupy the historian.) What interested Proust, as he says on a number of occasions, were general laws, and this is certainly consistent with the way he used observation as a starting point for the complex process of creative writing. He himself said that the characters in *A la recherche du temps perdu* were built up in an essentially composite manner, one having 'posed for the grimaces, another for the monocle, another for the fits of temper, another for the swaggering movement of the arm',[241] and the details which seem at first sight to be the product of apparently passive observation are clearly the result of a complex process of creative selection.

Thus although the Duchesse de Montmorency is related to 'the first barons of France', and well enough placed in the social hierarchy to give the reception for the King and Queen of England at which Marcel shows such exquisite tact in his acknowledgement of the Guermantes' greeting, she is quite prepared to meet Madame Swann as long as this is out of doors. Talking to her in the Zoological Gardens or in the Bois de Boulogne is one thing. Allowing her access to her drawing room is quite another, and the apparently observed detail is important because it fits into the overall pattern of Proust's depiction of this extraordinarily and comically hierarchical society. Odette is also most assiduous in conforming to the anglomania which was so noticeable a feature of Parisian polite society in *La Belle Epoque*. She denies that she is 'fishing for compliments', religiously speaks of 'Christmas' and never of 'Noël', has her invitation cards printed with the words 'to meet . . .' and even tries to have her husband give his name on his visiting cards as 'Mr Charles Swann'. When the Narrator meets her again, after a gap of many years, at the reception given by the Princesse de Guermantes in *Le Temps retrouvé*, her voice has not changed, being still 'exaggeratedly warm, caressing, with a trace of an English accent',[242] and her reply to his compliment on her youthful appearance contains the inevitable 'How nice of you to say so, *my dear*'. But she is not serving as a kind of dressmaker's model on which Proust is pinning a series of garments which he has noticed lying around. He is creating a particular character, building her up with details he may well have invented. Indeed, when he describes how 'cette cocotte illettrée' (this illiterate courtesan) makes the mistake of referring to the various members of the French aristocracy as 'Royalties',[243] it is tempting to use the Italian proverb and say 'se non è vero, è ben trovato'. This is, we feel, exactly how Odette would speak if she were a real person. One of the advantages which Proust derives from the length of *A la recherche du temps perdu* is the ability to show how characters evolve with the passage of time, and it is very satisfying to see him choosing – or inventing – the right detail to illustrate how this happens.

For Proust's 'mastery of reality' was an active quality, not a passive virtue. Monsieur de Norpois, for example, is a gentleman of the old school, a man so punctilious in replying by return of post to any letters addressed to him that it was 'as though he enjoyed at the post office the special and luxurious privilege of supplementary deliveries and collections at all hours of the day and night';[244] the detail is exactly right to illustrate the effects which his courtesy produces. It is no habit of accidental and automatic notation which enables us to learn that the 'utterly undistinguished' Madame Cottard wore 'a pair of white gloves straight from the cleaners'.[245] Oriane de Guermantes, Madame Leroi and even the rather less elegant Madame de Cambremer would, we are sure, have had a fresh pair every day, and Proust never puts a foot wrong in depicting the voluntary or involuntary signs whereby we reveal to others what we think or what we are, or which show the direction in which society is moving. We also recognise a correct as well as a creative eye for detail when he includes among the illustrations of Albertine's untruthfulness the example of 'the architect who promises you that your house will be ready at a date when it will not have been begun'.[246]

There is thus no gap between Proust's realism and his concern for general laws. The disadvantage of a literature based upon notation, as anyone who has tried to read the novels produced by the Spanish writers belonging to the school of *costumbrismo* will know, is that it gives an accumulation of extremely boring details which are totally meaningless outside their immediate geographical context. The apparently observed details in *A la recherche du temps perdu* are not like that. When Proust describes how some of Monsieur de Guermantes's cousins, 'like working-class parents, were never at home to look after their children', it comes as no surprise to us to discover why. It is that they go in for the arts, so that 'every morning the wife went off to the Schola to study counterpoint and fugue, and the husband to his studio to carve wood and tool leather'.[247] The habits of intellectuals have clearly changed little in the sixty or so years which have elapsed since Proust's death, and the advice which he gives about a choice of restaurant has lost nothing of its usefulness. For when we read of a Normandy innkeeper who carefully refrained from giving his hostelry the modern comforts of an hotel, and did not allow his millionaire status to deprive him of his peasant speech and air, we know that the tourist world of the 1890s was exactly like that of the 1980s. The dinner which this innkeeper serves is not only better than the one we might eat in the most luxurious hotel. It is even more expensive.[248]

This constant applicability of the realism of *A la recherche du temps perdu* to our own very different world is one of the most surprising, paradoxical and satisfying aspects of Proust's achievement as a novelist. It is not only that his equation of prestige with the power to exclude offers so immediate a key to an understanding of the reputation of some University Departments of English. By systematically refusing any association with the *hoi polloi* from physics, mathematics or modern languages, the members of these Departments add immeasurably to the reputation already won by their scholarly achievements, and the creative use which Proust made of his powers of generalised observation enabled him to foresee this particular phenomenon of social behaviour with an almost uncanny accuracy. Neither did the difference in time which lies between us and Proust prevent him from anticipating the way technology has changed our own experience of the world. He observes in *Sodome et Gomorrhe* how the invention of the motor car makes us realise that 'distances are only the relation of space to time and vary with it', and even modifies our conception of art. For 'a village which seemed to be in a different world from some other village becomes its neighbour in a landscape whose dimensions are altered', and the ability to travel at speed brings together places which were, in the past, 'as hermetically confined in the cells of distinct days as long ago were Méséglise and Guermantes'.[249]

Although Proust himself was one of the most prolific correspondents ever to profit from the efficiency of the nineteenth-century postal system, it is the telephone which is most frequently used as an instrument of communication by the characters in *A la recherche du temps perdu*. Marcel waits in such silent and motionless anxiety for Albertine to telephone him that he hears, for the first time in months, the sound of the clock ticking in his room, and it is easy to imagine the delight which Proust would have derived from the John Schlesinger film, *Sunday, Bloody Sunday*. He would have found almost as much truth in the dependence of the different characters on the telephone as in the rivalry between Alex Grenville (Glenda Jackson) and Daniel Hirsch (Peter Finch) for the affection of the bi-sexual, Morel-like character of Bob (Murray Head). Neither would Proust have been surprised to find that there has been no change in the experience we have when we speak for the first time on the telephone to someone whom we are used to seeing as we talk to them. When Marcel first hears his grandmother's voice on the telephone, he does not recognise it. He has, as he then realises, 'been accustomed to follow what she said on the open score of her face'. It is only as he listens that he both recognises who it is and hears new and different qualities in the voice, as his grandmother allows herself to express the tenderness for him which she normally keeps under control. When he then notices, for the first time, 'the sorrows which had cracked it in the course of a lifetime',[250] you are reminded of how frequently the same kind of thing happens even with our own more perfect instruments.

Proust is nevertheless describing a society which is quite

extraordinarily different from our own, and this difference is not limited to the fact that so few of the characters in *A la recherche du temps perdu* have to work for a living. They also all have servants, 'a strange breed', the Narrator tells us, whose members lead so abnormal a life that its ways are 'bound to produce certain characteristic faults'.[251] In *A la recherche du temps perdu*, these faults are gathered together – by the side of some great virtues – in one of Proust's most memorable characters, the servant Françoise. She is one of the first people we meet in the section of *Du côté de chez Swann* called 'Combray', and one of the first to make Marcel aware of the complexity and many-sidedness of the most apparently simple human being. For she is, on the one hand, the provider of the most delicious meals, the person who can make coffee with a perfect aroma and fill hot-water bottles that are really hot. But, on the other, she is also someone whom Marcel sees pursuing a chicken with such absolute ferocity that the 'meekness and unction' which he normally associates with her completely disappear. These qualities are nevertheless still there, and are very real, on the next day at dinner, when the same chicken 'made its appearance in a skin gold-embroidered like a chasuble, and its precious juice was poured out drop by drop as from a pyx'.[252]

Françoise offers comparable ambiguity in her attitude towards other people. When the kitchen girl, nicknamed Giotto's Charity by Swann because of the heaviness which her body takes on in pregnancy, is finally delivered of what one assumes to be an illegitimate child, Marcel's mother is so disturbed by her sufferings that she sends Françoise to check up on the symptoms in a medical dictionary. Françoise goes to consult the book, but does not return. Marcel is sent to look for her, and finds her moved to tears by the description which she is reading of these very symptoms. When, however, Françoise returns to 'Giotto's Charity's' side, she is totally unmoved, and merely comments that it is the girl's own fault for getting herself into trouble.

Françoise does not disappear with the death of Tante Léonie. She comes into service with the Narrator's family, bringing with her 'the country air, the social life of a farm of fifty years ago transported into our midst by a sort of reversal of the normal order of things whereby it is the countryside that comes to visit the traveller'.[253] She epitomises the extraordinary ability of servants to 'find out the business of their masters, those strange beings who converse among themselves and do not speak to them',[254] and

develops what one suspects may have been a well-justified
suspicion of Albertine. She also has an infallible ability to discover
among a pile of letters on the Narrator's desk the very document
which it is imperative that she should not see, and to replace it in a
visibly reproachful way on the very top.

But Françoise is far from being the only servant in *A la recherche
du temps perdu* to nourish our admiration for Proust's realism as
well as for his sense of humour. The violinist Morel is very nicely
used by Proust at one point in *Sodome et Gomorrhe* to bring out the
ignorance and pretentiousness of the aristocratic guests whom
Madame Verdurin has invited, along with her original, more
middle-class Faithful, to one of her musical evenings at her
country residence of La Raspelière, in Normandy, which she is
renting from the Cambremers. Madame de Cambremer turns
down the Narrator's suggestion that Morel should play César
Franck and insists on Debussy. However, after the first few bars,
Morel realises that he does not know the whole of the piece which
he has undertaken to play. So he slides unannounced into
something by the much more popular and – at the time – more
accessible Meyerbeer. This continues to evoke cries of ecstatic
admiration until Morel reveals what he has done. The real
identity of the musician whom everybody has so publicly admired
casts a certain chill over the assembled company.[255]

There often seems to be something characteristically French
about the aggressive undertones running through the humour in
so much of *A la recherche du temps perdu*. The passion which the
Narrator's father has for meteorology, and which leads him to
dismiss as an idiot any of his son's friends – Bloch, for example –
who cannot tell him what the weather has been like, makes him an
amiable eccentric on the lines of Mr Woodhouse in Jane Austen's
Emma. In Combray, you laugh at people because you love them,
and you love them even more because you can laugh at them. But
as you meet the Guermantes and the Verdurins, the laughter
takes on the more pessimistic tinge which it has in *Le Misanthrope*
or *Candide*. Madame Verdurin may make us smile when she shows
that she is a great hostess by taking part in all the conversations at
the same time. The inventiveness of Proust's comic genius may
even make us laugh when we read how 'under the influence of the
countless headaches which the music of Bach, Wagner, Vinteuil,
Debussy had given her' her forehead had 'assumed enormous
proportions, like limbs that become permanently deformed by

rheumatism'. We may appreciate Proust's wit when he describes how her temples, 'suggestive of a pair of throbbing, pain-stricken, milk-white spheres' thus proclaim, 'without any need for her to say a word: "I know what is in store for me tonight"'.[256] But none of this can make us forget that prolonged acquaintance with her is the kiss of death for the personal happiness of her guests. She and her husband publicly bully and humiliate the unfortunate Saniette until the poor man is reduced to tears, and Madame Verdurin's terror lest any of her 'Faithful' may escape from her tyranny has quite disastrous consequences for Professor Brichot. For when he is thinking of marrying his laundress, who has in fact been his mistress for some time, Madame Verdurin soon dissuades him – in his own best interest – to refrain from contracting such a *mésalliance*. She does the same when Brichot tries to take an interest in Madame de Cambremer, and the result is disastrous: Brichot's growing blindness and consequent loneliness make him turn to morphine, and he becomes an addict.

9
Models, Language and Perspective

The remark that *A la recherche du temps perdu* consists of long sentences about a little cake presents matters in the right order. It is Proust's use of language which is important in creating the autonomous world of his novel, not the actual incidents or real people that he may or may not have used as his models. It is certainly interesting, on an anecdotal level, to learn that the principal models for the Baron de Charlus were the Baron Jacques Doasan and the Comte Robert de Montesquiou. The first, as George Painter has shown, provided Charlus's portly physique and disconcerting habit of fixing his eyes on the young men who aroused his interest, while the second was the source for Charlus's interest in the arts, his tendency to deliver interminable monologues in a shrieking voice, and his taste for scatological comparisons. Montesquiou's remark that Madame Aubernon, described by George Painter as the 'chief original' for Madame Verdurin, 'looked like Queen Pomaré on a lavatory seat' is certainly in the same vein as Charlus's joke about Madame Verdurin's coffee cups being taken for chamber pots.[257] But it fades into insignificance by the side of Charlus's long speech, delivered in the lady's hearing, in which he insists that when Madame de Saint-Euverte opens her mouth to issue an invitation, it is as though somebody had just broken the lid of a cesspool.[258] When Charlus adds that if he had the misfortune to go to one of her receptions 'the cesspool would expand into a formidable sewage-cart', Proust's final creation takes on so terrifying a dimension that it is easy to agree with Roland Barthes's remark that we should say that 'there are elements of Charlus in Montesquiou',[259] and not the other way round. What matters is Proust's use of language. It is this which gives life to his creations

142

and it is this which goes beyond the individuals whom he happened to know and fulfils his stated ambition of illuminating general laws.

For the social distinctions which Proust and other people regarded as so essential an aspect of late nineteenth- and early twentieth-century France depended as much on language as they still do in England. Oriane de Guermantes, for example, is described as having 'a sort of almost peasant pronunciation which had a harsh and delicious flavour of the soil' and which reveals what the Narrator calls 'the ingrained habit of really distinguished people and people of intelligence who know that distinction does not lie in mincing speech'.[260] This way of speaking reflects the habit of the genuine nobility of fraternising more readily with their peasants than with the middle class, and for the connoisseur of the differences which still distinguish non-U from U speech in England, Proust is describing a familiar phenomenon. Because the English aristocracy has always kept close links with the land, its speech habits have tended to be imbued with the same earthy directness which characterises Oriane de Guermantes, and the list of U and non-U words in the 1978 edition of Debrett's *U and Non-U Revisited* shows that the distinction originally noted by Nancy Mitford in 1956 is still valid.[261] The upper-class speaker says 'scurf' and not 'dandruff', 'constipating' and not 'binding', and 'pregnant' rather than 'expecting'. Oriane de Guermantes has no hesitation in referring to Rachel as 'une cochonne' (a sow), and the Prince de Guermantes speaks to his peasants as though he were one of them.

Proust makes another interesting sociological point in the analysis which accompanies this account of how the most elegant lady of the Faubourg Saint-Germain speaks French. Oriane belongs to 'the one branch of the Guermantes . . . which had for long remained more localized, more hardy, wilder, more combative than the rest'[262] – in other words, to the type of aristocracy which had, by remaining close to its roots, managed to remain relatively independent of the domestication which the centralising policies of Louis XIV had imposed upon the rest of the French nobility. It is, one feels, this aspect of her family background which explains Oriane's outspokenness and independence of mind, and it would be intriguing to know whether this was a connection which Proust expected his readers to make. He also comments on the way Madame de Villeparisis still speaks, underlying how she rolls her 'r's, and must clearly, whatever his disclaimers about observation, have noticed some of the older aristocrats doing that instead of using the softer, Parisian, uvular 'r'.[263]

A la recherche du temps perdu does more than tell the story of how a little boy grew up to be a writer. It also describes how the son of a senior civil servant made his way into the top aristocracy, and Proust is very good at catching the speech intonations of those who are on the social make. Charles Morel, for example, speaks of his father as 'mon paternel' – the translation as 'the governor' has many of the non-U overtones[264] – and the very socially upwardly mobile Narrator is most illuminating on how the family servant Françoise taught him to speak when he was still a child. Since he learned peasant and therefore authentic pronunciation from her, and therefore discovered early in life that 'one did not say "the Tarn" (Le Tarn) but "the Tar" (Le Tar); not "Béarn" but "Béar" ', he did not need, when he went into society at the age of twenty, to learn that one ought not to say, like Madame Bontemps, "Madame de Béar*n*".[265] Perhaps because of his Germanic descent, Basin de Guermantes does not in fact speak very good French from a purely formal point of view. He thinks that the expression 'avoir maille à partir' – to have a bone to pick with somebody – means to break off relations, and that 'faire des embarras' – to show off – means to create complications.[266] But his rank puts him sufficiently above such contingencies for it not to matter, and he is, in this respect, like the other great noblemen mentioned in *Le Temps retrouvé* 'who had always worn the plainest alpaca cloth, and on their heads old straw hats which a man of the lower middle class would have refused to put on'.[267] As anyone who has cast an eye at the medical profession will tell you, it is the senior consultants who allow themselves to be seen in public in gardening trousers which their junior registrars would have given to a jumble sale, and Lord Emsworth's sister Constance is for ever critical of her brother's predilection for the oldest clothes in his wardrobe. Proust also raises some other English echoes when he comments on how the grandchildren of his vulgarly ambitious friend Bloch will be 'kind and modest almost from birth'.[268] The Public Schools, as is well known, are for the fathers and not for the sons of gentlemen. Had a miracle happened and Madame Bontemps succeeded in marrying her niece Albertine off to Marcel, any children born to the interesting couple would have found an excellent social position ready made for them.

In 1965, the publication of the second volume of George Painter's biography of Marcel Proust was followed by a lively correspondence in *The Times Literary Supplement* on the question of whether or not Marie Nordlinger, the girl from a well-established and highly cultivated Jewish intellectual family in Manchester who had helped Proust with his translation of Ruskin in the 1890s, had or had not served as one of his several models for Albertine Simonet.[269] This was certainly a step in the right direction from the traditional identification of Albertine with Alfred Agostinelli, but inevitably neglected the fact that the real Albertine – the one in the book – is at one and the same time a verbal creation and someone whose personality and actions are revealed to the Narrator by the way she speaks. For when Albertine comes to visit him in Paris, shortly after the death of his grandmother, he realises from the vocabulary she uses that she has become rather a different person from the young girl whom he had met the previous season at Balbec. She corrects her earlier statement about Elstir's stupidity by saying that he is 'really quite distinguished', and hints at the smartness of the Fontainebleau golf club by declaring that 'It's really quite a selection'. The sequence of events shows that Marcel is quite right to interpret these and other changes in her linguistic habits as a series of signs that Albertine has become more sexually available. For she does not repeat the behaviour at Balbec which led her to ring for help when he tried to kiss her, and their relationship – in spite of Françoise coming in with the lamp and thus conjuring up 'a picture of "Justice shedding light upon crime" ' moves on to a new stage. He is thus shown to have read the signs correctly when he noted that the word 'Selection', even when used in the context of a golf club, was 'as incompatible with the Simonet family as it would be, if preceded by the word "natural" in a text published centuries before the researches of Darwin'.[270] Albertine is changing, as we all change, in response to the different linguistic stimuli which follow any move into a different kind of society.

After moving on to a different stage partly as a result of a change in Albertine's language, the relationship between Marcel and Albertine is also helped towards its inevitable failure by the use she makes of a particular expression. No sooner has she said something capable of putting his fears and suspicions at rest by confessing that her earlier claim to have been brought up by Mlle Vinteuil's Lesbian friend is a pack of lies invented to make herself more interesting, than she accidentally opens up a whole new abyss of anguish for him. She dismisses his offer to pay for her to give a splendid dinner in order to impress the Verdurins with a phrase that he only half hears and which she does not complete. 'Spend money on them!', she declares. 'I'd a great deal rather you left me free for once in a way to go and get myself . . .' ('me faire casser . . .'). It is only after the phrase has continued to work its way through what he calls 'that curiously alive and creative sleep of the unconscious (a sleep in which the things that have barely touched us succeed in carving an impression, in which our sleeping hands take hold of the key that turns the lock, the key which we have sought for in vain)' that an appalling word, of which he had never dreamed, suddenly bursts into his mind. What Albertine was going to say before she interrupted herself was 'me faire casser le pot', a slang expression for 'to have anal intercourse'.[271]

It is not long after this conversation that Albertine leaves him. The evidence which he collects about her real or supposed Lesbian activities is never sufficiently conclusive for him to say whether or not she has ever been guilty of what he always calls 'le mal' (evil-doing). It was, he says, her use of this expression which revealed to him how 'it was this that she would have preferred', and you can see how the way she interrupts herself in the middle of this particular expression increases his suspicions, even though the imagination does boggle a little at the physiological implications. There is ever the temptation to wonder whether this particular passage is not one where the autobiographical basis of Proust's own relationship with Agostinelli is rather visible. Since he seems to have been quite happy for Agostinelli's wife Anna to live with her husband in the apartment where he tried to keep his chauffeur prisoner, his jealousy does not seem to have been aroused by Agostinelli's heterosexual activities. Affairs which Agostinelli might have had with other men could nevertheless have had quite a different impact and this could well have provided the starting point for the words which Albertine just manages to avoid saying. But such speculations fit better into a study of *A la recherche du temps perdu* as indirect autobiography than into any account of it as a novel, and from this point of view the revelations brought about by the expression 'me faire casser le pot' are rather different. They fit into a relationship which is deliberately presented to show how impossible it is to find out what other people are like – unless, of course, they happen to betray themselves by the way they speak.

One of the many curious features about the long account in *Le Temps retrouvé* of how the Narrator is now going to make sense of his experience by writing a book is that he nowhere comments on how he, as a writer, is going to use language to illuminate human behaviour. Just as the pages in *Le Temps retrouvé* which describe the book which the Narrator is about to write make no mention of the possibility that parts of it might be very funny, so there is a comparable absence of any suggestion that the attentive reader might profit from a glance at Odette's anglicisms, from the Duc de Guermantes's reference to the elegant Oriane as 'ma bourgeoise' (the missus) or from the really rather English habit which the Courvoisier family have of giving the word 'intelligent' the implication that the person to whom it was applied 'had probably murdered father and mother'.[272] Indeed, Proust's apparent indifference to these effects sometimes conjures up the rather worrying thought that *A la recherche du temps perdu* might not in fact be the work that the Narrator decides to write in the final volume. Proust would certainly have been unhappy if this possibility had been suggested to him, and it would clearly have little appeal for the more devout Proustians. But to the absence from the *ars poetica* of *Le Temps retrouvé* of any mention of homosexuality, of humour and of the use of language as a means of social or sexual communication should also be added the possibly rather pedantic point about Proust's apparent inability to tell the difference between metaphors and comparisons.

For the formal position in *Le Temps retrouvé* is quite clear, and is set out in what is rightly regarded as one of the finest passages in the whole of Proust's novel.

An hour is not merely an hour, it is a vase full of scents and sounds and projects and climates, and what we call reality is a certain connexion between these immediate sensations and the memories which envelop us simultaneously with them – a connexion that is suppressed in a simple cinematographic vision, which just because it professes to confine itself to the truth in fact departs widely from it – a unique connexion which the writer has to rediscover in order to link for ever in his phrase the two sets of phenomena which reality joins together.[273]

The problem arises when you turn from this magnificent description of Proust's aims to the language which he actually uses. For you then notice that instead of using what is normally thought of as a metaphor – 'John was a lion in the fight' – Proust is much more inclined to use comparisons – 'John fought like a lion'. For example, in two of the most famous passages describing how the taste of the 'petite madeleine' brings all his childhood memories back to life, Proust introduces his poetic illustration of what is happening by using the comparative conjunction 'comme'. In the first passage, this is translated by 'like', in the sentence which tells us that

> when from a long-distant past nothing subsists, after the people are dead, after the things are broken and scattered, taste and smell alone, more fragile but more enduring, more unsubstantial, more persistent, more faithful, remain poised a long time, like souls, remembering, waiting, hoping, amid the ruins of all the rest; and bear unflinchingly, in the tiny and almost impalpable drop of their essence, the vast structure of recollection.[274]

In the second passage, the fact that this is a comparison and not what a more literally minded critic would call a metaphor is again apparent from the translation of 'come' by 'as', when Proust writes that

> as in the game wherein the Japanese amuse themselves by filling a porcelain bowl with water and steeping in it little pieces of paper which until then are without character or form, but, the moment they become wet, stretch and twist and take on colour and distinctive shape, become flowers or houses or people, solid and recognisable, so in that moment all the flowers in our garden and in M. Swann's park, and the water-lilies on the Vivonne and the good folk of the village and their dwellings and the parish church and the whole of Combray and its surroundings, taking shape and solidity, sprang into being, town and gardens alike, from my cup of tea.[275]

Both of these passages illustrate what Proust says about style in *Le Temps retrouvé*: that it is 'a question not of technique but of vision'.[276] After reading them, we do see our own experience of time and memory in a different, more poetic way. It would also need only a slight stylistic adjustment to make them a more exact illustration of the point that Proust made in his essay on Flaubert. For he wrote there that 'only metaphor can give style a kind of eternity',[277] and these comparisons already do precisely that. But although this change would have to be made if these comparisons were to become genuine metaphors, there is once again a considerable advantage for Proust in not paying too much attention in his practice as a writer to what he says he is doing in his theoretical statements. For his remarks in *Le Temps retrouvé* are in no way an adequate guide to the extraordinary variety of scientific comparisons which give such wealth to the texture of his prose.

These occur very frequently in Proust, especially when he writes that 'to ask pity of our body is like discoursing in front of an octopus, for which our words can have no more significance than the sound of the tides, and with which we should be appalled to find ourselves condemned to live'.[278] For whatever his interest in the external, social world, Proust never ceases to be the novelist who takes us further inside the workings of the mind than any previous imaginative writer. Indeed at the reception at Madame de Villeparisis's in *Le côté de Guermantes*, his slow-motion internal camera gives a particularly good example of how the involuntary memory can work in a social as well as a personal and poetic context. The Narrator hears one of the more unfashionable guests, a historian specialising in the first half of the seventeenth century, ask Monsieur de Norpois if he 'hadn't thought of giving the Institut an address on the price of bread during the Fronde', observing that this 'might be an enormous success'. What this means, adds Proust, is 'give me a colossal advertisement', and he notes how the historian then smiled at the Ambassador 'with an obsequious tenderness which made him raise his eyelids and reveal eyes as wide as the sky'. Then, he suddenly remembers that he had seen such a look before 'in the eyes of a Brazilian doctor who claimed to be able to cure breathless spasms of the kind from which I suffered by absurd inhalations of plant essences'. This doctor had looked at the influential Professor Cottard with the same 'timid, suppliant and self-seeking' air, and this memory prompts the reflection that since the two men were not acquainted, there are psychological laws which have as general an application as physical ones. 'If the requisite conditions are the same', he writes, 'an identical expression lights up the eyes of different human animals, as an identical sunrise lights up places that are a long way apart.'[279]

It is an almost perfect example of Proust's originality in showing how the workings of the mind remain the same in a public and in a private context, and of how he uses scientific imagery in order to show the reader a new way of looking at experience. There is nevertheless a difference between Proust's comparisons with the world of science and his attitude towards art. For all his familiarity with the world of nineteenth-century science, he never expresses any of the optimism which led certain nineteenth-century thinkers to believe in the ability of science to produce all the answers. 'The unknown element in the lives of other people ('l'inconnu de la vie des êtres')', he writes in *La Prisonnière*, 'is like that of nature, which each fresh scientific discovery merely reduces but does not abolish.'[280] Although the Narrator may observe 'with the satisfaction of a zoologist' the similarities of appearance between Legrandin and his young nephew Léonor de Cambremer, Proust the analyst of human experience sees no way in which science will ever be able to really enable us to understand what happens to us. For that, we need to turn to art, and think of how the musician Vinteuil is as inspired as a Lavoisier or an Ampère in 'discovering the secret laws that govern an unknown force';[281] Proust's views on this particular issue show how misleading it would be to distinguish systematically between his views and those of his Narrator. For Proust himself wrote in his essay on Flaubert's style that it is possible 'by the entirely new and personal use which a man makes of the past definite, of the present perfect, of the present participle, of certain pronouns and certain prepositions',[282] for our vision of reality to be as revolutionised as it was by Kant's Categories, his theory of knowledge and of the reality of the external world. It is, for Proust as well as for his Narrator, only art which offers intellectual certainty as well as ultimate philosophical values.

It is consequently understandable that an author as enthusiastic about the visual arts as Proust should take so many of his artistic comparisons from painting. Like his hero and *alter ego*, Charles Swann, Proust had a great admiration for the seventeenth-century Dutch painter Vermeer. Swann, again like Proust, had a positive mania for artistic comparisons, as when he likens Odette to Botticelli's portrait of Jethro's daughter in one of the frescoes of the Sistine chapel, or says that Bloch looks like the Bellini protrait of Mahomet II with 'the same arched eyebrows and hooked nose and prominent cheekbones'. Swann would also see 'in a bust of the Doge Loredan by Antonio Rizzo, the prominent cheekbones, the slanting eyebrows, in short, a speaking likeness to his own coachman, Rémi', as well as 'in the colouring of a Ghirlandaio, the nose of M. de Palancy; in a portrait by Tintoretto, the invasion of the cheek by an outcrop of whisker, the broken nose, the penetrating stare, the swollen eyelids of Dr du Boulbon',[283] and this is to some extent his problem. In his relationship with Odette, he is unable to come to terms with a woman who cannot be kept prisoner in a picture frame. But he lacks the ability to create a work of art which is presented as the salvation for the Narrator Marcel, and is in this respect one of the characters whom Proust most obviously uses for didactic ends. But at the same time, he perfectly illustrates one aspect of the impact which Proust makes on his readers. After reading *A la recherche du temps perdu*, you cannot visit a picture gallery without instinctively comparing the faces on the canvases with the appearance of your friends.

The comparisons with the visual arts which run so consistently through *A la recherche du temps perdu* – and which create yet another resemblance between Proust's world and that of Anthony Powell in *A Dance to the Music of Time* – are nevertheless not limited to painting. Architecture is called in to provide what does, for once, come very close to being a metaphor, when Proust uses it to illustrate the change which comes over Robert de Saint-Loup at the outbreak of the First World War. For this enables him, the Narrator says, to rediscover his hereditary essence as a member of a warrior aristocracy: 'This man who throughout his life, even when sitting down, even when walking across a drawing room, had seemed to be restraining an impulse to charge, while with a smile he dissembled the indomitable will which dwelt within his triangular head, at last had charged. Freed from the books which encumbered it, the feudal turret had become military once more.'[284]

This description comes when Saint-Loup has in fact already been killed in action, and it is perhaps significant that Proust's language is once again at its most effective and moving in the presence of death. The Narrator describes how his mother, when faced with her mother's death, 'convulsed by every gasp of this agony, but at moments drenched with tears, stood with the unheeding desolation of a tree lashed by the rain and shaken by the wind'.[285]

One of the claims made for Proust as a writer by André Maurois, in his Preface to the 1954 Pléiade edition of *A la recherche du temps perdu*, is that he gave new life to the use of images in fiction by borrowing them from the contemporary disciplines of science, physiology and politics. This is, as I have tried to suggest, one of the most interesting aspects of his use of language, and I also commented in Chapter 4 on how the use of images and comparisons from the world of natural science in the opening section of *Sodome et Gomorrhe* has the advantage of leading him to present a less anguished and more tolerant view of homosexuality than his official opinion of it as a disastrous hereditary taint would normally allow. A comparable distinction is introduced between Proust's official beliefs and the implication of the words he uses if one looks at the full text of one of the images quoted by André Maurois, in which Odette Swann's gradual conquest of new social territory in fashionable Paris is compared to a colonial war. For just before the Narrator's mother makes the remark to the effect that 'Now that the Tromberts have been subdued, the neighbouring tribes will soon surrender', the point is made – in one of those groups of three adjectives of which Proust is so fond – that these new social connections which Odette is so determined to make were established in the 'summary, rapid and violent manner'[286] which characterised colonial expeditions. It is an effective piece of understatement which reminds us of the realities of late nineteenth-century European behaviour.

From being one of the first writers to sign an appeal in favour of Captain Dreyfus, the French officer accused of being a traitor on virtually non-existent evidence and principally because he was Jewish, Proust moved to a much more conservative position, and did so very largely in reaction against the anticlericalism which was to take on a particularly virulent form after the separation of Church and State in 1905. This had already led him, on 16 August 1904, to publish in *Le Figaro* a long article defending the artistic splendour and social role of the great churches and cathedrals of France, and he also introduces into *A la recherche du temps perdu* itself an amusing reminder of the quarrel between Church and State. A friend of the Narrator's mother regrets the way in which the presence at Combray of 'a Radical mayor who does not even lift his hat to the priest'[287] makes it impossible for her to discover the real truth about Gilberte Swann's forthcoming marriage to Robert de Saint-Loup. But this sympathy for the Catholic church, which was indeed subjected to a certain amount of persecution in the late nineteenth and early twentieth centuries, does not come out in the language in which Proust chooses to talk about religion itself. The comparisons involving religion are almost invariably comic, and this slightly irreverent note is not limited to the reminder by Jupien that a priest who has just enjoyed the facilities of his homosexual brothel should 'contribute to the expenses of the church'.[288] In one of the examples quoted by André Maurois, the Narrator describes how he kept common sense at bay during his infatuation with Gilberte Swann by banishing for ever from his mind, 'as a good Catholic banishes Renan's *Vie de Jésus*, the corrupting thought that their house was just an ordinary flat in which we ourselves might have been living', and the irony does not seem to be directed primarily against the sceptic. When he is invited to dinner at the Swanns' and sees that each of the male guests finds as he sits down to dinner that a carnation has been laid by the side of his plate, he watches to see what his fellow guests will do before slipping the flower into his buttonhole 'with the air of naturalness that a free-thinker assumes in church when he is not familiar with the Mass, but rises when everybody else rises and kneels a moment after everyone else is on his knees'.[289]

Since Proust's own religion was very much that of art – like Baudelaire and Mallarmé, he perfectly exemplifies Thibaudet's remark that the nineteenth century began, in Chateaubriand, with the poetry of religion and ended with the religion of poetry[290] – it is perhaps not altogether surprising that his use of strictly religious comparisons should occasionally verge on the irreverent. 'Ay, they're a great family, the Guermantes', Françoise is made to say when the Narrator and his family come to take up residence in one of the dependencies of the Guermantes's enormous house in Paris, and is described as speaking in a tone of respect which shows that she bases the greatness of this family 'at once on the number of its branches and the brilliance of its connexions, as Pascal founds the truth of Religion on Reason and on the authority of the Scriptures'.[291] Later on in the same passage, the

Narrator uses an even less respectful comparison when he speaks of how difficult he finds it to believe that the ordinary people whom he knows in day-to-day life suddenly begin to lead a magical existence when they are received by the Guermantes. Indeed, he writes, 'the presence of Jesus Christ in the host' seemed to him 'no more obscure a mystery than this leading house in the Faubourg being situated on the right bank of the river' and so near that he could, from his bedroom, 'hear its carpets being beaten'.[292] The frequency with which Proust uses religious comparisons to poke fun at people who take the world of high society seriously is a fairly clear sign that he has little respect for Catholicism or the Faubourg Saint-Germain. There is thus, for the agnostic, some mild satisfaction in being able to contemplate an author whose use of language precludes any take-over bid from the more proselytising literary critics who want to take everybody back to Pont Street or the Place Saint-Sulpice. A man who can describe how the general manager of a chain of hotels would bow to his more important customers 'as though he had found himself confronted, at a funeral, with the father of the deceased or with the Blessed Sacrament'[293] puts himself, by the very language he uses, beyond the reach of this kind of religious salvation.

Neither is Proust averse to reminding his reader, by the comparisons which he uses to describe certain attitudes, that other groups apart from the French radicals and freemasons of the early twentieth century can be guilty of intolerance. When Madame Verdurin, undoubtedly the least attractive character in *A la recherche du temps perdu*, expresses the obviously untrue opinion that not even the payment of an enormous sum of money would persuade her to welcome members of aristocratic families such as La Trémoille or Des Laumes as guests in her drawing room, she notices that Swann is not expressing unqualified agreement. Her long-suffering husband then sees with regret, and understands only too well, that she is now 'inflamed with the passion of a Grand Inquisitor who has failed to stamp out heresy', and this is not the only time that Proust uses religious comparisons of this type. Because other women show a certain reluctance to adopt Madame Verdurin's article of faith about the unspeakable dullness of any drawing room other than her own, she is forced to adopt quite a stern attitude towards them. Since their critical spirit and demon of frivolity 'might, by their contagion, prove fatal to the orthodoxy of the little church', she has even been obliged to expel, one after the other, all of those 'Faithful' who were of the female sex.[294]

It is unlikely that Proust would have been happy with the placing of an interpretation of this kind on his religious images any more than he would have been delighted with the parallel that another of his comparisons brings to mind with the style of the English writer who was his junior by only ten years. It is nevertheless tempting, when you read of the 'fiery glow' in the air in early spring evenings when the infant Marcel walked back with his parents to Tante Léonie's house, and are told how it associated itself in his mind with the glow of the fire over which, at that very time, 'was roasting the chicken that would welcome him on his return',[295] to think of how P. G. Wodehouse's Tuppy Glossop could not look at a sunset without thinking of how it reminded him of a slice of roast beef, just done to a turn. The Narrator has a comparably Wodehousian vision at Balbec. For there, he sees 'a band of red sky above the sea, compact and clear-cut as a layer of aspic over meat', and then, a little later, 'over a sea already cold and steel-blue like a grey mullet, a sky of the same pink as the salmon we should later be ordering at Rivebelle'.[296] Wodehouse's culinary comparisons are, of course, a shade shorter. Violet Waddington, in *If I were You*, has eyes which are large and soft and the colour of very old sherry.

Proust himself, in discussing Bergotte, emphasises the unexpected nature of the images which characterise his style, and is almost certainly thinking of himself when he says that 'any new form of conversation, like all original painting and music, must always appear complicated and exhausting'.[297] This is because, he next tells us, all novelty 'depends upon the prior elimination of the sterotyped attitude to which we have become accustomed, and which seems to be reality itself', and this closing phrase shows how fully Proust's theory and practice as a novelist anticipated the French literary theorists of the 1960s and 1970s. For it was an article of faith with them that what we call realist literature is merely a term applied to novels and plays which correspond to our idea of what is probable. The problems which Proust had in finding a publisher for *Du côté de chez Swann*, like the difficulty which a fair number of readers still have in getting beyond the first pages of *A la recherche du temps perdu*, show how right he was to insist on the slowness with which literary taste catches up with new developments in the art of writing. It is certainly for this reason that I have myself insisted on the more traditional aspects of Proust's work, and have come to realise how fully *A la recherche du temps perdu* is a book which reads the reader just as much as the reader reads it, and perhaps even more. When one of his pupils came to pay a call on Hippolyte Taine before going to visit England, the philosopher asked him what hypothesis he was going to verify during his stay there. The hypothesis which I have verified in this study of Proust is that he is most interesting when talking about the emotions and about sexuality, and when analysing the behaviour of human beings in society. I drew the courage to do this from the most iconoclastic and liberating of contemporary French thinkers, Jean-François Revel. It was when I read, in his *Sur Proust*, the rhetorical question 'quel lecteur de Proust ne prend la fuite, aujourd'hui, quand il voit se profiler au coin d'une rue, comme la silhouette menaçante d'un impitoyable raseur, les accablantes et inévitables aubépines',[298] that I realised why it is a mistake for people like myself to concentrate too much on the first volume of *A la recherche du temps perdu*. For it is there that the indefatigable hawthorns lurk most persistently to buttonhole and bore the reader who has not yet learned to accept that he will always prefer the analysis of people to the description of things. It is certainly because of my own tastes that I have tended to suggest that Proust is often a different and a better writer than his own theory of literature would allow, and am conscious of how many of the qualities I admire in him are not strictly literary ones. I have, in other words, like all literary critics, provided a self-portrait: that of a sceptically minded middle-brow Englishman, who realised too late in life that he should have studied politics, sociology or psychology and not modern languages and literature.

But if it is true that Proust's account of how childhood traumas perpetuate themselves in adult life, like his analysis of the acquisition and maintenance of prestige in an affluent society, does not constitute the strictly literary quality of *A la recherche du temps perdu*, this still leaves unanswered a question once asked by Jacques Derrida: what would literature be if it were only itself, that is to say, literature?[299] It is fairly clear, in the case of Proust, that the more strictly literary value of his work tends to lie in those aspects of *A la recherche du temps perdu* on which I have not concentrated; his poetic evocation of Combray, his description of the village church and of the hawthorn in full bloom, his meditation on the poetic associations of names, his picture of the blossom on the apple trees, his attempt to describe in words the effect of Vinteuil's music. To enumerate these aspects of his work, and to realise how many others one is omitting, is a reminder of how rich, varied and inexhaustible a world he created in what I have tried to discuss as a novel but which would be equally well approached as an essay in autobiography, a collection of prose poems, or an examination of the nature of perception.

For it is certainly true that Proust saw himself as an artist and not as a psychologist or social analyst. A more literary approach to his work – there are plenty of them – would undoubtedly bring out these more poetic and impressionistic qualities, which are evident on every page of the book. As a novelist, Proust will inevitably if not always rightly be thought of first and foremost for his views on time and for his depiction of those moments when a chance physical sensation brings the past flooding back to us. He was also one of the first to dispense with a conventional narrative framework, and to carry out what André Maurois called 'a Copernican revolution in reverse'. He did this by putting the individual mind back into the centre of the creative writer's imaginary universe, and consequently describing events from a highly personal viewpoint which affirmed the value as well as the inevitability of its own subjective vision. It is of course true, as I pointed out in Chapter 1, that the narrative viewpoint in *A la recherche du temps perdu* is not always a consistent one. This fact has led a number of critics to distinguish between Marcel, the character who undergoes the experiences, and the Narrator, who tells the reader about them, and there would be no need to limit the number of narrative voices to two. I have not found it possible or useful to do this, and recognise that my failure is linked to a purely personal inability to appreciate how great a service Proust performed for literature when he made it problematic. This is undoubtedly one of the great achievements as far as literary critics are concerned, and it certainly links him with the great calling into question of the very concept of literature which is so marked a feature of contemporary aesthetics. To readers whose interest – like mine – is in content rather than form, this calling into question can sometimes be slightly tiresome, but there is no doubt that it has played its part in ensuring that the problems raised by *A la recherche du temps perdu* remain at the forefront of literary discussion in the French-speaking as well as the English-speaking intellectual world.

Notes

A la recherche du temps perdu is quoted from the Bibliothèque de la Pléiade edition by Pierre Clarac and André Ferré (3 vols, Gallimard, Paris, 1954) and from the translation by C. K. Scott Moncrieff and Terence Kilmartin (3 vols, Chatto and Windus, London, 1981). The reference III 869;901 means that the passage in question is on page 869 of the third volume of the French edition; and on page 901 of the English translation.

Wherever possible, Proust's letters are quoted in Philip Kolb's edition of his Correspondance, published by Plon. Kolb IX, 1909, 112 means that the quotation is on page 112 of the ninth volume, which contains letters written in 1909.

Contre Sainte-Beuve is abbreviated to CBS, and quoted throughout in the 1971 Pléiade edition.

Marcel Proust. Choix de Lettres, présentées et datées par Philip Kolb (Plon, 1965), is referred to as Choix.

1 THE BOOK, THE MEMORIES AND THE MAN

1. See Beckett's Foreword to his Proust (John Calder, London, 1956). Beckett's essay was first published in 1931 by the Grove Press, Paris and New York. It is more informative about Beckett than about Proust. It refers to 'the abominable edition of the Nouvelle Revue Française in sixteen volumes'. It tells us on p. 87 that 'Proust's style was generally resented in French literary circles. But now that he is no longer read, it is conceded that he might have written even worse than he did.'

2. I 45;48.

3. II 755–7;783–4.

4. III 868;900.

5. III 869;901.

6. Less pure, III 898;935. Cement, III 267;1013. Style, III 889;925.

7. Kolb XII, 1913, VIII. The publisher in question was Alfred Humblot, head of the rather commercial publishing house of Ollendorff.

8. III 895;931.

9. Kolb III, 1902–3, 196. See also Selected Letters 1880–1903, translated by Ralph Manheim (Collins, London, 1983, OUP paperback, 1985), p. 284.

10. CSB 221–2. See By Way of Sainte-Beuve, translated by Sylvia Townsend Warner (Hogarth Press, London, 1984), p. 76.

11. See 'La mort de l'auteur', *Mantéia*, No. 5 (Marseilles, 1968), pp. 12–17.

12. II 789;817.

13. George D. Painter maintains in his *Marcel Proust. A Biography*, 2 vols (Chatto and Windus, London, 1959, 1965, Peregrine Books, 1977), II, p. 12, that Proust had a 'carnal relationship' with the actress Louisa de Mornand sometime between April and July 1904. Proust's letters during that period (Kolb III and IV) do not bear out this impression. They are taken up principally with his attempt to console her for the fact that her lover, Louis d'Albufera, had omitted to tell her that he was going to marry Anna Massena d'Essling. Perhaps wisely, Proust did not think he personally ought to marry, and wrote to Georges de Lauris in November 1909 that it would be a crime to make a young girl share his 'atrocious life', even if the prospect did not terrify her (Kolb IX, 1909, 216).

14. Kolb XIII, 1914, 214–24.

15. Kolb I, 1880–98, 42–3.

16. II 982;1014.

17. I 4;4.

18. See *Le Monde*, 28 Oct. 1984. Review by Bernard Alliot of Pierre Assouline's *Gaston Gallimard* (Ballard, Paris, 1984).

19. *Les Plaisirs et les jours* was republished in the *Pléiade* edition in 1971, in the same volume as *Jean Santeuil*. See pp. 119, 154. *Jean Santeuil* was translated into English in 1955, after its first appearance in French in 1952. In 1986, a new edition was published by Peter Owen, London, of Louise Varese's translation of *Les Plaisirs et les jours* under the title of *Pleasures and Regrets*, with an Introduction by D. J. Enright.

20. C. Hahn, Kolb II, 1899, 292. Not sleeping; Anna de Noavilles, III, 1902–3, 445, 447.

21. I 852;911.

22. II 758;785.

23. See *L'Evénement du jeudi*, No. 62 (9 Jan. 1986), p. 75.

24. *Temporary Kings* (Heinemann, London, 1973), p. 218.

25. III 1028;1084.

2 NARRATION, CHRONOLOGY AND TECHNIQUE

26. III 955;988.

27. Kolb XIII, 1914, 311. Although Proust said in the same letter that Agostinelli had behaved very badly towards him, George Painter (II, p. 85) writes that 'in all the evidence for Proust's relationship with Agostinelli . . . there is nothing for which this honest and amiable man can be blamed'.

28. I 515;554.

29. I 878;939. In a letter of 7 Dec. 1921, Proust told his American admirer Walter Berry that he agreed with Armand de Guiche's precept that one should 'avoid too much sensual pleasure and not intellectualise golf', and Odette remarks in I 621;668 that since, unlike several of her friends, she does not play golf, she lacks the opportunity to wear what she calls 'sweaters'. There is a rather sad note in *La Prisonnière* when Albertine is depicted in III 382;381 as leaning against the Narrator's bookshelves the shoulders which, in *A l'ombre des jeunes filles en fleurs*, I 828;888, had sullenly carried golf clubs. Had Marcel

behaved as Ferdinand Dibble in P. G. Wodehouse's *The Heart of a Goof* did towards Barbara Medway and 'folded her in his arms, using the interlocking grip', he might not have had occasion to write, in I 930;992, the unfortunately ambiguous sentence: 'Le golf donne l'habitude des plaisirs solitaires', 'Golf gives one a taste for solitary pleasures'.

30. III 605;618. For the possible similarity in this respect of Octave with Jean Cocteau, see Painter, II, p. 158.

31. Miss Hansford-Johnson's reconstructions were originally broadcast in 1957 on what was then the BBC Third Programme and published in book form by Macmillan in 1958. Although Bloch had escaped to America, Miss Hansford-Johnson underlines his ubiquitous immortality by mentioning how she had recently seen him in an hotel at Brighton 'dogmatically explaining to a friend that the Brontës had written only one novel worth the attention of any intelligent person: and that was *The Professor*'.

32. Derwent May, *Proust*, Past Masters (OUP, 1983), p. 5.

33. Kolb XII, 1913, 79 and Maurice Bardèche, *Marcel Proust, romancier*, 2 vols (Les Sept Couleurs, Paris, 1971), I, p. 238. See also Pléiade II 1174 for Proust's reluctance to call *Sodome et Gomorrhe* a novel and his preference for the title: Jalousie par Marcel Proust.

34. I 575;619. Husband's instructions, III 659;674.

35. I 17;18.

36. I 330;360. See also II 684;709 where both Monsieur de Bréauté and Général de Froberville appreciate the reasons lying behind Oriane's sudden discovery, on the eve of the Marquise de Saint-Euverte's party, that she simply must spend the day going to see the stained-glass windows at Montfort-l'Amaury.

37. I 77;83 for the cigarettes and I 466;503 for Norpois.

38. III 300;304 (Charlus, revolver). Norpois I 466;503.

39. III 300;304. I 315;344.

40. I 778–9;835.

41. For Genette, see *Figures III* (Editions du Seuil, Paris, 1972). There is also an English translation by A. Sheridan, *Figures of Literary Discourse* (Basil Blackwell, Oxford, 1982).

42. II 220;225. At II 239;246, Dreyfus is referred to as still being on Devil's Island, from which he returned in October 1898 to be retried at Rennes in August 1899.

43. For J. B. Priestley, see *Literature and Western Man* (Heinemann, London, 1962), p. 419. For Steel, see *Chronology and time in 'A la recherche du temps perdu'* (Droz, Geneva, 1979), pp. 223–34.

44. I 617;664.

45. III 952;995.

46. III 1020;1074.

47. I 367;399. II 834;863.

48. III 439;447. For money, see Bardèche, I, p. 293.

49. *TLS*, 14 March 1958. Anti-semitism, II 252;260. Unable to spell, III 300;304.

50. III 1031;1087. In an interview which he gave in 1913 as part of his very careful strategy for launching *Du côté de chez Swann*, Proust made exactly the same remark. *CSB* 557.

51. III 958;1001.
52. III 661;677.
53. III 957;1004.
54. III 985;1034.
55. I 512;551.
56. III 678;696.

3 FREUD, CHILDHOOD AND THE UNCONSCIOUS

57. Kolb II, 1899, 377.
58. I 350;382.
59. *CSB* 335–6. The 966 pages of the 1971 Pléiade edition of *Contre Sainte-Beuve* provide a good deal of information about Proust as a man and a literary thinker, not all of which is reproduced in the 201 pages of translation by Sylvia Townsend Warner, published by the Hogarth Press in 1958 and reissued in paperback in 1984. We learn that the fault which he felt most inclined to forgive, at the age of thirteen or fourteen, was the private life of men of genius; that, in his twenties, his favourite literary hero was Hamlet; that the military event he most admired was his own enlistment; his chief defect a lack of will-power; and his greatest need 'to be loved, or, rather, to be more accurate, to be caressed and spoilt, far more than the need to be admired'.
60. III 677;694.
61. III 10;2.
62. II 1121;1158.
63. *Eyeless in Gaza* (Chatto and Windus, London, 1936), p. 8.
64. *Metamorphoses*, 7, 21. Huxley, p. 9.
65. I 350;380.
66. I 36–7;39.
67. Jeremiah 17:9.
68. II 180;184.
69. I 288–9;315.
70. I 128;140.
71. Bardèche, II, p. 135.
72. *CSB* 336.
73. Jean-François Revel, *Sur Proust* (Julliard, Paris, 1960), p. 27.

4 LOVE, JEALOUSY AND LESBIANISM

74. I 513;522. III 900;937. III 820;848.
75. Painter, I, p. xii.
76. Rivière's lecture was published in 1926 by *Les Cahiers de l'Occident* under the title 'Quelques progrès du cœur humain'. It contains an extended comparison between Proust and Freud, especially in their attitude towards the unconscious. Rivière says that Proust may have heard of Freud and had some general idea of his doctrine, but ruled out any question of a direct influence. Other people who knew Proust agree that he did, as a man, share the pessimism about love expressed by his Narrator. These include Antoine Bibesco in 'The

Heartlessness of Marcel Proust', *Cornhill Magazine*, 983 (Summer 1950) and Valentine Thomson, 'My Cousin, Marcel Proust', *Harper's Magazine*, vol. 164 (May 1962). Proust also wrote a letter to Louis de Robert in May 1913 in which he described himself as having continually been unhappy in love (Kolb XII, 1913, 165).

77. I 696;749.
78. I 763;819.
79. II 156;158.
80. III 375;382.
81. See Jaroslav Vogel, *Leoš Janáček* (Orbis Publishing, London, 1980), p. 81.
82. See *Homosexuality and Literature 1890–1930* (Athlone Press, London, 1977), p. 60. The Lawrence letter was to A. W. MacLeod on 26 Oct. 1913. See *Collected Letters*, ed. Harry Moore (Heinemann, London, 1962), p. 234.
83. II 481;499.
84. II 479–80;497–8.
85. II 317;327. II 901;938. III 907;945.
86. I 230–1;252.
87. III 612;626.
88. Revel, p. 197.
89. Priestley, pp. 375, 329.
90. I 646;661. I 669;711.
91. II 593;616.
92. III 702;721.
93. I 817;875.
94. I 343;373.
95. III 643;658.
96. III 72;66.
97. III 405;412.
98. III 97;91.
99. *La Condition humaine*, 1933. See the 1946 Folio edition, p. 142.
100. See A. M. Tilley and Alan Boase, *Montaigne: Selected Essays* (Manchester University Press, 1934), p. xii, who point out that Montaigne's mother, Antoinette de Loupes, was 'of the French branch of the Jewish family of Lopes'. Some doubt was cast on this by Roger Trinquet in *La jeunesse de Montaigne* (Nizet, Paris, 1972), and Géralde Nakkam in *Montaigne et son temps. Les événements, les essais* (Nizet, Paris, 1982), pointed out that the Louppes or Loupes family was of the Christian religion. Dr Nakkam nevertheless concluded (p. 31) that the family probably was Jewish in origin.
101. 'Du Repentir', *Essais*, III:2.
102. Léa III 215;212. Morel II 910;941. Rachel II 167;170.
103. III 351;359–60.
104. III 90;84. Swann I 366;398.
105. *Colette. A Passion for Life* (Thames and Hudson, London, 1985), p. 124.
106. Painter, II, pp. 320–1.
107. See M. Bowie, *Proust, Jealousy, Knowledge* (University of London, Queen Mary College, 1978).
108. See *When We Were Very Young* (Methuen, London, 1924), pp. 30–4.
109. III 528;538.
110. I 794;851–2.

111. III 827;856.
112. III 371;378. I 794;851–2.
113. III 181;179. See Philip Rieff, *Freud. The Mind of the Moralist* (Doubleday, New York, 1961), p. 161, where Proust is described as 'the novelist of Romantic introspection' and as deserving comparison with 'Freud's sensitivity to the transitoriness of sensual fulfilment'.
114. *Horizon* (August 1945), pp. 101–10.
115. Kolb XIII, 1914, 119.
116. III 159;156.

5 HEREDITY, HOMOSEXUALITY AND SCIENCE

117. II 578;601.
118. I 892;953.
119. See Gide's *Journal* (Pléiade, 1949), pp. 692, 694, 705, 1067, 1322. The two writers exchanged a number of letters, published in *Lettres à André Gide* (Ides et Calendes, Neuchatel and Paris, 1949). Proust read Gide's *Les Caves du Vatican* with great enthusiasm, and in April 1914 asked in an untranslatable pun: 'Je voudrais bien savoir si tous les "oncles" de Cadio [=Lafcadio] sont des "tantes"' – a slang word for homosexuals.
120. Céleste Albaret, *Monsieur Proust* (Collection 'J'ai lu', Robert Laffont, Paris, 1973), p. 385.
121. II 615;638.
122. Wilde's speech is quoted from H. Montgomery Hyde's *Oscar Wilde. A biography* (Eyre Methuen, London, 1976), pp. 257–8.
123. *Journal*, p. 1322.
124. II 615–32;637–56.
125. III 661;677. It is later revealed (III 684;701) to be much less, but the couple are still fairly well off, and Robert spends quite a lot of money to provide additional luxuries for his mother-in-law.
126. III 683;701.
127. II 921;952. See C. N. Armstrong, 'Diversities of Sex', *British Medical Journal* (14 May 1955), pp. 1173–7; see also 9 July 1955, p. 141.
128. II 607;629.
129. II 664–5;689–90.
130. III 344–5;350. For Horace, see *Epistles*, I, X, 24. For 'great lady', see III 824;853.
131. Painter, II, p. 262.
132. Anthony Powell, *Temporary Kings* (Heinemann, London, 1973). Not that Widmerpool has any friends, of course.
133. Originally published by Thomas Nelson, London, 1967. Panther Modern Society paperback, London, 1969.
134. See *TLS*, 12 June 1981.
135. I 945;1008.
136. See Céleste Albaret, pp. 465, 252.
137. See Simon Raven, *The Rich Pay Late* (Panther, London, 1966), p. 26, and *Fielding Gray* (Panther, 1969), p. 58, both being volumes in the *Alms for Oblivion* ten-volume series.

138. See Jeffrey Meyers, *Homosexuality and Literature 1913–1930* (Athlone Press, London, 1977), p. 127. For King Fahood, see *The Essential T. E. Lawrence*, ed. Philip Garnet (Penguin Books, Harmondsworth, 1956), p. 12.
139. I 159;173.
140. I 113;122.
141. III 528;538.
142. Beckett, p. 18.
143. III 263;265.
144. I 346;376.
145. I 350;381.

6 LITERATURE IN THEORY AND IN PRACTICE

146. III 870;903.
147. *Les Paradis artificiels*, VI.
148. III 1031;1087.
149. See Paul Valéry, *Pièces sur l'art. Degas, Danse, Dessin* (Pléiade, Paris, 1962), II, p. 1208, for the remark by Mallarmé.
150. III 908;946.
151. 'Marcel Proust: the novelist of memory', *The Listener*, 20 Oct. 1955, p. 663.
152. Magnifying glass, III 1033;1089. Price-tag, III 882;916.
153. II 378;393.
154. I 759;815. II 270;279.
155. II 520;540.
156. II 141;143.
157. I 838;897.
158. Sévigné, I 653;703. Sherbatoff, II 858;887.
159. *Choix* 262.
160. III 124;119. II 986;1018. II 86;84. Madame Cottard, II 960;992. First rendezvous, III 186;184.
161. III 889;924–5.
162. III 815;843.
163. II 503;521–2.
164. III 1033;1089.
165. See Proust's letter to Gaston Gallimard in May 1919. *Choix* 244.
166. III 1035;1091.
167. II 453;470.
168. III 760;783.
169. See Bardèche, I, p. 223.
170. I 547;589.
171. I 710–12;763–4.
172. II 328;339.
173. III 914;953.
174. III 634;649.
175. III 980;1029. I 490;529.
176. III 877;911.
177. Beckett, p. 63.

178. III 895;931–2.
179. III 896;932.
180. This interview is available both in *CBS* 557–8 and in an appendix to *Choix*.
181. *CSB* 598.

7 EXCLUSION, SOCIETY AND ADVICE

182. II 1085;1121.
183. III 669;686.
184. II 79;77.
185. II 487;505.
186. II 312;322.
187. II 195;199.
188. II 224;230.
189. III 900;937.
190. II 942;974.
191. I 516;557.
192. II 662;687.
193. II 663;688.
194. III 246;248.
195. II 261;269.
196. This masterpiece was originally published in 1908 and has been continuously in print since then. The quotation is from p. 30 of the 1964 edition (Bowes and Bowes, London).
197. II 1097;1133.
198. III 217;214.
199. II 247;254.
200. I 191;209.
201. III 694;712.

8 HUMOUR, OBSERVATION AND REALISM

202. I 675;725–6.
203. *CSB* 337.
204. II 324;335–6.
205. II 796;825. See earlier I 499;537.
206. I 453;488–9.
207. I 458;494–5.
208. I 877;937.
209. III 750;783. III 783;809.
210. Revel, p. 124.
211. III 772;797.
212. II 463;480. II 678;703.
213. I 205;224.
214. III 241;242. In fact, Cottard reappears at the end of the book, another

inconsistency which Proust would presumably have ironed out if he had lived long enough to see the whole of his manuscript through to publication.

215. *Jean Santeuil* (Pléiade, 1971), p. 652.

216. I 652–3;701–2. There are a number of notations about drink in *A la recherche du temps perdu*, including a remark in I 811;869 about ordering more to drink not because of the well-being it will bring you but because of the euphoria produced by what you have already consumed. On 9 Dec. 1921, Proust drank a whole bottle of port from the Ritz. See *Choix* 267.

217. II 106;105–6.

218. II 264;273.

219. III 761–2;785.

220. III 729;749–50.

221. I 699;751–2.

222. III 613;626.

223. II 425;441.

224. II 427–8;444.

225. I 388;421. II 427;446.

226. II 108;108. II 147;148. II 425;444.

227. Painter, II, p. 308.

228. II 662;686.

229. I 73;78–9.

230. *CSB* 558. In a note explaining *Du côté de chez Swann*, and which served as a basis for an interview published in *Le Temps* on 12 Nov. 1913, Proust said that he would be quite prepared for his book to be seen as a 'Bergsonian novel' since 'literature has tried at every period in history to link itself – after having been written, of course – to the reigning philosophy'. However, he added, it would be incorrect to do this since 'my book is dominated by the distinction between the involuntary and voluntary memory, a distinction which is not only absent from Bergson's philosophy but is contradicted by it'.

231. II 1097;1133. II 200;205.

232. I 769;825.

233. See 'The Coherence of *Le Temps retrouvé*' in Larkin B. Price, *Marcel Proust. A Critical Panorama* (University of Illinois Press, Urbana, 1972), p. 118.

234. I 676;727. II 941;973. On taking notes, see Bardèche, I, p. 339.

235. I 781;838.

236. II 33;28.

237. III 976;1023. II 495;514.

238. III 1006;1058.

239. II 745;772.

240. Painter, II, p. 308.

241. II 900;939.

242. III 950;993. See also I 191;208. I 562;567. I 546;588.

243. I 544;586.

244. I 438;472.

245. I 374;407.

246. III 180;178.

247. II 32;28.

248. III 35;27.

249. II 997;1029.

250. II 135;135–6.
251. II 64;61.
252. I 122;132.
253. II 64;61.
254. II 824;835.
255. II 954;986.
256. II 906;936.

9 MODELS, LANGUAGE AND PERSPECTIVE

257. Painter, I, pp. 97, 94. III 268;270.
258. II 701;726.
259. *La Quinzaine Littéraire*, 15 March 1966.
260. II 485;503. II 494;513.
261. *U and Non-U Revisited*, ed. Richard Buckle, published by Debrett's Peerage (London, 1978). See also *Noblesse Oblige*, by Nancy Mitford and others (Penguin Books, Harmondsworth, 1956), for the view that upper-class speech habits are characterised by the avoidance of euphemisms.
262. II 494;513.
263. II 224;223.
264. II 265;274.
265. III 34;27.
266. II 667;692. II 237;246.
267. III 943;986.
268. III 969;1016.
269. *TLS*, 12 Aug.; 19 Aug.; 9 Sept. 1965.
270. II 356;369.
271. III 337;343. III 340;345.
272. II 580;603. II 441;458.
273. III 889;924.
274. I 47;50.
275. I 48;51.
276. III 895;931.
277. *CSB* 586.
278. II 298;308.
279. II 226;232–3.
280. III 391;398.
281. I 351;382.
282. *CSB* 586.
283. I 223;245. I 97;105. I 222;243.
284. III 851;881.
285. II 344;357.
286. I 515;555.
287. III 676;693. See *CSB* 141 for the text of the *Figaro* article.
288. III 829;858.
289. I 549;591. I 506;545.
290. Quoted by John Cocking, 'Marcel Proust. The novelist of memory', *The Listener*, 20 Oct. 1955, p. 663. The year 1955 was something of a Proustian year in

England, with the translation of *Jean Santeuil*, a special number of the review *Adam* and an exhibition at the Wildenstein Gallery. See also *TLS*, 7 Oct. 1955.

291. II 23;17.
292. II 30;25.
293. I 691;743.
294. I 188;205. I 259;283.
295. I 133;145.
296. I 803;861.
297. I 551–2;594.
298. Revel, p. 220.
299. See *Philosophy and Literature*, ed. A. Phillips Griffiths (CUP, 1984), p. 187.

Bibliography

One of the many advantages of late capitalist civilisation is that it makes almost all literary masterpieces, however apparently arcane, easily available in paperback. While it is convenient to refer to the 1954 Pléiade edition of *A la recherche du temps perdu* when providing notes, Proust's major novel can be equally well read in paperback. It has been in the Folio 'Livre de Poche' series since 1972. *Jean Santeuil* and *Contre Sainte-Beuve* are also in paperback. There are also two easily available selections of Proust's letters: *Choix de Lettres*, présentées et datées par Philip Kolb (Plon, 1965), and *Lettres choisies de Marcel Proust*, édition établie par Bernard Pluchart-Simon (Nouveaux Classiques Larousse, Paris, 1973).

Since 1983, Terence Kilmartin's 1981 revision of Scott Moncrieff's 1922–31 translation, *Remembrance of Things Past* (Chatto and Windus, London, and Random House, New York) has been available in Penguin, and since 1985 the same has been true of Gerard Hopkins's 1955 translation of *Jean Santeuil*. A number of the essays from *Contre Sainte-Beuve* were translated by Sylvia Townsend Warner and published by Chatto and Windus in 1958 under the title of *By Way of Sainte-Beuve*, and republished by the Hogarth Press in 1984. In 1985, Ralph Manheim's translation of *Marcel Proust. Selected Letters 1880–1903* (originally published by William Collins, London, with Doubleday and Company, New York, in 1983), appeared as an OUP paperback. The selection of letters was made by Philip Kolb from the masterly edition which he has been publishing of all Proust's letters since 1970, and the volume was prefaced by John Cocking.

Proust has always been popular with English-speaking readers, in spite of his own reservations about Scott Moncrieff's translation. He disapproved, as George D. Painter points out in vol. II, p. 344 of the Peregrine edition of his *Marcel Proust. A Biography*, of the way that the opening of Shakespeare's sonnet number 13, 'When to the sessions of sweet silent thought / I summon up remembrance of things past . . .', was used to translate the title, and wrote that it was 'no substitute for the intentional ambiguity of my *Temps perdu*, which corresponds to the *Temps retrouvé* that appears at the end of my work'. His reservations have been echoed by Germaine Brée in her *The World of Marcel Proust* (Chatto and Windus, London, 1967), who prefers the less poetic but more accurate title of *In Search of Time Lost*.

Remembrance of Things Past is nevertheless a translation which stands almost by itself as an original work of art, and it was apparently fashionable in some of the more advanced Parisian literary circles of the 1920s to read Proust in the Scott Moncrieff version. In 1941, the publishing house of Chatto and Windus hit upon an ingenious way of showing solidarity with occupied France. It republished, in twelve volumes priced at five shillings each (25 pence, 44 U.S. cents) the complete Scott Moncrieff translation.

Proust has proved as attractive to English-speaking scholars as he has to the ordinary reader. In 1982, Robert Gibson published in vol. IV of the *Cahiers Marcel Proust*, Nouvelle Série (Gallimard, Paris), an article entitled 'Proust et la critique anglo-saxonne'. This listed a total of 359 books, articles and unpublished theses written on Proust in English between 1913 and 1965. One of the more recent French writers on Proust, Jean-Yves Tadié, begins his eleven pages of bibliography with a reference to V. E. Graham's *Bibliographie des études sur Marcel Proust et son œuvre* (Droz, Geneva, 1972), which lists 2274 different titles (Tadié, *Proust*, Belfond, Paris, 1983).

Tadié's book is a good introduction to Proust for French-speaking readers, as is Maurice Bardèche, *Marcel Proust, romancier*, 2 vols (Les Sept Couleurs, Paris, 1971). Both give a detailed account of the different stages through which *A la recherche du temps perdu* passed between 1909 and 1922. Alison Winton's *Proust's Additions. The making of 'A la recherche du temps perdu'* (2 vols, CUP, 1977) is based on the sixty-two *cahiers* (exercise books) in which Proust wrote the first notes and drafts for his novel and which the Bibliothèque Nationale acquired in 1962 as well as on the more complete manuscript itself, the three typescripts, and those galley proofs which Proust did correct before his death.

In addition to George D. Painter's biography, there is a full account of Proust's life in Richard H. Barker, *Marcel Proust. A Biography* (Faber and Faber, London, 1958).

There are two excellent books illustrating what Proust, his friends and the society he lived in looked like: André Maurois, *Le Monde de Marcel Proust* (Hachette, Paris, 1960), and Peter Quennell, *Marcel Proust, 1871–1922* (Weidenfeld and Nicolson, London, 1971). In addition to Terence Kilmartin's *A Guide to Proust* (Chatto and Windus, London, 1983), there is also P. A. Spalding's *A Reader's Handbook to Proust* (Chatto and Windus, 1952, republished by George Prior, London, 1975). The Pléiade edition has an excellent index of both people and places.

Index

THE CANADIANS
HOW THEY LIVE AND WORK

Other books in this series

The Argentines: How They Live and Work
by Dereck H. N. Foster

The Australians: How They Live and Work
by Nancy Learmonth

The Austrians: How They Live and Work
by Eric Whelpton

The Brazilians: How They Live and Work
by R. A. Wellington

The Chinese: How They Live and Work
by T. R. Tregear

The Dutch: How They Live and Work
by Ann Hoffmann

The Egyptians: How They Live and Work
by Shirley Kay

The Finns and the Lapps: How They Live and Work
by John L. Irwin

The French: How They Live and Work
by Joseph T. Carroll

The Greeks: How They Live and Work
T. R. B. Dicks

The Irish: How They Live and Work
by Martin Wallace

The Israelis: How They Live and Work
by Brian Dicks

The Italians: How They Live and Work
by Andrew Bryant

The Japanese: How They Live and Work
by W. Scott Morton

The Mexicans: How They Live and Work
by Peter Calvert

The New Zealanders: How They Live and Work
by R. J. Johnston

The Norwegians: How They Live and Work
by Arthur Spencer

The Poles: How They Live and Work
by Marc E. Heine

The Russians: How They Live and Work
by W. H. Parker

The Spaniards: How They Live and Work
by Michael Perceval

The Swedes: How They Live and Work
by Paul Britten Austin

The Swiss: How They Live and Work
by Neil Alexander

The United States: How They Live and Work
by David M. Smith

The West Indians: How They Live and Work
by Basil E. Cracknell

The Canadians

HOW THEY LIVE AND WORK

Jessie and Wreford Watson

DAVID & CHARLES

Newton Abbot   London   North Pomfret (VT)

GRIFFIN HOUSE : TORONTO 1977

To Margaret and Jamie

Published in Great Britain by
David & Charles (Publishers) Limited
Brunel House Newton Abbot Devon

Published in Canada by
Griffin Press Limited
461 King Street West, Toronto, Canada M5V 1K7

Published in the United States of America by
David & Charles Inc
North Pomfret Vermont 05053 USA

Set in 11 on 13pt Monotype Baskerville and
printed in Great Britain by
Latimer Trend & Company Ltd Plymouth

Contents

Contents

List of Illustrations

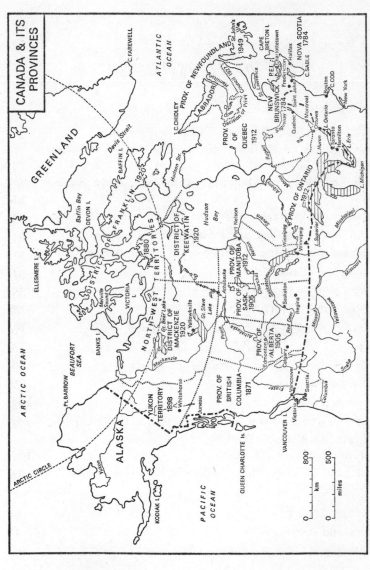

The provinces, capitals and chief towns of Canada, with the dates at which provinces or territories reached their present territorial extent

I

The People

THE beauty, richness, variety and freedom of Canada make it one of the most interesting and attractive of countries. Every year more than half a million Europeans visit or emigrate to Canada and as many as twelve million Americans cross the border to see it. What magnet draws them to Canada: what are they looking for and what do they find?

Many have friends and relatives in Canada and want to know how they live and work. They are often amazed at how many customs, religions and languages have been carried into Canada and are still active there. Canada is a truly multicultural country in which, though people have a distinct national outlook, respect is paid to past traditions. The native folk are found in every province, some of them living on their own, though not far from town, others mingling with the European immigrants. Of the latter, the French are the oldest and though they are dominant in Quebec, they have spread to all parts of the nation, carrying their language, schools and church with them. The British built the country, and are still the largest group in it: their parliamentary institutions everywhere prevail, and English is now the main tongue. The attempt to develop Canada as a bilingual country makes it different from its chief homelands, Britain and France, and also from its neighbour, the United States. Other languages, from Gaelic, through German, to Ukrainian, are also frequently used, and the visitor soon realises that Canada's rich heritage is still a very real thing. Cultures have not been melted down to form one image: in fact, the image of Canada lies in the preservation of many images. This is seen in the folk festivals or 'folklaramas' which are a part of every city.

These things are more obvious than might be thought, because most Canadians live close together in cities. The sophistication of city life, with high standards of housing and education, with splendid public buildings, major nationwide shops like the Hudson's Bay Co and Eaton's, excellent commercial services, and a high level of entertainment and the arts, can always be counted on to attract people. Moreover, Canadian cities are more than commonly clean, well run, free of corruption and crime, and pleasant places in which to walk around.

Yet no city is far from really quite wild countryside and to many visitors this is a delight. Scratch a Canadian and you will find a backwoodsman. In fact, millions of them go back to the woods every holiday, to ski in winter snows, or canoe on summer waters. Cities become emptied at the expense of cottage colonies or trailer parks. The settled part of Canada consists of narrow broken plains such as the basins of the Maritimes, the St Lawrence–Great Lakes lowland, the Prairie levels, and the lower Fraser Valley, separated from each other by the Appalachian ranges in the east, the Canadian Shield in the centre, and the Rocky and Coast mountains in the west. Thus it is everywhere easy to get into unsettled, untamed land.

The emptiness of Canada is one of its great attractions. There is a sense of room, lost in Europe and vanishing in America: room to breathe fresh air and to enjoy clean waters, room to get away from crowded conditions and to open up new developments. Canada still has an opening frontier. Beyond the restricted city base and the surrounding agricultural lands are the forests, waterpower, fuels and metals, now being tapped or still waiting to be exploited.

One of the fascinations of Canada is that it still is a country of exploits. The visitor or immigrant can not only see the great feats of yesteryear like the St Lawrence canals, the Canadian Pacific and Canadian National railways, the fisheries of the Maritime banks, the wheatlands of the Prairies, and the mines along the southern edge of Shield and mountain, all of which are themselves exhilarating to come upon, but also the great new hydro-electric works on the northern rivers like the Peace, the Churchill and the Hamilton; the big new mining areas in what were once empty spaces in Labrador, northern Manitoba and Saskatchewan, and in the far northern ranges of BC and the Yukon: even the prolonged silences of the outer isles, such as Baffin Land, or the uttermost archipelago, in the Sverdrup islands, are yielding to the prospector and the developer.

It is this excitement of things yet to be done, of the room to do them in, and the challenge of doing them, that must make Canada one of the most absorbing of countries to settle in or visit. It is rich both in natural resources and human endeavour. Firmly rooted as it is in the European past, it is nevertheless of the New World future. This dual role of continuing the great traditions of the Graeco–Roman civilisation, mediated through France and Britain, yet building a new consciousness and identity on them, out of the North American experience, gives Canada a unique place in relation to both Europe and America that compels attention and respect.

A nation of 23·5 million people (1975) Canada is a multi-racial, multi-cultural society, made up of many different stocks. Each of these has offered its distinctive contribution to the life and landscape of the country.

INDIANS AND ESKIMOS

Indians and Eskimos were the firstcomers to what is now Canada. Although later called native, they are of course immigrants just as much as the Europeans; they simply came in earlier and so appeared to European settlers to be native to the country. The Indians migrated to Canada from Asia at least 12,000 years ago, during warm phases of the last Ice Age, when the ice retreated from the Mackenzie and the Yukon for a while, and allowed people to cross over the Bering Straits and move into North America. The Eskimos arrived considerably later, about 5,000 years ago, after the Ice Age had declined, and the northern coasts were freed for human movement. Both groups belonged to the Mongoloid race, marked by narrow almond-shaped eyes, high cheek bones, straight black hair, and a yellowish-brown skin. They have been in North America long enough to have forgotten their Asiatic origins and to have developed their own ways of life. The Indians moved down from Alaska either along the Pacific coast to British Columbia or up the Yukon and across to the Mackenzie Valley into what are now the Prairies. They then entered the Great Lakes–St Lawrence system and so migrated east across the Ontario and Quebec of today to the Maritimes. The Eskimos kept chiefly to the arctic coasts across the Northwest Territories to Labrador.

In this wide sweep the early comers developed different cultures and separate languages. There are ten major language groups amongst the Indians: chief of these are the Algonkian, covering the Maritimes, northern Quebec and Ontario, and the northern Prairies; the Iroquoian, in southern Quebec and Ontario; the Siouan in the southern Prairies; and Athapaskan in the Mackenzie and Yukon basins. Small groups of languages occur in British Columbia. Because of language differences it has been difficult for Indians to acquire a sense of identity: many can only speak to each other in English.

Perhaps more significant than language has been their mode of life. By far the greater part of the Indians, and all the Eskimos, have by tradition been hunters and fishermen, living a semi-nomadic life following the migrations of the fish or animals on which they preyed. Many still continue in these occupations, though aided by modern tools. The Eskimos catch seals, white whales, walruses and arctic fish off the Hudson Bay, Arctic and Labrador coasts. They used to hunt caribou, but this is declining as the caribou have become depleted. The Pacific-coast Indians fish for salmon and crabs up the fjords of the west.

Prairie Indians have long ago ceased to hunt buffalo, some instead herd beef cattle: some still trap and fish in the western rivers and lakes. Finally, in the extreme south-east are remnants of the semi-agricultural and hunting people of the Lower Great Lakes and St Lawrence river, many of whom have taken up farming or work in the cities. They used to grow maize, squash, beans and tobacco on their village plots—crops which the whites took up and developed. Estimates of the Indian population at the time of the European invasion vary, but most put numbers at between 200,000 and 220,000.[1]

The impact of the early white invaders was masked to a certain extent in that they were fishermen, not interested in the land, or fur-traders, not anxious to clear the forests. Later, with the immigration of farm people who *did* want to cut the wood down and develop permanent sites for settlement, the conflict with the Indian really began. In some cases the whites wanted the very land the Indians were farming, in other cases they took over parts of the Indian hunting grounds—often those same valley sections which were valuable as wintering areas for the deer. Indians began to be driven back to marginal land or remoter areas: it was not unnatural that they should resist and that raids and counter-raids were made.

To resolve the situation a policy of separate development was adopted in which the Indians gave up their general rights over the land in return for specific reservations where they would be protected and would receive compensatory grants. Both the French and the British followed this policy. The reserves were laid out to allow for the fact that most Indians were hunters and fishermen, and needed space. Both French and British also reserved potential farm land for the Indians on reserves in the St Lawrence–Great Lakes lowlands, and later in the Red River Valley, the western Prairies, the Fraser delta, and lowlands on Vancouver Island. There was not a forced evacuation of Indians into the empty north, although, of course, since the whites did not spread north to any great extent, this did become the main refuge of both Indians and Eskimos who still form the majority of the population here.

'At the time of Confederation,' Battle points out, 'it was recognised that Indian affairs were of national rather than provincial concern and, consequently, a special provision was included in the British North America Act which placed Indians under the legislative jurisdiction of the Parliament of Canada.'[2] In 1876 an Indian Act was passed confirming Indians in their reservation rights, exempting them from taxes, providing an annual grant to them to recompense them for the loss of wider lands, and protecting their languages and customs.

They were in fact allowed to live on in their old ways within the new society, although they were prevented from the wider nomadic wandering to which many had been accustomed. Instead they were encouraged to farm, where possible, or adopt commercial fishing and trapping from fixed locations. The government established Indian schools and gave grants for livestock, seed, implements and equipment.

Subsequent to the two world wars, in which many Indians left their reservations to serve with the Canadian armed forces, a new Indian Act was passed in 1951, which gave the Indians much greater powers, enabling them to run their own reservations along the lines of county or municipal governments, to raise funds through taxation, and to administer the federal funds earmarked for public assistance. A federal Department of Indian Affairs and Northern Development was reorganised to help the Indians forward to integration with the rest of the country. An Indian Development Fund of nearly $30m has been set up for 'the encouragement of economic activity'. A major programme of school and further education has been launched and Indians who want to leave their reserves are helped to find work and homes in Canadian cities as ordinary citizens of the country. About a quarter of the Indians have given up their special treaty rights and, paying their taxes and claiming their vote, have assimilated with white communities, especially in the larger cities.

Recognised Indians, maintaining their treaty rights, number 295,215—that is more than the original number at Confederation. In fact, with an annual rate of increase of over 3 per cent per annum the Indian population is growing one and a half times more rapidly than the white. The Indians who have left the reserves, and especially those who have intermarried with the whites to become the Métis, may number as many again as the treaty Indians.

The registered Indians are grouped in 565 bands on 2,200 reserves and 59 settlements. The reserves cover 6·3 million acres (2·55 million hectares).

Indians have recently begun to group themselves into brotherhoods on both a provincial and national basis in order to achieve unity among themselves and present their case for a more fully-recognised status in Canada. The first brotherhood to be established was in Manitoba, in 1969. Now there are brotherhoods in most provinces and in the Yukon and Mackenzie territories. A nationwide brotherhood was set up at Ottawa in the early seventies and scrutinises all acts about to be passed that might affect Indian life. Indians now control an estimated $32 million of their own money. Recently, very considerable compensation has been given for loss of hunting grounds involved in the James Bay hydro-electric project, and in the Mackenzie Valley oil and gas strip.

Eskimos, now numbering 18,000, scattered in small communities from the Mackenzie delta to Labrador, have tried to overcome their isolation by forming a national Eskimo brotherhood known as the Inuit (Eskimo) Tapirisat of Canada (ITC). It has its headquarters in Ottawa and keeps a close watch on proposed Federal legislation. It also sponsors an Inuit Cultural Institute to help keep the old ways alive. Eskimos and Indians have, with some whites, joined together in a special organisation, the Committee on Original Peoples' Entitlement, to safeguard 'native rights' in the Mackenzie basin, caught up in the exploitation of the vast potential of oil and natural gas that now makes native areas so very important. They are asking that the land through which the pipe lines pass shall be recognised as theirs, and that they should collect royalties on the oil. In Alaska, Eskimos have received compensation for the land used by the oil companies.

THE FRENCH AND THE BRITISH

The French and British were, and are, the chief European elements in the country. Jacques Cartier, sailing into the Gulf of St Lawrence, claimed his newly discovered land, now Quebec, for the king of France on 24 July 1534. Cabot discovered Newfoundland for the British as early as 1497, only five years after Columbus had come upon the Caribbean, but it was not until 1583 that formal claim to Newfoundland was

made, by Sir Humphrey Gilbert, for Queen Elizabeth I.
Settlement came later still. The French established Port Royal,
NS, in 1605, and Quebec in 1608; the British set up a small
colony in St John's, Newfoundland, in 1613. In 1663, Louis
XIV organised his French Territories in North America into
two provinces, Acadia, in the Maritimes, and Canada in the St
Lawrence basin. He appointed Jean Talon as the first 'intend-
ant' or Secretary of State for New France in 1665, who, the
following year, made the first census of the colony, which had a
white population of 3,215. These were mostly traders, trappers,
fishermen and missionaries: they included virtually no home-
steaders. Talon induced Louis to send out settlers to open up
and work the land, but by 1700 there were still only 15,000 in
Quebec, and 2,000 in Acadia. In 1763 when New France was
taken over by the British there were only 70,000 white colonists,
including about 3,700 Acadians. Some 12,000 Acadians had
been lost by expulsion; 3,400 of them back to France. By and
large, the French were not active colonisers. Not more than
10,000 had immigrated from France during the whole of the
French period before the British takeover. Thus by far the
greater number of French in Canada sprang from natural increase of the original settlers. They were truly French-
Canadians.

The French-Canadian birth-rate was for long very high,
averaging between 30 and 40 per thousand. They were a Roman
Catholic people who placed emphasis on the family and did not
believe in the restriction of births. They were also a rural
people who counted on the family to supply the manpower for
cutting down the forest and clearing and cultivating the land.
At Confederation, they amounted to 1,082,940 people and
were increasing at the very high rate of 30 per cent per decade.
The Quebec birth-rate has exceeded the national average for
every census till 1961, when for the first time it fell below the
national level.

Coupled with the high rate of natural increase was a comparatively low rate of emigration. Consequently, although
Quebec did not receive much population by immigration it
kept up its share of the total population of Canada, even though

that population grew nearly seven times during the centennial period 1867–1967. Since the rest of the country was being built up by a considerable amount of immigration, it says a lot for the French-Canadians that they were able to hold their proportion so consistently.

Quebec has, of course, lost quite a number of French-Canadians, but these have been mainly to other Canadian provinces, though the loss to New England may have amounted to as many as 600,000. Its present population is 6·2 million.

The French-Canadians have spread throughout Canada and indeed have come to form a 'French belt' running from Cape Breton in Nova Scotia, through the north shore of New Brunswick and in Restigouche and Upper Saint John Valleys; across the whole of Northern Ontario, particularly in the Great Clay Belt, and in the mining and pulp-and-paper towns; in the Red River valley of Manitoba, across the whole of the northern Prairies from Le Pas (Man) to Prince Albert (Sask), Lac la Biche, the Lesser Slave Lake, and Peace River (Alta); to the Upper Peace River in British Columbia. There is a French-speaking community in every part of Canada. This is one of the chief differences between Canada and the USA, giving Canada its unique bi-cultural identity. It is interesting to note that between 1961 and 1971 in every province there has been a considerable increase in bi-lingualism (from 19 per cent in Saskatchewan to 14 per cent in Quebec). French and bi-lingual speakers are significant at least from Nova Scotia to Manitoba, and are represented in Newfoundland and the far west.

The British population was less than the French until after the American Revolution, when there was a large influx of Loyalists. Before that time, most of the 3,600,000 British immigrants to North America went to the American Colonies. The large influx of Loyalists to the Annapolis Valley, NS; the lower and middle Saint John Valley, NB; the Eastern Townships, PQ; and the St Lawrence–Lower Great Lakes was what really made early Canada British, and by 1867 the British had outnumbered the French, with a total of 2,102,000 (846,000 Irish, 706,000 English, and 550,000 Scots). They have never shown the rate of natural increase of the French, with averages of

B

about 20 births per thousand but have depended for their large and persistent growth on immigration. Had all these immigrants stayed in Canada, the British proportion of the total would have been much higher than it is, but about three-fifths left for the USA.

Newfoundland, England's oldest colony, was actually settled by both English and French, the French establishing themselves on the west coast and in Placentia bay. Placentia, set up in 1640, remained their chief centre to 1713, when they were deported. Thereafter, the British population became predominant, with many immigrants from the West of England and from Ireland. By the end of the eighteenth century, the island's population had grown to 20,000.

The emphasis had then shifted to the Maritimes and the St Lawrence–Lower Great Lakes. The port of Halifax was opened in 1749 as a major strategic base, and a rapid influx from both Britain and New England followed, with 6,000 people by 1751. When the Acadians were evacuated from the Annapolis Valley and Minas Basin in 1755, those areas were swiftly taken up by British from Yorkshire and also by New Englanders. Meantime the Highland clearances in Scotland led many Highland Scots to seek a refuge in Cape Breton Island and Prince Edward Island, while from Northern Ireland groups came to settle mid Nova Scotia. New Brunswick awaited the United Empire Loyalists for its main influx, receiving about half the 25,000 refugees who moved into the Maritimes. Loyalists were the main source of British migration into the St Lawrence basin in the late eighteenth century, moving into the Eastern Townships of Quebec, into Eastern Ontario, and into the Niagara Peninsula and Lower Great Lakes area. They were soon joined by Scots emigrants at Glengarry, Perth, Dumfries, and MacNab townships, at Guelph and in Bruce County. Galt, a well-known Scottish-Canadian, founded the British American Land Co to induce Scots and others to colonise S Ontario and the Eastern Townships. The war of 1812–14 saw a halt, but after it many soldiers stayed on in Canada, and British immigrants, disillusioned by the Napoleonic Wars, flooded in. Irish, fleeing the potato famine in 1846, began to arrive by the thousands from

1847, when they accounted for 70,000 of the 85,000 who came from Britain in that year. They settled mainly in S Ontario. In the mid-decades immigration ran at between 60–80,000 a year, until the American Civil War and its aftermath led to a slow down: altogether, over 800,000 British had moved into Canada between 1815 (after the war of 1812–14), and the mid-century.

Meanwhile the West was being slowly opened up. In 1812 Lord Selkirk induced Highland Scots to take up lands from his purchase on the Red River. Growth of population was slow until 1869 when the Dawson Trail from Port Arthur led to an influx of people from Ontario: Americans were also moving in, down the Red River. It was not until the Canadian Pacific Railway was built in the 1880s, however, that immigration became widespread. In that decade more than 900,000 people entered Canada, many destined for the west, where they were attracted by grants of free land (under the Dominion Lands Act, 1872). Most of these settlers were British, but from 1875–9, new elements, including Mennonites from Russia, and Icelanders arrived. A big wave of settlers in the nineties came from the Continent of Europe, and the next large onset, of over two and a half million immigrants between 1903 and 1914, had perhaps as many Americans as British entering Canada, with a large number of Europeans.

The tremendous intake of 1913 (400,000), changed the complexion of the Canadian population which grew distinctly more cosmopolitan. Even though the British continued to supply the largest single group they could not match the sum of other European migrants, particularly from Germany, Holland and Italy. Thus, although up to 1931 the people of British origin still formed more than half the total population in Canada, by 1941 they comprised just less than half the total population of 11,506,000. In 1971 British stock formed 44·6 per cent of the total, followed by French, 28 per cent, German 6·1 per cent, Italian 3·4 per cent, Ukrainian 2·7 per cent, and Scandinavian and Icelandic, 2·1 per cent. Poles, 1·5 and Jews 1·4 made up other significant groups. Indians and Eskimos together amounted to 1·5 per cent of the total.

OTHER EUROPEANS

Europeans other than British and French constitute altogether 23·1 per cent of Canada's population. Since their numbers are increasing more rapidly than the French or the British, they should soon outnumber the French and, possibly by the middle of the next century, equal the British: in that event they would be the dominant group and Canada would become truly multi-racial.

With the succession of the Hanoverians to the British throne, Germans, often as demobilised soldiers in the employ of the British, but frequently as settlers moving in by their own choice, began to be significant. In 1753 a group of Germans and German-speaking Swiss were settled in Lunenburg which they made into one of N America's most famous fishing and boat-building ports. Quite a number of so-called Pennsylvania Dutch—really of German extraction—followed the Loyalists into Ontario and settled in the Grand River Valley. Others moved into Eastern Ontario from up-state New York. By Confederation there were as many as 200,000 Germans in Canada—easily the largest of the 'other European' groups. Their strength was increased by a big influx of German-speaking Mennonites and, later, German Catholics, into the Prairies in the 1890s. After the two world wars many Germans were so disillusioned with Europe that they came in great numbers to Canada and became the largest group after the British in the post-war settlement, numbering nearly 200,000. Today they amount to over 1·3 millions, mainly in Ontario, but with a substantial number in the Prairies and BC.

The Ukrainians did not arrive until 1891, but as land-hungry people anxious to make the most of the Dominion land grant of 160 acres (64·75ha) per family (with a pre-emption allowance of another 160 acres [64·75ha] if required), they poured into the Prairies in the late 1890s and 1900s. In 1911 over 75,000 entered, fanning out over the three Prairie provinces. Although they were not allowed out of Russia after the

1917 Revolution, a few more got out during World War II. The major growth of the Ukrainian population which, in 1971, amounted to 581,000 was by natural increase.

The Icelanders came into the Prairies in 1875, settling the West shore of Lake Winnipeg, since when they have continued to move West; the Danes, by contrast, settled in the Saint John valley, NB, in 1872 and then went to London, Ontario, and Pass Lake, near Port Arthur; Swedes first entered with the Scottish settlers up the Red River, 1811, but did not arrive in substantial numbers till the 1880s when they moved in as Swedish-Americans from Wisconsin, entering the Prairies; the Norwegians also moved up from the USA, mostly from Minnesota, into the Prairies, some drifted west to BC and took up their initial way of life as fishermen of the fjords.

The other large groups, the Italians and Jews, entered Canada mainly during or after the two world wars and chose Montreal, Toronto and Hamilton as the chief targets for settlement. Some Jews, escaping from the Russian pogroms of the 1880s, took up farms in the Prairies, but most of their children migrated to Winnipeg or, to a lesser extent, Vancouver. Today Canada's five principal cities are the chief attraction for European immigrants, most of whom want to work in the city and not on the land. Indeed, in 1970, according to Dr Solandt, 50 per cent of all immigrants into Canada settled in greater Toronto.

NEGROES AND ASIANS

Negro and Asian immigrants have formed a growing proportion of the population. The black settlers arrived during the period 1775 to 1865, after the American Revolution and up to the American Civil War, as refugees from American slavery. The Canadian colonies, like those of New England, were strongly opposed to slavery, and offered political asylum to slaves who could run away as far as Canada. About 15,000 in all came into Canada, a third of these going to the Maritimes, and the rest to Southern Ontario. From this their number grew by natural increase to nearly 100,000 by 1945. After the war, Canada accepted a growing number of Negroes from the British West Indies when, on gaining their independence, these countries found they could not maintain their populations, and many Negroes left the Caribbean. In 1971, these formed 8·8 per cent of the total immigration into Canada, and were the fourth largest group of immigrants.

Asians are also on the increase. Chinese were welcomed as labourers to help open up the gold mines in the BC gold rush of 1865 and the Yukon gold rush of 1889. They were also brought in as labourers to help construct the CPR and other railway lines between 1882 and 1911. These early immigrants were mostly single males as Chinese families were not encouraged to migrate. Similarly East Indians were welcomed to work in the docks, on ships and in camps in BC, during the development of Victoria, Vancouver, and Prince Rupert, from 1880 to 1911. Again, these were mostly single men. Gradually, the rules were relaxed to allow women and children to enter the country, and today people from the Indian subcontinent with 5·1 per cent, and the Chinese with 6 per cent, of the total immigration are listed in front of any single European group, other than the British. Indeed the Asians as a whole formed the third largest immigrant group in 1971. Most are professional and business men, bringing in skills and capital much needed in the development of Canada.

All these immigrants came to speak the English language and consequently swelled the number of English-speaking peoples in Canada, swamping the French-speaking Canadians. Since even those continental European immigrants who have settled in the province of Quebec want English-language schooling, and since the major increase in population today is through immigrants anxious to speak English, the English language will doubtless become even more dominant. At present 67·1 per cent of Canadians speak English only; 18·0 per cent French only, and 13·4 per cent are bi-lingual. With present trends, over 80 per cent will be English-speakers only by the end of the century, though of course the effort to create a bi-lingual nation, if pushed hard enough, might offset this trend, and maintain a more even balance between the languages.

The ethnic distribution of people by their country of origins shows the Maritimes and BC to be outstandingly British; Ontario to be dominantly British but with a rapidly growing element of other Europeans; Quebec to be substantially French, and New Brunswick and Ontario to have a significant French 'mix'. The Prairie provinces are the most cosmopolitan area of Canada, followed closely by BC and Ontario. The least cosmopolitan areas are Quebec, PEI and Newfoundland.

OTHER DEMOGRAPHIC TRENDS

Emigration has always been a problem for Canada since it lives next to the USA—a large and dynamic nation where there is a wider range of opportunity. On occasions more people have left Canada than come in. Between 60 and 70 per cent of these emigrants have been native-born Canadians whose places were then taken by immigrants; quite a number were immigrants who, after staying in Canada for a while, moved on to the United States. Indeed, Canada lost about 8 people, some native-born, some immigrants, for every 10 immigrants added to her population. Had Canada kept all her people, her population in 1971 would have been 35 millions, rather than 23 millions. Natural increase has thus been the main factor in accounting for the growth of the Canadian population. The increase of births over deaths has always been considerable, from 0·6 million, 1851–61, to 2·7 million, 1961–71.

The geographical distribution of population in Canada is very uneven, and, moreover, it has changed with time. In the eighteenth century the Maritimes and Quebec dominated; there were few people in Ontario and next to none in the west. The nineteenth century saw Ontario spring to the lead—a lead which it still holds, though its dominance is not as great. The twentieth century witnessed the rise of the Prairies and British Columbia, although, in absolute terms, it saw further concentration in Quebec and Ontario. It is this unevenness of growth that has been so typical of Canada and which has posed so many problems. The favoured areas were picked out and centred on, the marginal regions were avoided, or only taken up slowly. In the Maritimes the plains bordering the Bay of Fundy and Northumberland Sound became populous and well developed, particularly the Annapolis Valley, the Lower Saint John lowland, and Prince Edward Island. In the eighteenth century these matched the population of the St Lawrence–Lower Great Lakes region. However, after Confederation they began to fall back, their place taken by the Central Provinces. Today they only account for 7·1 per cent of Canada's total.

It was really with the development of the St Lawrence and associated canals and the railways that the Central Provinces forged ahead, placing an emphasis on trade and commerce. Today they account for about 64 per cent of the country's total population, of which over three-quarters are in trade, transportation, manufacturing and professional services.

Dominant though they are in the nation's affairs, they do not quite have their former preponderance in numbers since, from the 1880s, the west has grown more and more significant. Not present in the initial Confederation, and only slowly developing after they joined, the western provinces awaited the arrival of the transcontinental railways and access to eastern and above all European markets before they really expanded. As late as 1901 they had barely passed the half million mark between them, and only accounted for 11 per cent of Canada's total, which was behind the Maritimes with 16·7 per cent, and well behind the Central Provinces with 71·3 per cent. Then things changed; the enormous immigration of land-hungry people up to World War I, and the rapid industrial expansion during and after World War II, the discovery of oil and natural gas and the use of a wider range of resources—all saw the west move ahead. Today the Prairie Provinces and BC make up 26·6 per cent of the Canadian people having far surpassed the Maritimes (7·1 per cent) and made a dint on the supremacy of the centre (63·4 per cent). Ontario with 1 out of 3 Canadians is still the most populous province with 8·35 million.

URBANISATION

Urbanisation has marked the biggest shift in Canadian population. After World War I, immigration, unlike the great waves of the 1880s and the 1910s, flooded into the cities. Not much new land was taken up, but many factories were built, and this was typical of the new trend. The same was true of the great boom in immigration after World War II: by far the largest number of immigrants moved into Canada's cities. As a result comparatively few of them went on to the USA. Here was a significant change: whereas 60 per cent or more of late nineteenth-century and early twentieth-century immigration, intended for farming, lumbering, or mining, went on to the US, less than half that number quit Canada when their main objective was city life and a city job. The cities of Canada were much better run, much less corrupt, much freer from racial strife, much less dominated by class division than American cities, and offered a better environment for mid-twentieth-century development. Hence Canada's population which was only 35 per cent urban in 1901 became 63 per cent urban in 1951, and in 1971 76·1 per cent—one of the highest in the world.

The urban revolution is currently the most notable thing in Canadian geography and is dividing Canada more and more into urban-based regions. This is a tremendous change. Whereas Canada could be effectively divided into its main physiographic divisions up to the mid-century, and one could speak of Appalachian Canada, the St Lawrence–Great Lakes Lowland, the Canadian Shield, the Prairies, and BC and the Yukon with some degree of relevance for Canadian life, after the great urban break-through of the sixties, Canada became dominated by the hinterlands of Montreal, Toronto, Winnipeg, and Vancouver, with Edmonton and Halifax playing lesser, though significant roles. The future of Canada lies with its great cities. Today, over three-quarters of its people live in towns, cities and city fringes. This is a marked change-over, and it is a change-over that is increasing. More and more want to be in or near city centres. In fact, there is now a move from the town to the city, and from the medium-sized city to the great metropolitan community, as urban living becomes the modern mode. Canada had few cities of any significance by 1901. But today Montreal is one of the world's great cities, with a worldwide reputation by any set of standards. And Toronto is a parallel attraction. Between them, these two cities account for nearly one quarter of the whole of Canada's population. Today, more and more people are crowding into fewer and fewer cities: we live in the age of metropolitan dominance.

The urbanisation of Canada since 1851 has been growing in every province, but has varied with the regions. BC was the first to be more urban than rural, with 50·9 per cent urban in 1911; by 1921 Ontario was 58·8 per cent urban and Quebec, 51·8 per cent; by 1941 Nova Scotia with 52 per cent urban was added to the list of citified provinces; by 1951, Manitoba joined this group; by 1961 Newfoundland (50·7) and Alberta (63·3) had followed suit. At the last census, 1971, New Brunswick had passed the 57 per cent mark, and Saskatchewan was just over 50 per cent, leaving only PEI still significantly rural (61·3).

The primary sector in the Canadian economy is declining and the tertiary and quaternary sectors are rapidly expanding. These are concentrated not only in cities in general but more particularly in the large cities. More and more people are crowding into already crowded centres, especially into those cities of more than half a million. These include Toronto (3 million); Montreal (2·8 million); Vancouver (1·1 million); Ottawa-Hull (·6 million); Winnipeg (·56 million); Hamilton (·51 million) and Edmonton (·51 million). Quebec city is close to this mark (·49 million).[3]

None of these cities is standing still. Attracting both the main amount of immigration and natural increase their rate of growth continues to make them major targets for more growth. Calgary is developing at the prodigious rate of over 20 per cent every five years; Toronto comes next with 16·3 per cent followed closely by Edmonton, 16 per cent; Vancouver, 14·9 per cent; Ottawa-Hull, 12·7 per cent, and Hamilton with 10·2 per cent. Thus Ontario and the west are growing very fast. Quebec city (9·3 per cent) and Montreal (5·8 per cent) are less vigorous, as a result of the lower birth rate in French Canada and much lower immigration into the province of Quebec, but are still expanding at over 1 per cent per annum (which means an addition of 28,000 to Montreal—or a small-sized city—every year). Actually, Toronto is now growing three times faster than Montreal, and surpassed its rival at the end of 1976 to reach about 3 millions when it became the largest city in Canada.

Whole citified regions are emerging. Toronto is but a part of the development round the head of Lake Ontario, known as the 'golden horseshoe' which, with Hamilton and other cities, already has a population of about 4 millions and may well reach 8 millions by the end of the century. Another rapidly growing citified region is the lower mainland of BC along the Fraser, from Chilliwack to Vancouver. These, and examples from the lower Red River and the Ottawa–St Lawrence junction, image forth a Canada of tremendous dynamism, developing communities of the first order, not only on a national, but on a world scale. Projections of great city population for 2001 show interesting trends:

City	Pop (rounded)	Rank 2001	Rank 1976
Toronto	4m	1	2
Montreal	3½m	2	1
Vancouver	1¾m	3	3
Calgary	1½m	4	9
Edmonton	1½m	5	6
Ottawa-Hull	0·9m	6	4
W'peg	0·8m	7	5
Quebec	0·8m	8	8
Hamilton	0·7m	9	7

The peopling of Canada has reflected both history and geography. Historic ties with Europe have made it a major target of immigration. Its history of struggle and competition with the United States has lost Canada many of its incomers. The very uneven geography has created a distinctly uneven distribution of population, with nearly two-thirds in the Central Provinces, more than one-fifth in the west, and less than a tenth in the east. More and more Canadians are wanting to live in cities, especially in large metropolitan cities.

2

The Nature of the Country

CANADA is an immense country with strong regional differences. Many of these differences were exploited by the French and the British in separate colonies. To give scope for their continued development, provincial government was established, replacing the old colonies. To unite the differences into one country was the work of confederation. A federal government attempts to unite differences into one fabric and so enable regional variety to contribute to national strength. The nature of the country, the history of its settlement, and the government evolved to run it are, therefore, all bound together.

SIZE

What first strikes the traveller is the size of Canada. If he drove by the Trans-Canada highway from St John's, Newfoundland, to Victoria, a distance of over 5,000 miles (8,000 km), the journey would take twelve days. Flying from Gander in Newfoundland to Whitehorse in the Yukon would be farther than crossing the Atlantic. The latitudinal spread is also considerable, from Pt Pelee in the south, on Lake Erie, 41° 41', to Cape Columbia in the north, 83° 07', on Ellesmere Island: this is greater than the distance from Madrid, Spain, to the North Cape, Norway.

Indeed, Canada is the second largest country in the world, covering an area of 3,845,774 square miles (9,960,555sq km). This is larger than both her neighbour, the United States, with 3,608,653 square miles (9,346,411sq km), and the giant of Asia, the Chinese People's Republic, with 3,759,191 square miles (9,736,305sq km). It is only exceeded by the Soviet Union, with 8,598,701 square miles (22,270,635sq km).

To be a giant is often an embarrassment. A great deal of energy and more than the usual resources are needed to keep one going. Canada's bigness has stretched costs and ingenuity to the limit. Largeness, in terms of only a moderate population, has meant sparseness, and has forced the people to spread out thinly, isolating one community from another, or straining resources to keep people in touch.

However, the fact that Canada has vast areas of still untapped forest, fuel, water and mineral wealth should, if proper conservation methods are followed, enable the country to play an ever-growing part in the economy of the world as a whole, and particularly in the well-being of the United States, of Western Europe, and of Japan.

LOCATION

Her location is another telling feature about Canada. She is a distinctly northern land in a world where geography and history have conspired to emphasise the north. Most of Canada lies north of the Fortieth Parallel and is thus in one of the most strategic positions of the world today being the only country directly between the two super-powers, the USA and the USSR. At the same time she faces the densest populations of the world in the temperate lands of Western Europe and of Japan and northern China. This has already given Canada her most useful and profitable contacts: she is at the very centre of things—a fact reflected in her wide network of trade and her web of foreign relations.

THE SIGNIFICANCE OF SHAPE

The shape of Canada is such as to increase her geographic involvement in surrounding areas. Broadly speaking, it is like a diamond, with points thrusting well out from its main mass. A deep salient extends southward through Peninsular Ontario into the heart of the United States. The Lower Great Lakes region of Ontario is south of at least eight states in the USA and pushes right into the centre of the American manufacturing belt. With such an inter-penetration of their geography it is no wonder that, historically, America and Canada have been so closely knit in so many ways.

Canada forms the easternmost thrust of North America, in the Maritimes and Newfoundland. This first attracted the British, under Cabot, and the French, under Cartier, to her shores, and has been an important factor in maintaining her strong ties with those two great mother countries. Newfoundland and Nova Scotia ports were chosen for the convoying of Canadian and American ships to Britain in both world wars because they commanded the shortest crossings to Britain.

Canada's extension to the west is less marked because of Alaska. Nevertheless, so far as the populous parts of North America are concerned, Vancouver is the nearest major port to Japan, and Canadian–Japanese trade is very much on the increase.

STRUCTURE AND RELIEF

The structure and relief of Canada show both a simplicity and a variety that are striking. Canada is made up of four principal structures, from a great central upland or 'shield' of old, hard rock, through interior lowlands, sloping down from the shield in basins that then rise to marginal fold mountains, which finally sink to a continental shelf.

The Canadian Shield, which is at the heart of the country, covers 1,850,000 square miles (4,791,480sq km), or more than the whole of the European Economic Community—indeed, of Western Europe. It includes some of the oldest rocks of the earth, dating back over $4\frac{1}{2}$ billion years. It is made up of huge lava tablelands, of swarms of granitic domes, ranges of tightly folded metamorphic rocks and shallow basins of sandstones and limestones. It was once much higher than it is now; most of its

ridges are just the worn-down but stubborn cores of ancient
mountains. It has been planed by prolonged erosion into a
plateau-like surface, about 1,400ft (427m) above sea-level.
Tilted at its edges in the Torngat Mountains (6,000ft or
1,830m) on the east, the Laurentides (2,400ft or 732m) on the
south, and the Snare and Nonacho ranges (2,000ft or 610m) on
the west, it sinks down in the centre under the seas of Hudson
Bay. It has a knubbly uneven surface that has made road and
railway construction very difficult. Its rough hardness, together with its width, has formed a barrier between east and
west, overcome only at great cost. It was long considered a
forbidding area and is still largely unsettled, but though the
greater part of it is unfit for agriculture, it is rich in forest—a
much-needed resource today. It is also rich in metals, with
major deposits of iron, nickel, lead, zinc, copper and gold. The
wealth from mining has made the Shield a central part of the
Canadian economy with the mining towns acting as a major
market for eastern machinery and western food.

Flanking the Shield are Canada's interior lowlands, consist-
ing of the Great Lakes–St Lawrence plains on the east, and the
Canadian Prairies to the west. They form belted plains of hard
and soft beds of sedimentary rock gently sloping back from the

----

Young Indians at a social club in Yellowknife, North West
Territories, an important gold-mining centre. Increasingly both
Indians and Eskimos have abandoned hunting and fishing as a
livelihood for work in mines, lumber camps, ranches and towns

Scottish-Canadians compete at the annual Highland Games at
Antigonish, Nova Scotia. Canadians of British origin are most
numerous in the Atlantic Provinces, but are spread throughout
Canada

NB, and finish along the outer maritime edge in a series of rounded ridges at about 800ft (244m) with elongated basins, like the Annapolis Valley, NS, between them. The whole structure has been fractured and drowned by the sea, so that it is a mix of great ocean inlets (the St Lawrence Gulf and Bay of Fundy) with peninsulas between them. Groups of islands stud the waters, notably the gem of the Maritimes, Prince Edward Island, and the much larger island of Newfoundland. Here sea is as important as the mountains: both put even small plains at a real premium.

The Western Cordilleras are much more massive, continuous, and lofty. They run in strong north-south belts, starting with the high fault-cut and ice-torn Rocky Mountain system, 10–12,000ft (3,000–3,660m) on the inner side; then a series of mountain stumps, steep-sided but broad-topped plateaux and deep-gouged troughs in the centre; followed by the superb coastal range, lifting its jagged crest to eternal snows in Mt Waddington, 13,104ft (3,996m) and Mt Logan, 19,850ft (6,050m). These plunge down dramatically to the stretch of walled-in sea known as the Inner Passage, running from Puget Sound to Alaska, beyond which is a broken sea-invaded insular arc, including Vancouver Island and the Queen Charlotte Isles. The relief here is at its strongest and creates the greatest variety of climate, soils, farming, forestry and recreation in the whole country.

The Inuitian Mountains run through the Parry Islands and Ellesmere Island in the extreme north of Canada. They consist of a series of close-packed pitching folds and low domes which, though bare of vegetation and with little life, including people, have considerable reserves of oil and natural gas and add appreciably to Canada's fuel wealth.

The continental shelf is very widely developed off the Island of Newfoundland and Nova Scotia where swirls of cold and warm currents include the famous fishing grounds of the Grand Banks. Oil and natural gas have also been discovered in this great structure, though not in easily accessible areas. The Pacific shelf has been faulted down and deeply drowned along the coast, but between the Queen Charlotte Isles and the mainland it may hold oil and gas in the Hecate Basin. The Arctic shore slopes gently down to a broad continental shelf which, off the Mackenzie delta, is very rich in natural gas, and also has significant pools of oil.

RIVERS AND LAKES

The rivers of Canada have done a great deal to help unite the country along an east-west axis, from coast to coast. They comprise some of the greatest rivers of the world. The St Lawrence links up the Great Lakes on the southern edge of the Canadian Shield with the Gulf region of the Maritimes, forming the main artery of settlement and trade through Ontario and Quebec. Its immense supply of water is used for hydro-electric development on a big scale and for Canada's chief industries. The western edge of the Shield sheds waters into the Red River and Lake Winnipeg: these are joined by the great system of the North and South Saskatchewan flowing across the Prairies from the snow-capped Rocky Mountains. The whole complex of rivers and lakes then empties via the Nelson River into Hudson Bay, in the hollow of the Shield. Both Shield and Rockies feed the tributary rivers and lakes that make the Mackenzie one of the continent's mightiest waterways. Finally, in the West, the water-rich Rockies throw off the Columbia, Fraser, Skeena and Yukon rivers which wind through the Central BC and the Yukon Plateaux, before finding their way to the Pacific, in the case of the Fraser through a profound gorge in the Coast Range.

Thus, although the Appalachians, the Shield, and the Western Cordilleras do create marked barriers to routes from one part of Canada to another, they also shed rivers that have drawn movement up them and through the passes to link one region with another. The St John affords an easy connection between the Maritimes across the Appalachians to the interior; head streams of the Great Lakes, like the Pigeon and Rainy rivers, mesh with the Winnipeg River and so link the Central with the Prairie provinces; the Saskatchewan headwaters go back to the Yellowhead and Kicking Horse passes through the Rockies, to lead down to the Thompson and Fraser, linking up

the interior with the Pacific coast. Thus the rivers have overcome the longitudinal grain of the continent to strengthen the
latitudinal trend in Canada's history and growth.

THE CLIMATE

Climate is very much part of the Canadian character. As
Stephen Leacock, the humorist, once said, life in Canada consists of preparing for winter, enduring winter, and recovering
from winter. It is a winter-dominated country. Kipling's title
for Canada, 'our lady of the snows', is very appropriate. Yet the
summers, though brief, are strong and vital. Plant growth is
rapid and luxurious, and the heat brings on the crops to make
Canada a wealthy agricultural land.

Seasonal contrasts are marked and form a major characteristic of Canadian life. As winter approaches virtually every
householder puts up storm windows and doors to protect his
home against high winds, snow, and ice. As the snows descend
snow ploughs emerge from their depots to keep the roads clear.
Cars don snow tyres. Many industries lay in large stocks of coal
and oil against the intense and prolonged cold. Central heating
plants start to operate. Women wear fur hats and coats and fur-
lined boots; men get out their topcoats and over-shoes. Hot food
is served at home and in restaurants. Ski resorts open up, and
frozen canals and lakes ring with the blades of skater and ice-
yacht. The 'roaring game', curling, comes into its own. Otherwise, outdoors quietness rules, as most of the birds fly south. In
the country, the cattle are brought in from the fields, which remain empty from mid-November to mid-May. Then as spring
comes, the whole rhythm of life is reversed. Cattle low in the
fields. Birdsong rings through the air. Great skeins of geese make
the flightways of the sky alive. Central heating is turned off; air-
conditioners begin to hum. Storm windows are taken down.
Screens to keep out flies and mosquitoes are fitted to windows
and doors. Women appear in summer dresses, men in open-
necked shirts. There is a weekend rush to cottages by river and
lake. Cars are seen with canoes strapped to the roof, pulling

boats cradled in trailers, or crowded with bathers. Iced drinks and salads are the order of the day. An almost tropical style of life obtains—until the first touch of autumn colour reminds, by its vividness, of the winter about to come back. Holidays finish. School takes up. The thanksgiving festival is done. Central heating clicks on. Our lady of the snows again puts on her furs . . .

The climate is dominated by four main air masses: the polar continental, cold and dense: the tropical gulf, volatile and turbulent: the maritime polar pacific, strong and penetrating, and the maritime polar atlantic, raw and changeful. Of these, by far the most influential is the polar continental air mass which overspreads most of the country for most of the year.

Cold, dense air is nursed by the ice-caps and the permanently frozen soils of the Canadian archipelago and the northern mainland where it resides all year. Early in September it begins to spread south over the Canadian Shield. Its front is marked by polar cyclonic storms where cold salients push into the warmer southern air and undercut it in swirling conflicts full of rain or snow. A line of September storms curves down from the lower Mackenzie past James Bay across to Labrador. By November, polar air has conquered most of the Shield, and the storm-line runs from Alberta through the Great Lakes down the St Lawrence and across the Maritimes. By December all of Canada except the Pacific shore is covered by the polar continental mass, which goes on advancing through January until it is brought up in February against the southern Appalachians and the Ozarks. By this time the storm tracks are well south of Canada, through Texas and Alabama. Canada is gripped by intense cold with arctic streams sweeping the country.

The tropical air then becomes re-activated and, in late February, starts to move north out of the Gulf of Mexico. It spreads up the Mississippi and the Ohio, fighting the cold air right across the interior lowlands, in storm upon storm. Sudden salients of warm air will bring winter thaws to southern Canada in March, although the ice does not melt in the lakes or the snowfalls cease till the end of April. The Alberta lows are revived again and sweep east down the Great Lakes–St Lawrence, bringing warm-front weather to end the winter. Polar air breaks up and grows weaker, and tropical air surges in, finding no barrier to prevent its rapid expansion up the Ohio and down the St Lawrence, or across the Canadian prairies and down the Mackenzie. Very warm weather takes over the southern parts of Canada in late June and lasts through July and August, often accompanied by thunderstorms and heavy showers. The soil, moist with winter thaws, is activated by spring rain and summer heat; plant growth is all but fantastic, bare deciduous trees grow verdant crowns in a week or two, corn is waist high by August, and harvested by September. Warmth dies after golden October days, the James Bay storms deepen, snows drive down from the north, and the polar continental air mass strengthens and re-asserts itself.

While the march and countermarch of continental cold and heat form the main drama of Canadian weather, the invasion of maritime air across the Pacific and Atlantic coasts adds considerably to the climatic stir. Off Canadian shores lie the Aleutian and Icelandic low pressure systems, sucking in flows of air over the Pacific and Atlantic oceans. The air drawn into the Pacific low sweeps across the islands and up the mainland valleys of British Columbia. It is mild, wet, unstable and active, keeping the winters warm and rainy, with comparatively little snow. The far west keeps green in the winter, characterised as it is by forests of Douglas fir and sitka spruce and, where these are replaced, by rich pastures or by winter wheat. Summers too are cool, with showers interrupting sunny spells, except for the interior basins, which are hot and dry. These are cut off from most of the rain-bearing winds by the high mountains of the Coast. The Rockies also comb out the wetness from western winds leaving a dry rain-shadow area over southern Alberta and Saskatchewan—Canada's dry belt. However, high air streams passing over the Rockies are often caught in a down draught that then kicks off a wind swirl forming a lee-cyclone: this Pacific air, as it moves across the Prairies, will bring refreshing rain.

The maritime influence of the Atlantic is not as strong as might be assumed. The air is drawn off the continent into the Icelandic 'low', well to the east. Consequently, continental conditions often spread over Newfoundland and New Brunswick, especially in winter, when rivers and lakes and even much of the sea is frozen. Ice grips the shores of northern Newfoundland and of the St Lawrence gulf: air drawn over it is chilled and made dense, as though passing over snow-covered land. Maritime influences are restricted to the southern coasts, though fortunately mild conditions there are enough to keep the ports of St John's, Newfoundland, Halifax, NS, and Saint John, NB, open. In spring and early summer warm air from the Gulf Stream is drawn into depressions travelling across still chilly land, and fog swathes the estuaries and bays. In summer, warm-front storms blow along the retreating edge of the polar continental air and bright hot weather prevails, broken by occasional showers.

An air mass, the tropical continental, off western Mexico, which does not often penetrate Canada does, nevertheless, have strong effects when it invades southern BC and the south-west Prairies. It is dry and hot, and carries critical spells of drought into areas already in the rain shadow area of the Coast and Rocky Mountains. Periodic droughts in the grain growing regions of Alberta and Saskatchewan can be crippling.

SOILS AND VEGETATION

Soils and vegetation reflect and reinforce the influence of climate. Canada is a green land made up of a huge arc of unbroken forest from the Atlantic to the Pacific, lying between the grasslands of the south-west Prairies and the mosslands of the Arctic. The forests are in the humid and temperate regions swept by the struggles between polar continental and tropical gulf air, or crossed by polar maritime storms. In the north, where cold polar air predominates, they consist mainly of conifers. In the south, bathed in summer airstreams from the Gulf of Mexico, they are made up of broad-leaved deciduous trees. Further north, trees thin out to mosses and lichens in tundra too dry and cold, under the polar 'high', for woodland. In the southwest, they give way to prairies in the rainshadow of the Rockies or where the tropical continental air makes its sallies.

There are three major forest zones, the boreal, the eastern

warm summer, and the western mild winter types. The boreal
forest stretches across northern Canada from Queen Charlotte
Islands to Newfoundland. There are only a limited number of
species. The sitka spruce is common in the western islands, the
white spruce in the Yukon and Mackenzie, and the black spruce
from Ontario eastward. A poplar belt fringes the conifers along
the northern front of the Prairies. Other species are balsam fir,
jackpine, hemlock, birch, willow and aspen. The whole region
has been glaciated, much of it is underlain by at least winter-
frozen soils if not permafrost, and as a result of winter-melt,
spring rains and autumn storms it has wet, acidic, podzolised
(or leached) soils. Little land is fit for agriculture, but is ideal for
forest, well suited to pulp and paper operations. Forest products
are amongst Canada's chief exports.

The warm-summer deciduous forest occurs in the Great Lakes
–St Lawrence region and in the Maritimes. It has responded to
low plains in a southern latitude with, for Canada, fairly long
growing seasons, and humus-rich deep grey-brown soils. In
southern Ontario oak, hickory and chestnut create a broad-
crowned, summer-green woodland, with species like the black
walnut, the locust, the tulip-tree and other exotics spreading
from still further south. In Quebec and the Maritimes the sugar
maple, beech, yellow birch, ash and pine are more common.
The fountain-like splay of elm-tops used to give a touch of grace
to all the eastern plains, but Dutch elm disease has left nothing
but gaunt arms, as in a war-blasted scene. Excellent hardwoods
for house and furniture-construction come from Canada's deciduous woods. Most of the woodland has been replaced by
some of Canada's best mixed-grain silage-grass, dairy and beef-
fattening farms.

The forests of the West (its mild winters created through the
influence of Pacific maritime airs), benefit from Canada's longest growing season to produce hardwood conifers like the giant
Douglas fir, western cedar, and western hemlock. Rich, brown
soils have built up from the decay of the fallen forest monarchs.
Quite rapid changes in forest and soil types follow changes in relief. On the wet, cloudy, mild, western slopes are the sitka
spruce, Douglas fir, and red cedars, growing to great heights to

give the impression of towering cathedrals. On the higher slopes, the forest changes to Engelmann spruce and lodgepole pine better able to withstand wind, frost and acidic soil. In the interior, where rainfall declines markedly, are the open woodlands of aspen, ponderosa pine, and glades of tall grass. As aridity increases, the soil becomes a desert-brown, and bears sage brush, short grass, and cactus. The western forest is now Canada's main source of construction lumber—where cleared—on low river terraces or coastal plains: its deep and rich soils have formed the basis of a corn, oats, barley, hay and silage-grass rotation, ideal for dairy farming.

The grasslands of Canada are in the dry interior, either between the lofty western ranges of BC, or in the southern parts of the Prairie Provinces. To white explorers bursting out of the eastern or northern forests they seemed all but barren, yet today they have been replaced by Canada's finest areas of wheat and barley production, and by improved grass for Canada's ranching empire. The parts still under grass are small, since so much range has passed to crop-land. Thus, while there once stretched broad belts called the tall-grass prairie to the north and east, and the short-grass prairie to the southwest and south, now virtually all the northern zone is under the plough, and indeed even most of the southern zone has gone over to agriculture. 'Nevertheless, standing on the slopes of the Cypress Hills and looking out over southern Alberta or south-west Saskatchewan, one may recapture again something of the awe with which early settlers gazed across the seemingly endless plains with their open, sweeping horizons, with no trees to bar the view, the eye being led by the windswept billow of swale upon swale of grass to the immensities of space itself.'⁴ Here the skyscape comes into its own as the supreme element in the scenery.

The soils created under the grassland by rotting roots and decaying grasses are amongst the richest in Canada. They have formed themselves into three belts: the black earths to the north and east, the light or yellow-brown soils to the south and west, and the chocolate-brown soils between. The black earths are without question the most fertile soils in Canada. Extending from Winnipeg through Saskatoon to Edmonton they mark the lushest fringe of the tall grass prairie in a subhumid zone swept by the Alberta 'lows' of spring and early summer. Here the summer surge of tropical gulf air has its maximum effect against the polar continental air. A dense sod of tall grasses and low brushes shed a thick humus that turned the surface soil black. The humus was broken down by summer rain and heat and carried deep down into the soil, making it rich in plant nutrients. The chocolate or chestnut-brown soils occur in a transition zone from subhumid to semi-arid conditions where tall grasses gave way to short. These are neutral soils and amongst Canada's best for wheat raising. The light brown soils grew up in Canada's drought belt often called Palliser's triangle, after Captain Palliser who was sent by the British to survey conditions in the Prairies before settlement. He claimed that this triangular area from Medicine Hat to Moose Jaw to Estevan was not suited to agriculture. Though some of it has been ploughed up for barley, oats and rye, much of it still remains in short-grass range. Where irrigated, however, the light brown soils have produced excellent crops of barley and alfalfa.

In conclusion, although Canada is on the northern margin of the habitable world, with two thirds of its land still empty, it is able to multiply its resources with space. Growth has been slow and moderate because of the difficulties and limitations of the environment, especially in contrast with the United States, but through the industry and ingenuity of its people it has made steady progress and now has one of the highest standards of living in the world.

3

How the Country is Run

CANADA is a country with eleven governments—the federal one at the centre, and one in each of the ten provinces. There are also councils in the Yukon Territory and the Mackenzie District of the Northwest Territories. The Provinces are in turn divided up into counties and municipal districts each with their councils. In Ontario the counties and municipal areas have been reorganised into regional administrations. Thus Canadians are, for their numbers, one of the most governed of all peoples.

HISTORICAL DEVELOPMENT

Historically, Canada is a fusion, rather late in time, of different colonies, each with a distinctive social and economic tradition. This has to be borne in mind by the visitor who is at first only aware of the things that make Canada as a whole a reality. Yet even to the casual visitor, provincial flags on flagpoles as well as the Canadian maple must make regional loyalties very evident. Soon he will realise that the eastern provinces, Manitoba, and British Columbia all had a life of their own before Canada came into existence. If Sir Humphrey Gilbert's assertion of the British claim to Newfoundland in 1583 was the beginning of that province's story, then it existed as a separate British Colony for 366 years before it joined the Canadian confederation in 1949, and has had a very short life as part of Canada. If Quebec's origin goes back to 1534, when Cartier set up a cross, thirty feet high, bearing the Arms of France on it, or at least to 1541, when de Roberval, made Governor of Canada by Francis I of France,

sent five ships with settlers, stock, and tools to found a colony,
then it was between 326 and 333 years old before it joined the
Canadian confederation in 1867. It has been part of the Can-
adian nation for only a quarter of its history. Consequently,
French Canadians have a profound sense of their own nation-
hood, which makes them speak of the Pays or State of Quebec,
defining Quebec as 'the National State of French Canadians'.[5]
Pierre Trudeau, though the Prime Minister of Canada and a
Federalist, occasionally refers to 'the Quebec State'. As for Nova
Scotia, its charter goes back to 1621, when King James the
Sixth and First gave Sir William Alexander, later Earl of Stir-
ling, the commission to colonise and develop it. Thus it had a
separate identity for 246 years before Confederation brought it
into Canada in 1867. Furthermore, Nova Scotia had the proud
distinction of being the first colony to win for itself the right of a
legislative assembly, elected by the people in 1758.

These strong local traditions divided up what was to become
Canada into areas with personalities of their own. Ontario began as the upper part of the French colony of 'Canada'. According to the Quebec Act of 1774, 'Canada' included not only the
traditional areas of French settlement in the St Lawrence basin
but all the land south to the Ohio and west to the Mississippi.
This huge extension beyond the lower Great Lakes fell to the
Americans after the revolutionary war. The rump of 'Canada'
then ran from Lake Erie to the Gulf of St Lawrence, still a considerable area. Loyalists from the new American republic streamed
there around the ends of the lower lakes, Erie and Ontario, settling in the Windsor and Niagara peninsulas and at Kingston.
These essentially British settlers soon objected to conditions in
'Canada'. For one thing the French land system was still based
on feudal rents and dues, under their seigneural régime, whereas
the British wanted to hold land in free and common socage, as
they had been accustomed to do. Moreover, unfortunately for
them, the Quebec Act denied the new colony the right to elect a
popular assembly. British though the loyalists were, they were
also North American, and had participated in colonial assem-
blies. In 1785 they petitioned the crown to split 'Canada' in two
so that a separate portion might exist under laws of due repre-

sentation and 'with an exemption from the French tenures'. In 1791, the British government divided 'Canada' into Upper (Ontario) and Lower (Quebec) provinces.

In the meantime new developments were taking place thousands of miles to the west. A year after Upper Canada (Ontario) was constituted, Captain Vancouver began his momentous journeys round Vancouver Island and up the British Columbia coast, lasting to 1794. He made a formal claim to all the land from 45°–58°N. This reinforced Cook's claim of 1778. From the landward side, exploration was also active: Alexander Mackenzie, acting on behalf of the Hudson's Bay Co, widened his discoveries by moving up the tributaries of the Mackenzie River across the Rockies and, in 1793, reached the Pacific Ocean. The Hudson's Bay Co then began trading on the Pacific Coast, and extended British interest down the Fraser and Columbia rivers. From these beginnings there grew the separate colony of British Columbia.

An important break from the Hudson's Bay Co occurred in Manitoba where, in 1811, Lord Selkirk was granted 116,000 square miles of former Company territory in order to settle emigrants from Scotland in the fertile plains of the Red River Valley. Highlanders cleared from the glens were given the chance in 1812–13 to create a new colony. Until 1836, this colony was given its own administration in the form of the Assiniboia Council, which met at Fort Garry, now Winnipeg. Settlement grew swiftly until in 1870 the separate province of Manitoba was created.

Land owned by the Hudson's Bay Co, after having passed to Canada, became the North West Territories. This was soon eaten into and broken up. In the east, portions were transferred to Quebec and Ontario whose boundaries thus ran to the Bay. In the west, pioneers, moving into the Territories in ever greater numbers, wanted to govern their affairs like settlers in other provinces. In 1905, Sir Wilfred Laurier, the Prime Minister of Canada, introduced legislation to set up the two provinces of Saskatchewan and Alberta. Thus all the major parts of Canada came into being. The Territories shrank to those lands north of the Sixtieth Parallel, on the west side of Hudson Bay, together with the islands of the Canadian Archipelago. The Yukon was given special status as the Yukon Territory, with its own Council, waiting only for more settlers and fuller development for provincial powers.

Thus for a considerable time the history of Canada has been one of marked provincial loyalties, as people have wanted to solve their local problems in their own way. This is still an important aspect of Canadian life.

PROVINCIAL POWERS

Provincial powers are very considerable. Since Quebec had been given distinctive rights under the Quebec Act of 1774 (including its own law, church and educational system), an example had been set which in large measure had to be followed. The British North America Act of 1867 divided the powers of government so that (Section 92), 'In each Province the Legislature may exclusively make Laws in relation to Matters' of primary interest to the province. These interests are in the economic, social, education, and administrative fields. They give each province its own police force and judicial administration; its own civil liberty and property rights; its own university, school, prison and hospital system; its own public works and parks programme; its own licensing laws, ranging from marriage to automobiles and liquor; the sale and management of its own public lands; the control of its own natural resources, although in the case of water and agriculture this is shared with the central government; and its own rights to taxation, including personal, corporation and sales taxes. A large budget facilitates this provincial administration, and indeed the larger provinces like Ontario, with over 8 million people, and Quebec with over 6 million, can match many a European country.

Provinces have been flexing their powers more and more. Quebec has passed Bill 22 making French the normal business language in that province, although English is not displaced as a language used in Federal business; Ontario gave a tax discount on provincial-made cars in 1975, in effect an import duty on foreign-made cars; and Alberta has taken the lion's share of royalties on gas and oil production. Some provinces have entered the international scene with the establishment of their own official representatives in London and Washington; Quebec also has a special relationship with Paris, and with the 'Agence de Coopération culturelle et technique' which acts in and for all French-speaking states.

Each province is governed by an elected Legislative Assembly based on universal adult suffrage. Each has a lieutenant-governor who proclaims, prorogues and dissolves the Assembly. No provincial government can stay in power for longer than five years without calling a provincial election. The lieutenant-governor, appointed by the central government, can refuse to give his assent to any provincial bill, or he may 'reserve it for the governor-general's pleasure'. A reserved bill cannot come into force unless within a year it has been approved by the governor-general in Council. If the lieutenant-governor does assent to a bill he must still send it to the central government which could disallow it if the interests of Canada in general were affected. Altogether 112 provincial acts have been disallowed, since Confederation. Thus, although provincial governments do have considerable say, this can be qualified by the government at the centre.

A train emerging from a pass through the Rockies at Windy Point, Jasper, Alberta

The Canadian Shield, with its abrupt edge facing the St Lawrence and Great Lakes, is featured by many waterfalls making Canada rich in hydro-electric power. Here Montmorency Falls, near Quebec city, supply power for the textiles industry

FEDERAL POWERS

Federal powers give the balance of decision to Canada as a whole. It must be remembered that, as Senator Forsey says, 'Canadian federalism was born among the Civil War agonies of American federalism. Macdonald (the first Canadian Prime Minister) and his colleagues were close students, and in many respects, great admirers of the American constitution. But to them it seemed clear that it had one terrible flaw, which might prove even fatal—States' rights. "The Americans", said Macdonald, "[had] commenced at the wrong end." They had given the central government a narrow list of specific powers, and had explicitly left everything else to the States and to the people. The Canadian Fathers of Confederation deliberately did the opposite; they gave the provinces a narrow list of specific powers, and stipulated that everything "not distinctly and exclusively conferred on the local governments and legislatures shall be conferred upon the general government and legislature . . . We thereby strengthen the central government and make the Confederation one people and one government." They explicitly

---

Canada's largest plains, the Prairies—lying between the Rockies and the Canadian Shield—are extensively developed by large wheat farms in the more humid parts

Ranching is a typical way of life in the short-grass range of the drier parts of the Prairies. With irrigation and the planting of sheltering forests, the number and quality of cattle reared have been greatly developed

D

conferred on the "general government all the great subjects of legislation ... all the powers which are incident to Sovereignty."'

The central government is responsible for these very important issues: the maintenance of Canada as a bi-cultural nation, with both English and French as its official languages—this makes Canada quite different from either Britain or the United States and gives it an identity of its own; the armed forces, to preserve its independence, and the Royal Canadian Mounted Police, over and above provincial police forces, to keep peace and order across Canada; the criminal law, so as to sustain the same justice throughout the nation; banking, currency, weights and measures, patents and copyright, to preserve basic standards of values; the raising of money by taxation and borrowing by use of the public credit; shipping and navigation, canals, ferries, telegraphs, the postal service, radio and TV communications, to knit the country together; the subsidisation of housing, family allowances and unemployment insurance to equalise social conditions; immigration, naturalisation, and civil rights, to control the levels and nature of Canadian citizenry; and Indian and Eskimo affairs, to protect and develop the native communities.

In addition, the federal government has major internal and external powers. Internally, it has the power 'to make laws for the peace, order and good government of Canada'. If a province does anything that endangers Canada or prejudices its basic interests then it can be checked and countered by the central government. For instance, the lack of provincial legislation to prevent air and water pollution, which meant that pollution passed from one province to another, was offset by all-Canada action as Canada passed the Clean Air and Clean Water Acts, offering protection to all citizens. Canada also has the right to 'regulate trade and commerce' across Canada and abroad. A province may do largely as it likes with its own resources but once it tries to trade these with other provinces or with foreign countries it comes up against federal regulations. A notable example of this has been oil. Though Alberta has the chief control over the licensing, exploration, and development of oil, and can fix oil prices within the province, it has nothing to say on oil crossing its boundaries. In effect, this has given Canada the say over the prices for oil traded across the country as a whole, and outside the country. Here is a real indication of the strength of the central government.

The federal government also has the right to regulate external relations. Under the constitution, the Dominion parliament and government were given 'all powers necessary or proper for performing the obligations of Canada, or of *any province thereof*, as part of the British Empire towards foreign countries arising under treaties between the Empire and foreign countries'. The government has used this right to regard the ownership and/or management of mineral and biological resources on the continental shelf off Canada as its own. The Canadian claim for a 200 mile off-shore limit to give maritime countries if not the ownership, at least the regularisation, of developments on the continental shelf, will in effect benefit the country as a whole; even inland provinces will share in the profits from off-shore activities.

Frequently there are clashes of interest between provinces and central government. Attempts to reduce conflict has led to frequent dominion-provincial conferences, where problems are thrashed out and solved. This has resulted in what Trudeau calls 'co-operative federalism'. Such co-operation has spread widely, especially in administrative fields. Thus though municipal affairs and housing are provincial matters, the federal government subsidises low-cost public housing. Constantly, federal and provincial ministers or top officials meet to organise co-operative programmes in their particular spheres. Federal-provincial committees then work out ways of implementing the joint agreements, or 'understandings'. Forsey points out an example. 'Prince Edward Island can legislate for the marketing of potatoes inside the province. The parliament of Canada can legislate for the marketing of potatoes in interprovincial and international trade. So the Island Legislature sets up a marketing board to deal with marketing inside the province, and the parliament of Canada provides that this provincial board shall, for purposes of interprovincial and international marketing, be deemed to be an agency of the Crown in right of Canada. So the

single board becomes both dominion *and* provincial: the same
members act under two pieces of legislation which, between
them, cover the whole field.'⁷ Canadian pragmatism often
comes to the aid of the Canadian constitution!

THE STRUCTURE OF GOVERNMENT

The forms of government are essentially those inherited from
Britain. It is a proud distinction that Canada is the only monarchy in the New World, and the only country in North America that operates a parliamentary system with a prime minister
and cabinet responsible to parliament. These things make Canada unique on the continent and distinguish it from the United
States and Mexico. They form a major part of the 'Canadian
identity'.

The executive power in Canada is vested in the Crown, as represented by the governor-general, and is exercised by the prime
minister and a cabinet of ministers of his selection. The royal
title in Canada today runs, 'Elizabeth the Second by the grace
of God, of the United Kingdom, Canada, and her other Realms
and Territories Queen, Head of the Commonwealth, Defender
of the Faith'. The Queen's personal participation in Canadian
affairs is not great: she does not now even appoint her own representative in the governor-general but acts on the advice of the
prime minister. Nevertheless, she does pay quite frequent visits
to Canada, during which she may open parliament, as at West-
minster.

The Crown is, however, a very real thing in Canada. Public
land is known as Crown land, and the disposal or care and
management of Crown land is a most important activity of both
provincial and federal governments. One of the main strengths
of the provinces is their ownership and control of Crown lands,
and of the forests, rangeland, waters, metals and fuels found on,
in, or under them. Management is often through Crown agencies, such as Crown corporations or Crown boards.

Crown corporations are 'agents of Her Majesty in right of

Canada' and are responsible to Parliament. Major Crown agencies are: the Bank of Canada, founded to 'regulate credit and currency in the best interests of the economic life of Canada'; the Canadian Commercial Corporation 'to assist in the development of trade between Canada and other countries'; the Export Development Corporation, to help finance Canadian exports; the National Harbours Board, the St Lawrence Seaway Authority, the Canadian National Railways, Air Canada, the Canadian Broadcasting Corporation, and the National Film Board of Canada to ensure adequate transport and communications across the nation; and the National Museums, the National Research Council, the Science Council, the Medical Research Council, the Economic Council, and the Canada Council to further research and help develop science and the arts throughout Canada. Government also gives partial support to the Royal Society of Canada. Marketing and development boards, such as the Canadian Wheat Board, the Fisheries Support Board, the Canadian Dairy Commission, and Uranium Canada have assisted in the growth of special parts of the Canadian economy. Atomic Energy of Canada is responsible 'for research into and peaceful uses of atomic energy'—a matter of utmost import to all Canadians.

The governor-general and commander-in-chief of Canada acts on behalf of the Queen and is in a sense the symbol and protector of the Crown-connection in Canada. His presence is another sign of the great difference between Canada and the United States, where the President is not only Head of State but Head of Government. Canada, like Britain, keeps these functions separate. The governor-general exercises 'on the advice of his Canadian ministers, all Her Majesty's powers and authorities (as Head of State) in respect of Canada'. The Rt Hon Vincent Massey, appointed in 1952, was the first Canadian to be made governor-general, a precedent that has been followed ever since, with the Rt Hon Georges Vanier appointed in 1959, the Rt Hon Roland Michener, in 1967, and the Rt Hon Jules Léger, in 1973. The governor-general is not involved in Canadian politics although he summons and dismisses Parliament, and must sign the Bills of Parliament before they become law.

His true role is to act as the symbol of unity in Canada and of the continuity of its traditions and its sense of identity.

The Prime Minister governs the country by reason of having won a parliamentary election. He is the leader of his political party, and rules according to the policies put to the electorate by that party. To this extent he is like an American president who is a party political leader and contestant. But there the similarity ends. He is not elected for a statutory period of years, like a president, but only for as long as he holds the confidence of the house. Should a vote of no confidence be carried, or should any major policy of his fail to get the required majority in the house, he must resign. Like the president he can choose his own cabinet, but unlike the president he must choose them from elected members of parliament. Both he and his cabinet are responsible to parliament; neither he nor his ministers have executive privileges, such as President Nixon tried to assert in the United States, that would put them above parliament or the law. When the prime minister resigns, his government falls, and all his cabinet ministers go out of office with him. The prime minister, however, has duties beyond the parliamentary function. He recommends the appointment of the governor-general, of the provincial lieutenant governors, privy councillors, the speaker of the senate, the senators themselves, all the justices of the superior courts, and certain senior public servants, such as deputy ministers of government departments, and the heads of Crown agencies. He also recommends to the governor-general those citizens of Canada who should receive the honours of the country.

The cabinet is made up of ministers each speaking for a department of government, but undertaking collective responsibility, with the prime minister, for the total government of the land. From the points of view of these ministers, joint decisions are reached on the policies to be presented to parliament for approval. If a minister cannot agree with his colleagues and, above all, with the prime minister, he must resign. The ministers are responsible through their departments to carry out the will of the house, once a bill has been approved. Ministers without a departmental responsibility (ministers without portfolio) may be appointed to help the prime minister for special purposes.

Much of the work of the cabinet is done through standing committees on groups of subjects and on areas of policy.

In Canada, with its two official languages, its many cultures and its wide geographical variations, it is a difficult yet necessary task for the prime minister to choose ministers representing both English-speaking and French-speaking communities, and also the major geographical sectors of Canada. If this is done justly and with skill it helps enormously to give a sense of unity to the country.

The all-Canada legislature is different from that in each Province, except in Quebec, since it operates through two chambers, the house of commons, an elected body, and the senate, an appointed one. Bills involving taxation or the use of public money must originate in the house of commons; this gives the elected members the main power, and ensures that people at large can have a say in how Canada is developed. Private bills, however, usually originate from the senate. The senate can amend bills put from the house, or even refuse to pass them, but after they have been looked at by the house of commons again and sent up, they must be approved. The house represents the will of the people. Parliament cannot continue in session for more than five years without a national election. Parliament must recognise the party with the second largest vote in an election as the official opposition, whose leader holds the constitutional position of leader of the opposition. Other minority parties must have a say in debates and a vote on bills presented.

The Canadian parliament is of course limited by the constitution to concern itself mainly with federal matters. It nevertheless has the right and indeed the duty to look at provincial legislation and to declare *ultra vires* those provincial bills contrary to peace, order, and good government in Canada as a whole.

THE ADMINISTRATION OF FEDERAL GOVERNMENT

Federal Government administration is enormously important in helping to maintain equal standards across the country and in giving Canadians a sense of real, working unity. The administration is done through departments and also through programmes. The departments include those dealing with people—Native Peoples, Immigration, Labour, Health and Welfare; those concerned with resources—Agriculture, Energy, Mines; those controlling development and communications—Consumer and Corporate Affairs, Industry, Trade and Commerce, National Revenue, Public Works, Regional Economic Development, and Transport; and finally, those involved in general good government, like Defence, Finance, and Justice.

Of special importance are federal programmes to offer Canadians better living conditions and fruitful lives across the country. On employment for example, there are more than 400 Canada Manpower Centres across Canada, directed from five regional offices in Halifax, Montreal, Toronto, Winnipeg, and Vancouver. In these offices skilled counsellors give information and advice on job-opportunities and help people to find jobs. The Job Bank was set up in 1973 to match jobs with workers. To help people get jobs, training courses are run by the Government under the Canadian Manpower Training Program (CMTP). The CMTP is most valuable for immigrants and those made technologically redundant, by giving them a knowledge of new methods and machines. Language training, educational upgrading, skill development and training on the job are all most useful aids. Another important agency in a country as wide as Europe is the Canada Manpower Mobility Program, which assists people in travelling to even remote parts of the land to take up employment.

Two of the exciting new developments are the Local Initiatives Program and Opportunities for Youth both of which help those who are anxious to help themselves, or others. LIP underwrites programmes initiated in local communities to provide jobs, while OFY gives young people a chance at joining summer projects useful to their community. Another imaginative programme, Outreach, delivers manpower programmes to those that find it difficult to contact them locally, as for example on native reserves, or in prisons or mental homes.

Housing has long been a problem in a country which has a

fairly high rate of natural increase and, in addition, tries to make room for immigrants. The Central Mortgage and Housing Corporation—a Crown agency—attacks the housing problem first by insuring housing loans granted by banks and insurance companies, and second by making direct loans to individuals. In addition, it operates a Home Improvement Program and—what is uniquely important in a land of long and bitter winters—a winter warmth scheme, to enable householders to put in central heating. The CMHC has seventy city offices, grouped into the five main regions of Canada. A very important new service has been the underwriting of better housing for Indians and Eskimos. Natives on low incomes can get adequate housing through direct grants. Band councils have been helped by loans to create new housing or improve old housing on Indian reserves.

Federal health services augment provincial ones. Very valuable is the federal power to see that foods and drugs must meet national standards of quality and serviceability. The federal government also makes sure that local health insurance benefits are postable outside of any province should the beneficiary move, and in other ways supplements provincial schemes.

A big contribution towards social equality amongst Canadian regions has been the Federal Family Allowance programme, to supplement family incomes and rid the country of poverty. A further recent development was the Canada Assistance Plan, to give special assistance to all persons in real need. Canada also runs an Old Age Security programme, since all provinces, except Quebec, have passed this field of service over to the federal government. Quebec has its own pension plan.

Old age and youth are given special help by the central government. Senior citizens, in addition to being eligible for the Canada Pension or for Old Age Security, can combine their pensions, from whatever source, and social security payments, through a Guaranteed Income Supplement. This takes the fear out of those years when people can no longer work and earn. At the other end of the scale, youth is given enormous assistance and encouragement. The Government Educational and Research Program offers loans to students to extend their education beyond school at centres of further education and at universities. The Canada Student Loans Plan provides a substantial loan, where a province issues a loan-eligibility certificate to a student about to be admitted to a recognised institution. The federal government also runs student summer employment and other programmes through Student Community Services, enabling voluntary organisations to improve their local communities by student help; language training, to make young people fully bi-lingual and thus able to get employment in Federal and other public services; drugs rehabilitation, to combat the non-medical use of drugs, and help drug addicts get back to work in the framework of their community.

Finally, the 'Arts and Recreation' programme of the central government encourages Canadians to create and to make more of cultural pursuits. Although most provinces have art galleries and museums and provide help to artists, their efforts are un-equal and, of course, are not aimed at developing a national culture. The central government, therefore, has set up major agencies to do this. Some of these are basic, such as the National Archives, the National Library, and the National Museums. Here are the maps, plans, public records and the papers of pub-lic men, along with the artefacts of Indians, explorers and early settlers that give a marvellous view of the growth and develop-ment of Canada. The National Library contains a copy of the holdings of 300 other libraries in Canada, and helps people lo-cate the books they need, which can then be obtained from the library concerned on inter-library loan. The National Arts Centre in Ottawa has encouraged the performing arts to a great extent, with its own national orchestra and theatre company: it is host to many provincial orchestras and theatres and so has quickened the arts everywhere. This is also the function of the Canada Council, founded 'to foster the study and enjoyment and the production of works in the arts, humanities and social sciences', mainly through grants. Very generous awards are given to creative artists to give them the time, free from other claims, to devote to their art. The 'Aid to Artists' programme is one of the finest anywhere. Another far-sighted federal activity is the Explorations Program offering grants to spark off new forms of creativity and to discover new insights into the national heritage.

As for recreation, a programme called Recreation Canada 'is especially pre-occupied with the growing importance of recreation in a post-industrial society' and encourages citizens of all ages to have some form of recreational activity. To assist in this, the federal government has provided a superb series of National Parks across the country—a matter that will be taken up in Chapter 8.

Canada is a unique amalgam of strongly regional sentiments and increasingly national feelings. Provincial autonomy has long been a feature and gives to the different regions of Canada the chance to work out problems in their own ways and to develop their own traditions. In Quebec this has led to a separatist movement. The need to create a Canadian identity and to get out from under Britain yet stand up to their giant neighbour, the United States, has strengthened the centralising forces striving to forge a nation with reason to be proud of itself.

The central government speaks for Canada in foreign policy. To take account of Quebec this is partly francophile; Canada has strong ties with French-speaking countries. But foreign policy is mainly centred in support of the Commonwealth and of the United Nations, and also in strong association with the USA. Canada took a leading role in linking America and Western Europe in the North Atlantic Treaty Organisation (NATO) and co-operates with the US in the North American Air Defence Command (NORAD). Canada belongs to 13 specialised permanent agencies and 18 ad hoc bodies of the UN —taking its part on the Committee on Peacekeeping Operations seriously enough to have joined UN peace efforts in the Congo, Kashmir, Palestine, Cyprus and Indo-China. Recent developments include a General Exchanges Agreement with the USSR, the recognition of the People's Republic of China, and the initiation of special relations with Japan. Finally, through the Canadian International Development Agency it has helped developing countries.

4

How They Live

GEOGRAPHICALLY, there is more open land and sparse settlement in Canada than compacted, dense development; nevertheless, sociologically most of Canada is urban, crowding into already crowded cities. Thus, although when travelling across it one thinks of the country as rural, while living in it one realises how urban it has become.

Nevertheless, rural life opened up the country and led to its division into administrative units that have affected routes and settlement ever since. Early systems of land survey have continued to influence the landscape. The traveller through Quebec cannot help noticing the long narrow fields, the nearness of the farms to each other, and the frequency of villages, their gleaming spires dominating the scene. Crossing to Ontario, he will find few villages, but many big isolated farms set comparatively far apart from each other in broad, square fields. These differences are very real and go back to the strong contrasts in Canada's bi-cultural development.

FRENCH RURAL PATTERNS

The French-Canadian land system originally consisted of the seigneury and its tenant farms. The seigneur was expected to build a church and a mill as well as his own manor house, and thus provide the nucleus of a village for the early settlers. The people who took land from him had to pay rent for it, and also a fee to use his mill. Tenants had the right to sell and to pass on their land, and their descendants the right to inherit and work it. Thus there was sufficient security of tenure for the tenants, or *censitaires*, to bid for farm holdings.

Both seigneuries and tenant farms were orientated to the rivers, and formed a pattern of fences and fields at right angles to the river-front that is still very much in evidence. In early days, of course, almost all traffic used the river—in summer by boat and in winter by sled. The best site for a manor house or farm was on a river bluff clear of floods, but near a landing. Consequently, seigneural boundaries consisted of a geometrical array of rectangles going back from the riverside into the bush. Modern administrative boundaries have adopted this system. Because the river-front was so valuable, rent was based on the farm frontage. Hence, farms tended to be narrow, but long—running back from a narrow frontage well into the land.

They became even narrower through subdivision. 'The law required both seigneurs and censitaires to leave their estates fairly divided among their children, a somewhat larger share, with the title and manor-house, going to the eldest son. As large families soon came to be the rule in Canada, estates grew small by ceaseless subdivision. The dividing lines continued to be run at right angles to the river, in order that all might maintain an equal share in the advantages of a waterfront.'[8] Even though the seigneural system was abolished in 1855, and was replaced by consolidated districts, subdivided into parishes, the earlier lot-lines remained to influence roads, fences, and farm boundaries. Most French Canadians live in narrow houses on long narrow lots, or in village and town, in tightly packed housing rows.

THE URBAN INFLUENCE OF FRANCE

French-Canadian villages and towns are unlike their Anglo-American counterparts in being centred on religious and cultural institutions. Driving into a French-Canadian settlement the traveller will pass along streets with a mixture of houses and shops, until he comes to a large square at the centre, where his gaze will be attracted to the high spire of the church, flanked by the tower of the parochial school. These institutions, along with the hôtel de ville are at the heart of the community. The inns and cafés, the *caisses*, the insurance agents and the gasoline stations mingle with the houses towards the village outskirts. Even in Quebec, French-Canadians see the Bishop's Palace, Laval University and the Courts at least vie for the centre with hotels and office blocks. The great banks are outside the wall. In Montreal, though the cathedral at Dominion Square is now over-shadowed by insurance blocks and banks, this is because the traditional French centre has been displaced by Anglo-American forces.

BRITISH RURAL PATTERNS

English-speaking Canadians, especially those of British stock, dominated by British or Anglo-American ways, live in a quite different manner. Those British who had come from the old country had been used to a secular landscape where mills and inns and shops and offices had become, or at least were becoming, as important as manor house and church. The manorial system had either been breaking up or had turned commercial, out to make a profit from the land. The church was divided, with villages peppered by competing chapels: the parish church was not necessarily the main, and certainly not the sole, village institution. This was even more the case in New England and New York from where the Americanised British came. There a highly individualised scene occurred, with scattered farms and mills, and villages structured as business service centres.

The land-system that came to prevail, and is now dominant in the Maritimes and Ontario, is derived from the township system of New England and New York, but operated in different ways.

Although townships varied in size, they took the same shape, aiming at being square. A base line was surveyed along a strip of lakeshore or riverside, and then boundary lines stretched at right angles from each end of the base. Concession lines parallel to the base were drawn at a distance of about a mile apart, while lot lines parallel to the sides of the township were laid off, thus creating an even, geometric grid.

However, the geometrical regularity of their location is only in respect of the local base line: these base lines altered in direction and length, so that a certain irregularity occurred across the countryside as a whole. This came to typify the early British settlement. Settlers arrived at quite different entry points to the Maritimes or Ontario. They surveyed the base lines for their townships quite independently of each other. If a leader and his group arrived on a sector of the sea coast or the lakeshore trending, let us say, from east to west, they would have a township squared off east–west by north–south. Another group might come on the shore where it changed its trend to north-east by south-west. This would then be paralleled by the base line, and the sides of that township and all its lot lines would then run north-west–south-east.

THE PRAIRIE 'GRID'

In the Prairie Provinces, the grid is, by contrast, much more regular. Sir John A. Macdonald, the first Prime Minister of Canada, who guided the opening of the West, boasted of 'one vast system of survey, uniform over the whole'.[9] The prevailing flatness of the land and the openness of the grassy vegetation lent themselves to a 'drawing board geometry' of land lay-out. The easiest way of developing the region was to run mathematically surveyed lines across it and then to follow with an even grid of roads and farms. The international boundary followed a line of latitude (the Forty-ninth Parallel north); the interprovincial boundaries, when set up, ran along lines of longitude. What more simple than to divide the Prairies into squares bounded by latitude and longitude.

The grid was composed of standard units, to which the eastern name of 'township' was applied, although the townships of the west were much more rigidly defined. Each township was a uniform six miles by six miles in extent. Each was divided into thirty-six sections, of one square mile (2·59sq km), or 640 acres (259ha). Each section was divided into quarter sections of 160 acres (64·75ha). Every settler could claim a quarter section and the pre-emption of another quarter section. In time the richer and more efficient farmers bought out others and amalgamated their holdings into whole sections or combinations of sections. Thus, farms from the first were spaced well apart, with pre-emption quarter sections in between, and as large-scale farming developed and smaller holdings were amalgamated, farms became even further removed from each other. Today it is sometimes difficult for a farmer to see his neighbour. This is a far cry from Quebec, where every farmer is, so to speak, at the other's elbow.

A traveller flying over the Prairie Provinces is thus struck by the astonishing regularity of straight roads, straight fences, squared-off farms, and grid-pattern settlements that extend from the Canadian Shield to the Rockies. The only breaks in the uniformity are the narrow lots of erstwhile Scottish Highlanders coming from long-lot crofting townships in the Scottish Highlands, or the even narrower long-lots of the French Canadians and the Métis (half-breed Indian and French) along riversides opened for settlement in the tradition of Quebec.

Since the Prairies were at first claimed and developed by the Hudson's Bay Company, this great trading company, on passing possession over to the Canadian government (15 July 1870), retained, first, a block of sections round each of its trading posts, and, in addition, one out of every twenty sections across the plains, from the Forty-ninth Parallel north to the Saskatchewan River (north branch). This allowed the Company to keep 6,639,059 acres (2,688,819ha) for its own use or for re-sale. As a result the Company's stores characterise almost all western towns, and the Company is active in land and water developments, farming, mining, and transportation, as well as fur trading.

The Prairies could not have been developed so rapidly and on such a massive scale without railroads and so, to encourage the Canadian Pacific Railway company to put its capital at risk in building a whole net of railway lines, the government gave the

CPR a right to alternate sections in a belt of land 24 miles (38·64km) deep on either side of its main line. Later branch lines also acquired land, and as a result, the CPR came to own 26,055,462 acres (10,552,452ha). Much of this it has developed as farm land by lease or by sale. It has been particularly successful in the drier south-west in promoting irrigation farming, especially for winter feed for sale to western ranches.

Finally, since many of the immigrants to the Prairies spoke little English, and were poorly educated, schools had to be quickly established. The Dominion Government therefore reserved two sections (nos 11 and 29) in each township for rural schools. This is one reason why, very unlike the French system, where schools are part of the institutional centre of village and town, the western grid sees a scatter of schools out in the rural districts. This worked well when people rode or walked to school. It is unnecessary in the days of the car and the bus and, consequently, consolidated school districts have been set up, with large new centres replacing the old one-roomed schools. But even these, to which the children are bussed, may still be at a central part of the open township in the countryside, and not in town.

ANGLO-CANADIAN TOWNS

Anglo-Canadian towns are distinct features of the Canadian landscape, differing significantly from French-Canadian ones. The traveller going into them is first impressed by the extreme regularity of their lay-out in a grid system of roads at right angles to each other. His next impression will probably be that every town is dominated by a central business district. The main roads meeting at the centre are fronted by shops, hotels and offices. This is quite different from the French-style town where they meet in the Cathedral square. In Toronto, for example, churches have had to take a peripheral position outside the centre. They are sited on Church Street, well to the side of Yonge Street, which is thronged with shoppers going from one huge multiple store, like Eaton's, to another, like Simpson's, and still further over from Bay Street, in the per-

E

petual shadow of enormous banks and insurance companies. In fact all the main institutions of the city—the churches, colleges, magistrates courts and even the city hall—are on the edge of, not in, the central business district. City Hall, Toronto, the most powerful institution of its kind in Canada, marks the northern boundary of the banking district, and the western limit of the large multiple stores. The Ontario Legislative building, the university, the city hospitals, the art gallery and the museum are even more peripheral. These things are not as central to Anglo-Canadian life as trade and commerce. It is business that can afford the highest land values and therefore command the point of maximum access in the city.

THE GROWTH OF THE CITIES

Metropolitan explosion now characterises Canadian life. Most people live in large cities or, rather, huge urbanised areas. As has been indicated Toronto and Montreal have both about 3 millions in their built-up areas, Vancouver about $1\frac{1}{2}$ millions, and Ottawa, Winnipeg, Hamilton, Edmonton, and Quebec over half a million. More important than these totals is their proportion of the overall population of the provinces. More than 1 out of 2 people in British Columbia and Manitoba live in Vancouver and Winnipeg: close on 1 out of 2 Quebec folk live in Montreal; and more than 2 out of 5 in Ontario, at Toronto. Indeed, more immigrants are swarming into the Toronto area than to the rest of Canada, and by the end of 1975 it had become Canada's biggest city, and one of North America's major metropolitan communities. Canadians love city life and not only that, but big city life. Here are the job opportunities, here the sports, the theatre, music, art, the rich social life, the competition and the co-operation which they enjoy. Immigrants, especially, can find a home from home, a bit of Scotland, or Little Italy, or Chinatown, or the Hebrew quarter which will offer them a helping hand, and make integration into the Canadian way of life much easier.

In fact, one characteristic of the Canadian city, shared with

America, is that most people have 'ghetto-ised' themselves, they have come to live among their own race, or in their own class, or among their own profession, or in the circle of their own religious group. The city is thus a patchwork quilt of very different neighbourhoods, distinguished by quite separate life styles.

STANDARDS OF LIVING

Standards of living, even among the so-called poor, are remarkably high. Only 2 per cent of the housing in Toronto is low-cost public housing—what the British would call 'council housing'. Among the 2½ millions of Clydeside, an urban region similar in size to Toronto, only 26 per cent of the dwellings are *not* council houses! In Canada as a whole, 59·5 per cent of the people live in private, detached housing. In Scotland, 54 per cent live in Council housing, built in multiple blocks. Such are the profound social differences between the old and the new country. However, in Quebec almost 60 per cent of the dwellings are multiple-type units. Here again, the contrast between the Anglo-Canadian, loving to live apart in his own home, and the French-Canadian, brought up to live close to neighbours, in triplexes and duplexes, reflects Canada's bi-cultural structure in the urban landscape itself.

Metropolitan life in the mid-70s has seen an increase in tenancy and apartment living, from 34 per cent of all dwellings to 39·7 per cent. In the large towns a forest of high-rise, middle-class apartment dwellings has sprung up, just on the outer edge of the central business districts. Many middle class are moving back from the suburbs to mid-town or even down-town life. This has livened up the whole of the inner city, which is no longer a place to work in by day and leave empty by night: instead, though suburbs still attract the greater part of the middle class and are sprawling into the countryside, mercilessly gobbling up good agricultural land, the inner parts of the city are seeing a tremendous revival—urban renewal now rivals suburban sprawl in Canadian city growth.

People pay from 23 to 27 per cent of their income for a home, and strive to have a roomy and comfortable place, with plenty of 'personal space' for each member of the family. The average Canadian family has 3·7 people to 5·4 rooms. Crowded dwellings, in which the number of people exceed the number of rooms, have decreased from 16·5 per cent (1961) to only 9·4 per cent (1971) of the housing stock. On the whole Canadians have one of the highest dwelling standards in the world.

Their homes are well equipped and sanitary. Over 91 per cent have a bath or shower, 93 per cent a flush toilet, and 96 per cent hot and cold running water. To meet the severity of winter most houses have central heating; 48 per cent are heated by oil, and 32 per cent by gas. Only about 2 per cent now use coal although, with the high price of oil, more homes are going back to coal-fired furnaces. About half the homes rely on electricity for their hot-water supply; the rest get their hot water through their central heating system, using oil or gas. There is strong competition between oil and electricity. Oil is more restricted in its place of origin, coming mainly from Alberta, but has been pumped through pipelines to Vancouver on the west, and the Toronto area on the east. From Montreal east, oil is shipped in fairly easily from Venezuela or Nigeria. Electricity has a much wider spread, with hydro-electric plants on every major river from the Fraser in the west to the Saint John in the east. As the oil crisis deepens, more people are switching to electricity.

This is, of course, the main power source for the many household labour-saving devices: 98·7 per cent of all homes have an electric refrigerator, 54 per cent electric dishwashers, and 78·8 per cent electric washing machines and clothes dryers. Nearly 50 per cent of households use power mowing machines to cut their lawns and since 95 per cent have telephones, 96 per cent TVs, and 97·6 per cent radios, demand on electricity is high.

Material comforts are now firmly a part of Canadian home life. Nearly half the houses have wall to wall carpeting. Over 90 per cent have double glazing, or storm windows and doors which are put up in the autumn and replaced in the spring by window screens and screen-doors, and 83 per cent of homes have repair work or some redecorating done every year.

Most middle-class Canadians have a second home or a

trailer (caravan) where the family will spend at least a month's holiday together: women and children usually stay on longer, after the father has returned to work. Every weekend from Victoria Day (24 May) to Labour Day (first Monday in September) there is a mass evacuation of every city, as millions go off to their second home or to a trailer camp, beside lake or stream in the bosom of the forest. The longing of most Canadians to 'get back to nature' is a very real part of Canadian living.

They get back to nature in a car. They travel to holiday, to work, to shop, and to church by car. Public transport is not greatly used, although the combination of suburban trains and the 'underground' keeps public traffic going strong in Toronto. But where possible, people move about by car: 78 per cent of Canadian households have a car, and nearly 20 per cent have two or more. The car has transformed Canadian cities, leading huge freeways right into the centre and demanding more and more central space for parking.

The car has had other impacts on Canadian life. It is now the fourth killer in Canada's annual death toll, with nearly 30 deaths per hundred thousand of the population. The death rate as a whole is very low, amounting to only 6·1 per thousand of all ages. This is partly because the Canadian health programme is so good. Most deaths are due not from infectious disease in youth but from the diseases of protracted old age. Both in home and in health Canada has a very high standard of living.

Health is both a federal and provincial responsibility. The Federal Department of Health and Welfare is directly responsible for the medical needs of Indians and Eskimos, has powers of search and research, and maintains standards. Canada passed a Medical Care Act in 1966 to inaugurate a Federal-Provincial 'medicare' scheme, by which the central government pays half the per capita costs and also gives capital grants. Medicare is administered provincially and ensures every citizen of basic hospital, medical and surgical care. Quebec developed its own scheme in 1965. Altogether 5·1 per cent of the GNP and 6·4 per cent of personal income are spent on health. With a doctor for every 637 people Canada offers one of the best medical coverages in the world.

5

How They Work and Get About

CANADA long earned her living from her primary products—furs, fish, the forest, the farm, metals and fuels. However, she developed these products for others, particularly Britain and America, to turn into consumer goods. This gave other people the main profits from Canadian resources. She then began to develop her own industries, particularly after the National Policy of Sir John A. Macdonald, in 1878, though this mainly involved the processing of resources for others to finish off. It was not really until World War I, when Canada made a major contribution to the arming of the Allied Forces, that she became a manufacturing power. During World War II this industrial strength grew tremendously. After that, Canada began to export manufactured goods as well as primary products. Banking and insurance were needed to support this new industrial country, and with their introduction, Canada grew into a financial and commercial nation. Her standards of living then advanced to such a degree that she spent a lot of manpower and money servicing home developments. She has now moved to the post-industrial society where her main aim is not to make goods, but to enlarge amenities, not make a living, but enjoy the good life. Hence primary production has sunk, secondary activity is on the decline, and tertiary progress is very much to the fore.

Between the mid-sixties and the mid-seventies, agriculture and other primary industries had declined from 13 per cent of all employment to 8·4 per cent, and manufacturing industries from 24·3 to 22·3 per cent; trade and finance, on the other hand, had shown marginal increase, from 20·9 to 21·5 per cent, while services had expanded quite appreciably, from 26·3 to

33·0 per cent. These trends are still continuing, widening the gap between the primary and tertiary sector of the economy. In terms of occupations, farmers had declined from 10·3 to 6·9 per cent of the major occupational groups, skilled factory workers from 24·9 to 24·7 per cent, and labourers from 4·8 to 4·2 per cent, whereas clerical workers had increased from 13·4 to 15·4, service jobs from 11·1 to 12·3 and professional positions from 10·6 to 14·2. Canada now has twice as many managers (9·8 per cent) as labourers (4·2 per cent); and nearly five times as many salesmen (7·0 per cent) as fishermen, trappers, loggers and miners put together (1·5 per cent). These figures represent the big changes in ways of living that have brought Canada to the forefront of the modern world.

PRIMARY PRODUCTION

Primary production still characterises much of Canada as a country, though fewer people are involved in it. Fur-trading is a main occupation in the north where the forests and northern shores still harbour fur-bearing animals. With her long winters, Canada needs fur coats and hats. These can, however, be made either from natural skins produced from the fur farms of Prince Edward Island and northern Alberta, or from artificial fur fibres. Hence there is less need for the Eskimo, Indian and white trapper today than before. Fishing is more important, and is a main way of working the rich sea resources of the Atlantic and Pacific.

Off the Atlantic shore the continental shelf widens out enormously and on it rise the Nova Scotia and Newfoundland banks, covering over 70,000 square miles (181,000sq km), or more than the whole of England. Here the mixture of the cold Labrador current and the warm Gulf Stream stimulates many forms of marine life: tremendous catches of cod, haddock, and herring are made, not only by Canadian but by American and European fishing boats. In the west, long fjords lead up great rivers to lakes well in the mountains where

salmon spawn by the million. Salmon-netting off or in the
fjords, and salmon-trapping up the rivers, exploit what is the
largest salmon fishery in the world. This too is fished by foreign
fleets, mainly American, Japanese and Russian. Here is a real
problem for Canada. The threat of overfishing off Canada's
coasts led Canada in 1976 to put in a strong plea for the revision of the Law of the Sea which would allow the country to
manage and control fishing to a 200 mile (322km) limit. As it is,
Canada has been the prime mover in international fishing
agreements such as the preservation of the halibut fishery of the
North Pacific, the convention for the protection of sockeye
salmon, the conservation of North Pacific fur seals, the international convention for the North-West Atlantic fisheries, and
the convention between Canada and the United States in respect of fishing in the Great Lakes. Canada is a major fishing
nation with landings of fish amounting to over $2\frac{1}{2}$ million
pounds weight a year, employing about 57,000 fishermen. Newfoundland alone catches nearly 1 million pounds. However,
there has been a decline in the number of fishermen as more of
the fish are caught from trawlers which are highly automated
and employ a small crew, and less from smacks and dories that
required many hands. The total value of the fisheries has none
the less grown and is running at over $550 millions a year.

Of course, Canada, with its huge area in sub-arctic and cool-
temperate climates, is basically a forest country. Agriculture,
only suited to the southern fringe, has not cleared most of the
trees away, as in Britain or the United States. Logging, saw-
milling and pulp and paper-making are traditional occupations
in every province and territory. There are three main ways of
working the wood. Veneering is done by peeling back the wood
in a very thin long sheet from sections of the log. In the west,
this is done with Douglas fir or Pacific cedar to make plywood,
sold for lining buildings. In the east, in Southern Ontario,
veneering exploits the hardwood forests of oak and maple to
make veneer furniture. Saw-milling is common everywhere but
is commercially most profitable in the giant hard conifers of the
Pacific coast, where the cedar, fir, spruce and pine are squared
for support timbers in construction or are planed to make clap-

board for outside walling on houses and sheds. There is a huge
export of over a billion dollars worth of construction timber from
British Columbia every year, mainly to the United States
which, having cut its forests ruthlessly away, is now short of
wood. Canadian conservation laws are trying to prevent the
same thing happening, especially as more and more of its forests
are being exploited by American companies. Pulp and paper-
making is the prime use of the spruce and fir of the boreal
forest. While it is flourishing in the Pacific west, and along
the northern fringe of the Prairies, it is most important round
the fringes of the Shield in Ontario and Quebec and among the
Appalachian ridges of the Maritimes and Newfoundland.

Both provincial and federal governments have strong laws to
keep forests worked on a long-time basis as a renewable resource. The Canadian Forestry Service does much research
work, keeps an inventory of resources, advises on use and development, and aids in forest management programmes. Each
province has its own Service which is concerned with fire protection, with reforestation, and with conservation. Quebec has
the largest forest area with over 260,000 square miles (673,400
sq km)—more than the total area of France: British Columbia
has 215,000 square miles (556,850sq km)—more than twice the
area of Britain. A great deal of their production is for export,
giving Canada valued earnings in foreign exchange.

Farming earns nearly twice as much as forestry, with between 4½ and 5 billion dollars worth of food and industrial
crops a year. Animal husbandry, contrary to most people's
image, is the mainstay of Canadian farming, earning over
$3 billion from all its activities. Cattle are the biggest earners,
bringing farmers more than $1 billion a year. A lot of beef is
exported to the United States. Most of the milk and butter are
consumed at home, but quite a bit of cheese is sold abroad, especially to Britain. Dairy products net between $¾ and 1
billion, and pigs about $½ billion. The huge growth of stock
farming (making use of the admirable summer grazing to
which the temperate climate with warm humid summers is so
well suited), has tempted grain farmers to go in more for forage
crops and feed grains than for wheat. Consequently wheat, the

main grain for human consumption, is in somewhat of a decline, and only earns about $¾ billion a year, where it used to
top a $1 billion. The wheat acreage is falling. In the mid-
sixties it used to amount to 30 million acres (12 million ha);
by the mid-seventies this had dropped below 20 millions (8
million ha). This was offset to a certain degree by a higher yield,
due to more fertilisers and better cropping, going up from 23
bushels per acre to about 28 bushels per acre. Perhaps more
significant is a decline in the number of operators and the widespread amalgamation of farms into huge wheat estates, so
highly mechanised that they might be called factory farms.
Many of them are, in fact, company farms, no longer operated
by a single owner, but run by a manager for a big commercial
organisation. This has meant that the rural population, thinly
spread though it is across Canada, is getting thinner. But it
also means that the few who are left are running bigger farms
for bigger profits, giving farmers a higher personal standard of
living. Thus although the agriculture acreage in Canada between the mid-sixties and mid-seventies fell from 174 million
acres to 169 million acres, or roughly 3 per cent, the income per
farmer rose by 46 per cent. Even taking inflation into account,
this was a significant gain.

Since Canada is so large it covers a wide range of farming
types. Different regions specialise in products best suited to
them. Prince Edward Isle with its red sandy soils has gone in
for potatoes; the Annapolis Valley in Nova Scotia, protected
from frosts, is famous for apples; the Montreal plain, long
associated with hay crops to feed the horses of horse-drawn
trams in the early city has used its rich pastures for dairy production; Peninsular Ontario, Canada's most southerly area, and
between three lakes, has hot humid summers ideal for tobacco,
peach trees, wine grapes, and market-garden produce; the
Prairies, naturally grassland, have either replaced the grass
with small-grain crops like wheat and barley or, in drier areas,
have used the rangeland for grazing cattle; in British Columbia,
the dry interior valleys of Kootenay and Okanagan irrigated
from river and lake, are world-known orchard strips, while the
Fraser delta with rich silty soils, mild winters, and Canada's

longest frost-free season, has its green meadows studded with dairy herds.

Government services and aids to farming are considerable. Federal assistance includes general price support (Agricultural Stabilisation Act, 1958); aid to animal husbandry (Canadian Dairy Commission, Livestock Feed Assistance); grain farming help (the Canadian Grain Commission, the Canadian Wheat Board, the Canada Grains Council, the Prairie Grain Advance Payment Act); farm credit programmes (the Farm Credit Act, Farm Improvements Loans Act); farm insurance coverage (the Crop Insurance Act) and marketing aid (Farm Products Marketing Agencies Act in 1972). In these ways a stable farm economy has been assured.

Mining is the most profitable form of primary production, with annual return in the mid-seventies of between $6 and 7 billion. Canada is fortunate in being rich in both metals and fuels. The Canadian Shield with 1,850,000 square miles (4,791,480sq km) forms more than half the country. Railways pushing west from Montreal and Toronto helped in the development of the great nickel-lead-zinc complex at Sudbury. A metalliferous belt ran from here through the gold mines of Timmins and Porcupine, N Ontario, to the copper mines of Rouyn-Noranda and Chibougamou, NW Quebec. Silver at Thunder Bay tempted miners to the head of Lake Superior where later they found the large iron reserves of Steep Rock. Larger iron bodies still were discovered in the Ungava trough far to the east and were mined at Schefferville and Gagnonville, NE Quebec, and Labrador City, Newfoundland. Big copper finds at Lynn Lake, Saskatchewan, were seen to be part of a metal-rich area extending to Thompson, Manitoba. Further north and west the gold rush to Yellowknife prompted explorations that came across big lead deposits at Pine Point, Alberta, and uranium at Uranium City, Athabasca.

Metal mining is also important in both the Appalachians and Western Cordilleras where, in the core of these mountains, crystalline and metamorphic rocks, veined with ore, have been the basis for the lead and zinc mines of the Buchan Plateau, Newfoundland, and of the Bathurst massif, NB, in the east; and the lead, zinc and copper mines of the Kimberley-Nelson-Trail region of interior BC and the great copper, zinc and iron mines of the enormous batholiths underlying the coast ranges of south-west BC and Vancouver Island. These western structures have been found in the Yukon to be rich in silver, lead, zinc and copper. Nickel is by far the most valuable Canadian metal, earning between $800 and 900 million: indeed Canada produces about two-thirds of the world's supply. Copper is a close second, with $800 million, followed by iron, over $600 million, and zinc with $500 million. These are important foreign currency earners for Canada.

Uranium is another example of metal mining with international importance. Shipments are still going from Ontario and Saskatchewan to the United States and Western Europe, though sales for nuclear installations are subject to Federal control.

Great though Canada's metal production is, it has not reflected the growth in non-metallic mining. Canada is the world's largest producer of asbestos, shipping 90 per cent of its produce to over seventy countries; 81 per cent is mined in Quebec, the rest coming mainly from BC.

Potash has recently been a main item of Canadian exports. Canada's installed annual capacity is the world's largest, coming from Saskatchewan. Sulphur, too, is on the increase, made from the sour natural gas of Alberta. Since 1968 Canada has become the world's largest supplier of sulphur.

Fuel-rich structures are also present in Canada. Coal is found preserved in basins between the more gentle folds of the Appalachians and Rockies. In Nova Scotia it has been virtually worked out, though the towns to which it gave rise, like Spring-hill and Inverness, have continued. In western Alberta, and in the Crow's Nest and Kootenay areas of British Columbia, large-scale development still continues, as the basis for steam-generated electricity plants. New mining in north-east BC visualises greater demand.

Oil challenged it, particularly since Canada was seen to have a cheap and plentiful supply. All along the eastern margin of the Rockies from the USA up to at least the Peace River country, large basins occur, some stretching even as far as southern Manitoba across Saskatchewan, which have in the distant past trapped and preserved, for present use, large pools of oil and of natural gas. Both Calgary—Canada's 'oil capital'— and Edmonton have benefited from these with the creation of large refineries. Oil is also piped to Vancouver and to Sarnia, Toronto, and Ontario, for refining. Natural gas is likewise piped both to Vancouver and to Toronto and is widely used for industrial purposes, where it has been an immense boon to chemical, glass, ceramic and metallurgical processes. The transportation of oil and gas has meant that the industrial areas in Ontario and Quebec, that used to rely on US or Maritimes' coal, were able to go on and expand even when coal was in short supply or was used less. However, the oil reserves in Alberta, as for example in the south and west, are near depletion, but others, in northern BC, are still in an early stage of development. Much further north, in the Mackenzie delta, very large reserves of gas and significant amounts of oil await development, forming a major back-up to Canadian oil resources. A major source of oil lies in the Athabaska tar sands, near Ft McMurray: the cost of separating the oil from the thick bituminous tar has been high and has so far prevented large-scale exploitation, but as the price of oil goes up, that cost will no longer seem prohibitive. Already tar-sand oil is beginning to flow and is being piped to Edmonton for refinement. Altogether Canada produces 250 million tons of oil a year, worth three to four times her iron production.

MANUFACTURING INDUSTRIES

Manufacturing has been stimulated in Canada by the need to refine and process its oil, metals, wood, fish and farm products, and now it adds enormously to the value of Canada's raw materials—bringing in over ten times the amount earned by metal and fuel extraction.

The success of Canadian manufacturing is due to a happy combination of circumstances: firstly, Canada has immense resources of raw materials, fuel, water and power to act as a base of supplies: secondly, she has a large market in the United States to the south, and traditional marketing connections in Britain, Western Europe and Japan; thirdly, she has a growing labour force, much of which is today highly trained: and finally, she can get capital either from her own growing stock markets or from New York and London, with which she has had long-established links.

These advantages, however, have not been spread evenly. The Great Lakes–St Lawrence basin has 60 per cent of the people of Canada, concentrated mainly in a narrow band between Quebec City and Windsor. Both eastwards in the Gaspé and the Maritimes, and westward in the Prairies and BC, the population thins out very much, with settlements separated from each other by great stretches of barren Shield, or difficult mountainous terrain, or semi-arid grassland. Ontario and Quebec, by contrast, are floored by a fertile plain, have cheap water transportation along the St Lawrence Seaway, have plenty of hydroelectric power, forest and mining resources in the Shield to the north and the Appalachians to the south, and penetrate deeply into the heart of the USA, being close to New York, Buffalo, Detroit and Chicago. These attractions drew the French, the United Empire Loyalists, and British immigrants to the area, and later became the chief target for a much wider immigration bringing in capital and skill from many parts of Europe. This cultural mix has been of great importance, offering the best from many traditions. Ontario and Quebec produce 81 per cent of all the goods made in Canada, Ontario making 53 per cent and Quebec 28 per cent. In fact, within the Commonwealth this region ranks second only to England in manufacturing.

The chief Canadian manufactures, each producing over a billion dollars worth of goods a year, are: food and beverages ($3\frac{1}{2}$ billion), transportation ($2\frac{1}{2}$) paper and allied products (2), primary metals (2), metal fabrication ($1\frac{3}{4}$), petro-chemicals ($1\frac{1}{2}$), electrical products ($1\frac{1}{2}$), machinery ($1\frac{1}{2}$), printing and publishing ($1\frac{1}{4}$) and textiles (1).

Food and beverages are processed from Canada's wealth of animal products, grain, and fruit. These are by no means manufactured where the raw materials are, but where the market is.

Meat-packing, flour-milling, the preparation of dairy products, brewing and distilling are concentrated to a remarkable extent in Ontario and Quebec. Over 90 per cent of the distilling, 80 per cent of the brewing, 68 per cent of the dairy products, 66 per cent of the fruit and vegetable canning, 55 per cent of the meat processing, and 50 per cent of the flour-milling are done between Windsor and Montreal. Produce is sent from the Prairies and other parts of Canada to be processed here, where there is not only a rich local market but a big American market nearby and within easy contact, via the Seaway, Western Europe. Transportation would almost of necessity be a major Canadian occupation with such tremendous distances to be covered, both overland and along the coast. Shipbuilding at Sorel and Montreal, railway rolling stock at Montreal, motor-car and truck manufacturing at Oshawa, Oakville, Hamilton, London and Windsor and the manufacture of aircraft at Montreal and Toronto are all very active, making use of the Seaway to assemble raw materials and export finished goods. Paper products, including newsprint, form a profitable way of exploiting the immense forests and the wealth of hydro-electric power found across Canada. Once again, the benefits of industrial 'agglomeration' mean that the central provinces dominate, with great pulp and paper works at Quebec City, Three Rivers, Ottawa, Thorold (on the Welland Canal) and Thunder Bay (Ft William and Pt Arthur). British Columbia, New Brunswick, and Newfoundland are also very dependent on their pulp and paper industries.

Metals and metal fabrication are a reflection of the enormous metal concentrations in the Canadian Shield and the large quantities of cheap electric power developed along the edge of the Shield and in the St Lawrence system. Big refineries occur at Pt Colborne (Welland Canal) and Pt Hope (L Ontario), and large steelworks at Hamilton, with other works at Toronto and Montreal. Metal fabrication from Welland City, Hamilton, Toronto, Montreal and Shawinigan (St Maurice valley) provides the sheets, tubes and bars of high-grade steel, copper, and aluminium needed in the metal-using industries. Machine-manufacturing of all sorts, to support other industries, marks a distinct improvement on the pre-war days when Canada imported many of its tools and machines. Canada has gained an enviable reputation for the sophistication and quality of its mining and pulp and paper-making machinery. Most of this is made in southern Ontario. The petro-chemical industry is the most rapidly developing one in Canada. This too is found mainly where the market is, in S Ontario, to which the raw materials, oil and gas, are piped. Sarnia, the first terminal of the pipe, and then Burlington near Hamilton and Clarkson near Toronto, developed huge refineries. Chemical derivatives are made in the Toronto region and Montreal. Electrical machines and goods have sprung up to exploit the extraordinarily rich resources of hydro-electricity in Canada, especially along the St Lawrence or the edge of the Shield. The making of electrical turbines and transformers, and of telephone and telex equipment, along with the manufacture of electrical goods, such as stoves, refrigerators, radio, TV, calculators and computers, form big business in the St Catharines, Hamilton, Toronto, Peterborough region in S Ontario. Textiles also make use of the cheap and plentiful supply of electricity to factories near Montmorency Falls and the Falls of St Francis, in Quebec, and at Welland near Niagara Falls. Montreal is noted for its clothing industry and is the fashion

---

Fishing is the oldest industry in Canada. Petty Harbour, Nfd, clings to the rocky edge of the Canadian Appalachians in an inlet facing the Newfoundland Banks, one of the world's chief fisheries

Forestry is another long-established occupation. It has of course modernised its methods as evidenced by this loader at Duncan, BC, each log containing 9,500 board feet. The cool humid climate makes most of Canada a land of trees

centre of Canada. Printing and publishing are yet another activity of note. Originally many of the publishers were branch offices of British houses, handling books printed and published in England or Scotland, but since World War II Canada has developed a home-based publishing business of considerable distinction and value. This is chiefly centred at Toronto and Montreal.

Government aid and control are important in industry. The Canadian government regulates standards, patents and copyright, and prevents restrictive trade practices through anti-combines legislation. The Department of Industry, Trade and Commerce stimulates the growth and efficiency of manufacturing through various programmes, chief of which are the Advancement of Industrial Technology, Industrial Research, the subsidisation of Capital Equipment, Building Equipment and Materials, and Industrial Productivity, Industrial Design, and Export Market Development. Assistance is offered to the automotive, shipbuilding and chemical industries. One service is unique, namely Counselling Assistance to Small Enterprises (CASE). Various provinces have set up development corporations, including the Newfoundland and Labrador Development Co, the Industrial Enterprises Incorporated of PEI, the Industrial Estates Ltd of

---

The St Lawrence Seaway brings ocean navigation as far as Lakehead, in the heart of Canada. Much internal and external trade is done by lake, river, and ocean-going boats. Here a freighter, 730ft (222m) long, carries 1,000,000 bushels of grain past Cardinal, Ont, the product of 50,000 acres of farmland!

Oil and gas pipelines are important new ways of fuel transportation in Canada, stretching from Alberta to Montreal in the east, and to Vancouver in the west (Cranbrook, BC)

Nova Scotia, the Quebec Industrial Development Co, the Ontario and the Northern Ontario Development Corporation, the
Manitoba Exports Co, the Saskatchewan Economic Development Co and the Alberta Opportunity Co.

THE COMMERCIAL SECTOR

Trade, commerce, and finance are crucial to Canada since, as
a small nation in a country of huge resources, it cannot absorb
all it produces, but must export more than a third. Canada is also a big importer, buying tropical or subtropical foods, fibres
and other products it cannot grow itself, and also a lot of sophisticated machinery and many consumer goods. Quite often imports have been greater than exports and Canada has had to
rely on its 'hidden exports' of bank and insurance earnings abroad—which are considerable—to balance its budget. The largest customer by far is the United States, and this is increasingly
so. While in the mid-1960s just over half its total trade, exports
and imports, was with the United States, in the mid-seventies
this rose to more than two-thirds. In fact many Canadians feel that
they are now economically too dependent on America. Exports
to the United States form more than two-thirds of all exports,
while imports form about three-quarters. Canada's next largest
trading partner is Britain, but this trade has been falling—from
16 per cent of Canadian exports in the sixties to 8 per cent in the
seventies; imports from Britain fell during this decade from 10·7
per cent to 5·4 per cent. Perhaps it was as well that Britain joined
the EEC; it could not count on its oldest dominion to any extent: Canada is now actively expanding its trade with Japan,
and SE Asia.

The Canadian government helps Canada's trade considerably. It has an anti-Dumping Act to prevent excessively cheap
goods from undercutting its own manufactures; a Financing and
Aid branch of the Department of Industry, Trade and Commerce, an Exports Development Corporation, and a programme
of Export Credits insurance, together with the insurance of Foreign Investments. Canadian tariffs help protect home indus-

tries but there is a British preferential rate to attract imports from Britain: this is to offset over-dependence upon the United States.

Canadian banks and stock exchanges play a major role not only in home industry but in foreign investment and trade. There are two government and nine private (chartered) banks. The Bank of Canada is really the bankers' bank; it was set up 'to regulate credit and currency in the best interests of the life of the nation', which it does largely by determining the total amount of cash reserves in the chartered banks, and the flow of currency to the country. An Industrial Development Bank was set up in 1944 to give aid to new businesses, especially where this would in turn help to develop a region in need of growth.

Of the nine chartered banks, five have their head offices in Montreal, testifying to the leadership Montreal has long given to the business life of Canada. Four of these banks, the Bank of Montreal (Canada's oldest, founded on 3 November 1817), the Royal Bank of Canada (Canada's leading bank), the Provincial and the Mercantile are English-speaking, representing the strong Anglo-American hold on the life of Quebec: only the Banque Canadienne Nationale is French-Canadian, a reflection of the limited role of the Quebecois in their own affairs. Two of the other banks, the Toronto-Dominion and the Canadian Imperial, are Toronto based, showing the rise of Toronto as a competitive money centre. The Bank of Nova Scotia, and the Bank of British Columbia represent the peripheral regions, but the former has nationwide and, indeed, international significance.

Six exchanges handle Canada's stocks, including two in Montreal and others in Toronto, Vancouver, Calgary and Winnipeg. By far the largest of these is the Toronto Stock Exchange, which has two-thirds of the total value and two-fifths of the total share volume of all listed trading in Canada. It was founded as early as 1852, and specialised in the support of mining, oil and gas, and industrial stocks. Of the eighteen principal stock exchanges in N America, Toronto ranks fourth. The Montreal Exchanges have dealt more in transportation and property, Vancouver and Calgary with resource development. Winnipeg is mainly a regional exchange. Keen competition between exchanges, banks, trust and insurance companies has led to a shift in Canada's money centre from St James Street, Montreal, to Bay Street, Toronto—often called the Wall Street of Canada. The value of shares handled by Toronto is more than twice that of all the other four exchanges in Canada put together. This has helped to confirm Ontario's extraordinary lead in Canada's industrial and business life.

FOREIGN AND CANADIAN INVESTMENTS

Canadian development has long depended on the import of foreign capital which has been used for the exploration and exploitation of natural resources, and for transportation and industry. In recent years Canada has exported a great deal of capital for enterprises abroad.

Up to World War I, Britain was the chief investor in Canada, and helped to develop her canals, railways, mines, forests and farm industries. By the mid-1920s, the United States took the lead, especially in mining, fuels and manufacturing. Many American businesses built branch factories in Canada. These changes were accelerated by World War II. Prior to that Britain still accounted for 40 per cent of the investment in Canada; this fell sharply to the current level of about 10 per cent while the American share rose dramatically to 80 per cent. Recently Japanese investment has been pouring in to develop the coal, iron, copper, potash, oil and other products needed for Japanese industry. Today, over 60 per cent of the capital in Canadian manufacturing is subject to foreign control; 80 per cent of the capital behind oil and gas development and 70 per cent of that in mining are foreign controlled, and some Canadians are concerned that too much of their economy is under foreign domination.[10]

Yet this is not a one-way matter. Canadian investments abroad are considerable, and amount to about a quarter of foreign holdings in Canada. Of the total, government aid to Commonwealth and francophone foreign countries accounts for over half. Private investment makes up 45 per cent, and is strongest by far in the United States, followed by Britain, Western European and Commonwealth countries. Some of this is in the form of branches of Canadian industry abroad, like the plants of Massey-Ferguson, Weston, and Carling; most of it is in banking and insurance transactions. The Royal Bank of Canada, the Canadian Imperial Bank of Commerce, the Bank of Montreal and the Bank of Nova Scotia are active in most metropolitan centres abroad, as are Canada Life, the Sun Life of Canada, and Great West Life insurance companies.

THE LABOUR FORCE

The labour force in Canada as a percentage of the total population is very high, amounting to nearly 60 per cent. This is partly due to the large number of immigrants coming in at ages between 20 and 45 when they swell the work force. It is also due to a great increase in the number of women going to work, now more than 50 per cent higher than in the mid-1960s. The service industries, shipping and business have increased the scope for women very considerably. Women now make up two-fifths of Canada's employed. However, the general rate of employment is rising more slowly than that of the population as a whole, and is less than 1 per cent per annum. Much of the work in Canada's primary and secondary fields of production is mechanised, and in less need of manpower. Consequently, unemployment stands at between 6 and 8 per cent, which is 2 to 3 times higher than in Great Britain, though about the same as in the United States. Trade and commerce, finance, transportation and the service industries—the tertiary sector of the economy—accounted for 64 per cent of the employed in the mid-1970s, which is only a little below the level for Britain and the United States. Employment in the goods-producing industries fell to 36 per cent. These figures would seem to suggest that Canada has now moved forward to being a post-industrial society. The average weekly wage is nearly twice that in Britain, but only about nine-tenths that in the United States. It is high enough to attract many immigrant workers from Europe, but rather too low to prevent loss of workers to the United States.

Union membership is low compared with both Britain and the United States. Less than one-third of the total labour force is unionised. Much non-union labour is used in the primary sector, and amongst women in all sectors. The Canadian Labour Congress, dominated by clerical and artisans' unions, has nearly three-quarters of the union membership. About two-thirds of its members are in unions affiliated with the American Federation of Labour. Quebec has unions of its own in addition to national and international ones, and its Confederation of National Trade Unions (CNTU) has nearly 10 per cent of Canada's union membership: these are mostly French-speaking workers. Labour relations are less settled than in Britain or America, and as a result there are significantly more strikes. The Canadian government is trying to overcome this through its very sensible and workable Labour Code. This provides that both employees and employers may organise for collective bargaining; that unions may be certified as sole bargaining agents if they have a majority of the unionised work force; that unions and employers must bargain in good faith; that no strike may be called until after a cooling-off period; and that arbitration must be resorted to and respected in the case of a deadlock in negotiations. Fair employment practices, prohibiting discrimination because of race, religion, or national origin, are enforced, and work standards, especially with respect to hours, are maintained. Overtime must be paid for more than 8 hours a day and 40 hours in a week. Equal pay for women has been established, and there are provisions for pregnant women who wish to return to their jobs after the birth of their children. All provinces have legislation providing for compensation in case of accidents and disablement at work.

Occupational pension plans are offered by most companies, and 40 per cent of Canadian workers participate in a pension plan. All public servants are covered, two-thirds of the miners, and over one-half of those in the secondary sector are protected. All regularly paid workers must now contribute to the Canada Pension Plan, supported by the Federal Government. In 1940 the government passed its Unemployment Insurance Act, revised in 1971 to 'cope with interrupted earnings resulting from unemployment'. A claimant can draw benefits for up to 51 weeks provided he has worked for at least 12 weeks in the last 52. Sickness benefit is available for a maximum of 15 weeks, and maternity benefit for 8 weeks before confinement. The benefit rate is two-thirds of the average insured earnings in the qualifying period to a maximum, in the mid-seventies, of $100.00 a week.

TRANSPORTATION

Transportation plays a vital role in the Canadian economy, not only in the assembly of raw materials and distribution of consumer goods, but in the geographical mobility of the work force and the opportunity to find work across Canada. In the seventeenth and eighteenth centuries riverways made the country; canals were vital in the early nineteenth century; the Seaway, in the twentieth century, has carried on their effectiveness; railways did more than anything else to help open up and develop the country in the late nineteenth and early twentieth centuries; the highway came into its own after the world wars and the airways have grown to tremendous importance since World War II.

As Harold Innis showed in his history of the Canadian fur trade, and proved in the field, canoe journeys of great lengths used Canada's astonishingly well-linked system of riverways from the Rockies to the Gulf of St Lawrence. The Saskatchewan and the Red passed into Lake Winnipeg and subsequent connections through the Lake of the Woods and Lake Superior allowed the fur trader to progress down the Great Lakes–St Lawrence waterway to Montreal. This is not merely history: many of the portages around rapids have become canals, others, between rivers, grew into portage roads and influenced later macadamised roads and railroads.

The 1820s to 1840s saw a fury of activity in building the Welland and St Lawrence river canals, including those around the Long Sault (from Prescott to Cornwall) and the Lachine rapids.

The Soo canal was also crucial, around the rapids between Lake Superior and Lake Huron. Meanwhile, the Americans had been busy linking up the Great Lakes with the Mohawk–Hudson, the Ohio and the Mississippi rivers. Canadian businessmen were in a very competitive position, able to contact the Mississippi through the Chicago canal, the Ohio down the Wabash canal, and the Hudson and New York through the Erie Barge canal, as well as Montreal and the St Lawrence Gulf down the St Lawrence canals. This is still the situation, except that the St Lawrence system has had all its canals deepened and widened in the Seaway, permitting ocean-going vessels to sail directly in and out of interior ports like Toronto, Hamilton and the lakehead.

The Seaway is the greatest single canal system in the world. The canals in it are 30ft deep (9·14m), and the locks are 730ft long (222m). These have power lifts and can raise or lower a ship within half an hour. Seaway construction by-passed the old Lachine and Cornwall canals with the modern Beauharnois and Eisenhower locks. The Welland canal has been redesigned to by-pass Welland City—a former bottleneck. The Americans have deepened and lengthened their locks on the Soo system. The result is that an enormous amount of traffic has been generated over the 1,212 miles (1,950km) between Montreal, at the mouth of the system, and Thunderbay, at its head. Between 4,000 and 4,500 ships use the Seaway every year, up-traffic amounting to about 30 million tons, and down, about 45 million. Ocean-going vessels, carrying international trade, make up approximately one-third of the traffic; the other two-thirds is domestic, carried in lake-boats. Bulk commodities comprise 80 per cent of the traffic, mainly iron from Labrador moving up to Hamilton, Buffalo, Cleveland and Detroit, coal from the Erie ports (handling Pennsylvania or Indiana coal) down to Toronto and Montreal, and wheat from the Lakehead downstream through Montreal to Europe. Containerisation is now the main method by which non-bulk goods are carried. 'House to house' containerload services run between the Lakehead, Toronto and Quebec City and the UK and European ports.

The one drawback of the Seaway is that it is frozen over in

January and February. Halifax, NS, and Saint John, NB, are ice-free, however, and become Canada's winter ports. They too have containerload services. In the west, Vancouver has expanded rapidly as a port, not only exporting the products of BC mines and forests, but acting as a major exporter of Canadian wheat and oil from the Prairies. So much wheat is now being sold by Canada to the Soviet Union, Japan and China, that Vancouver surpasses the Lakehead as Canada's wheat outlet.

Railways are so important to Canada that they may be said to be the basis of its economy. With the development of the Intercolonial line between the Maritimes and Montreal, and of the Grand Trunk system between Montreal, Toronto and Windsor, eastern Canada was well supplied. Moreover, excellent connections between Montreal and New York, and Toronto with both New York and Chicago linked the Canadian network with the American. It was not until the 1880s that Canada had a transcontinental system, when the Canadian Pacific Railway, completed in 1885, tied up Saint John, NB, with Vancouver, BC. A group of other lines was taken over by the Canadian government as a public transportation service and amalgamated to form the Canadian National Railways, running from Halifax, NS, to Prince Rupert and to Vancouver, BC. Altogether, Canada has 44,153 miles (71,055km) of operative track. Although railway passenger traffic has dropped appreciably in the last decade, except between Montreal and Toronto, railways are still the great carriers of bulk freight overland. Montreal is the main rail hub. From there to Vancouver it is 2,914 miles (4,690km), and to Halifax, 840 miles (1,352km). The Canadian National Railways carry about 52 per cent of the rail traffic; they have also branched out into other activities, with railway hotels in every major city, a chain of resort hotels linked by branch lines or by road, a fleet of inland and ocean-going vessels to join rail with water transportation, and a highway trucking system, to connect rail with road terminals. It also has a nation-wide and an international telecommunications system. In all these respects it is paralleled by the CPR with CP steamships and the CP airways, together with CP hotels. Thus Canada benefits by keen rivalry between its huge publicly owned and an immense privately owned transportation system. Government aid has always been considerable and the National Transportation Act of 1967 has been particularly helpful in giving payments 'for losses incurred on branch lines and passenger-train services operated in the public interest'. Altogether over 230 million tons of goods a year are hauled on Canadian railways, of which crude materials, ore, oil, wood products, and non-metallic minerals make up half, and food products, principally wheat, a quarter.

Roads are now not a mere adjunct to, but a serious competitor of, railways, having taken away most of the passenger traffic, and most of the short-range freight traffic from the railways. But though Canada's road network is enormous, much of this consists of rural, mining and logging roads without a hard-top surface; 241,622 miles (388,856km) of the federal and provincial roads have a gravel or earth surface, while 160,846 miles (258,859km) of municipal roads are non-macadamised. Of course, the fact is that, since Canada is so sparsely populated, roads have to go over vast lengths with virtually no settlement to give them local trade and support. This is a high burden on provincial and municipal taxation, and forms a major problem for Canada. Indeed it was not until World War II, when the federal government took the unusual step of getting into what had been a provincial sphere and put up money for a Trans-Canada Highway, that there was a hard-top road from coast to coast. Even this had gravel-topped surfacing for long stretches across the Canadian Shield until the fifties. But this highway now links up every province and every main city from St John's, Newfoundland, and Halifax, NS, through Montreal and Ottawa to Winnipeg, Edmonton and Victoria. Another, and a still more used highway is the Macdonald-Cartier freeway from Montreal to Windsor, through Toronto, with the Queen Elizabeth Highway running off it from Toronto through Hamilton to Buffalo. A highly used freeway also connects Montreal with Ottawa, by the Ottawa Valley through the Shield, and with New York, using the Champlain-Hudson gap through the Appalachians. Strong ties with the United States also occur between Saint John and Boston, Windsor and Detroit and Chicago,

Winnipeg and Minneapolis, and Vancouver and Seattle. The Alaska Highway and the Mackenzie Highway north from Edmonton have been invaluable in opening up the Yukon and the North West Territories.

Over 9½ million motor vehicles are registered, which, for a population of 23 million, gives a very high ratio. Of these about 6 million are registered in Ontario and Quebec, and another 1¼ million in BC—Canada's chief industrial provinces. Nearly 7 million of the vehicles are private cars, ie about 1 car to every 3 people in Canada, or more than 1 car for every family. This is an exceptionally high percentage even for an industrialised nation and shows the reliance Canadians put on private transport to get from place to place in their huge country. No wonder passenger-train services are dropping off. Canadians are wedded to private transport, as can be seen by the enormous areas taken up by private-car parking in every city, and the way in which freeways loop themselves right into the city centre. This has favoured extensive commuting between ex-urban settlements, the suburbs, and central shopping and business districts. Large commuter flows go in and out of every city each day: Canadians think nothing of commuting between 35 and 50 miles to work. There are over a million commuters driving into Montreal, Toronto, Vancouver and Winnipeg every day.

Air transport is offering both road and rail stimulating competition. Time is money in Canada, yet very valuable time is lost in covering the long distances between cities by either rail or road. From Toronto to Winnipeg it is 1,217 miles (1,959km); to Edmonton, 2,011 (3,236km); to Vancouver, 2,776 (4,468km); to Halifax, 1,175 (1,891km). Airways contract these distances in terms of time and therefore save businessmen a great deal of money. Moreover, airways are often the only means of making contact, especially in the North, where there are so few rail or road connections.

There is a fantastic network of airways in Canada, both public and private, both transcontinental and regional. The trans-Canada and international airlines are the public Air Canada, and the private CP Air. Together these earn 75 per cent of the total air-carrier income of Canada. Another 12 per cent is earned by 5 main regional carriers, Eastern Provincial, Quebecair, Nordair, Transair, and Pacific Western Airlines. The final 13 per cent of income is derived from 500 local carrier lines. In addition, foreign airways have pick-up rights in Canada where they connect Canadian cities with the USA, Western Europe, Latin America and Japan. No less than 31 international airlines link with the Canadian airways network. Scheduled flights are made every day to the United States, Mexico, Britain, France, W Germany, the Soviet Union, Japan, Hong Kong and Australia. Air Canada, the principal carrier, operates over 89,000 route miles (143,200km) and carries over 8 million passengers a year. CP Air carries about $1\frac{1}{2}$ million passengers. Pacific Western, owned by Alberta, flies another million people. Quebecair takes some $\frac{1}{2}$ million, and Eastern Provincial, $\frac{1}{3}$ million. Nordair links southern towns with the northern territories; Transair was started in Winnipeg to serve the Prairie provinces, but now operates in the north and also to the Caribbean. Canada has 174 national and municipal airports, handling from 6 to 7 million aircraft movements a year. Toronto is the leading air traffic centre, followed closely by Montreal. Vancouver, Winnipeg, and Ottawa are next in importance in that order. It is interesting that over 40,000 people in Canada hold private licences. Private flying is becoming increasingly important, and some businessmen now commute to work by plane rather than by car.

Canada now plays a major role as a business and industrial country. Her output of goods and services is growing at the rate of 5 to 6 per cent per annum, which is above the UK growth rate and is equivalent to the United States' expansion. Canada has been pre-eminent in attracting world capital, and is also important as an investor abroad—both a reflection of Canada's stability and her power to develop. About $25,000 million of direct investment in Canada from abroad, and over $11,000 million of Canadian money in foreign countries have helped stimulate the economy enormously. All this has affected Canada's trade, making her the sixth largest trading country in the world after the USA, the UK, Japan, West Germany and France. This is a substantial contribution to world economic development. In addition, Canada is now the fifth largest contributor of foreign aid, after the USA, France, the UK, and West Germany, with the second highest per capita aid programme in the world. Thus, as far as her economy is concerned Canada has certainly come of age, and is now one of the world's most developed countries.

6

How They Learn and Express Themselves

EDUCATION is a passion with Canada. Although shrewd judgement and hard work can get a man far, he can get still further armed with ideas. Many people have come to Canada to get on. Poor and in need, the immigrant longed to make good, and live securely. Even if he had means, he wanted to make more of them, and hoped in the New World to find greater scope than in the old. In either case, education seemed the answer.[11]

It should also be noted that many came to educate: among the French, the Jesuits, the Récollets, the Oblate fathers and the Ursuline nuns were highly schooled people whose mission was to set up schools as well as churches. The Seminary at Quebec, that became Laval University, was going only 11 years after the town was founded. The British too had a strong educational tradition, and it was not more than a generation after the founding of Halifax, 1749, Kingston, 1783, and Toronto, 1793, that universities were established. Scots settlers, especially, pressed hard to have high schools and universities as soon as possible; among the earlier institutions, they founded Dalhousie (Halifax), Queen's (Kingston) and McGill (Montreal). Many other settler communities stressed the need for education, including the Icelanders and Ukrainians in the west.

STRUCTURE OF EDUCATION

Constitutionally, education is a provincial matter, and so it has varied from one province to another. Each province has its own department of education with a minister in the provincial cabinet. In Ontario, Manitoba and Alberta there is also a department for advanced education, including universities. Provincial departments also run reform schools, agricultural schools, forest-ranger schools, and apprenticeship programmes. Each province has its own system of certification of teachers and validation of school courses. Schools are run on local rates as well as provincial grants. Local school boards hire teachers and are responsible both to local ratepayers and the provincial authorities. Schools supported by public money are known as public schools; they account for 95 per cent of the school population. Private schools are few, but are important; they are usually well staffed and equipped. Some public schools are run as separate schools —these are denominationally based institutions, such as Protestant schools in Quebec, or Roman Catholic schools in Ontario. In Quebec they are run by separate school boards, one for all Catholic and one for all Protestant public schools. Virtually all schools are comprehensive, some running as three-streamed schools, that is a collegiate, a commercial, and a technical school all in the one institution, others as non-streamed general schools.

There is latitude for experimentation between and within local authorities. For instance, some authorities still stress formal teaching in the traditional type of buildings, others have built the open planned no-walls, no-timetable, no-bell schools, focused on a learning-resource centre where groups of students do their own research on projects agreed on between student and teacher. A number of authorities have also encouraged fast stream schools to take the fast learner out of the ordinary comprehensive school and 'stretch' him in a highly selective and competitive system, dedicated not so much to 'citizenship education' but intellectual prowess. Thus Canadian schools have many patterns—to take account of a nation with strong regional differences and a multi-cultural tradition.

The rise of the consolidated school in the enlarged school district is now creating both a cultural and social mix. This is particularly the case in cities where the re-alignment of school districts has used sectors stretching across class zones, bringing children of different ethnic origins and economic levels together.

Thus schools are helping to ameliorate class divisions in Canada, and to produce a more equal society.

Levels of education provide various combinations of nursery, primary, secondary and post-secondary schooling.

PRIMARY AND SECONDARY SCHOOLS

Public nursery schools for the 3–5 year olds are by no means nationwide or even all-provincial. They are only common in the bigger cities, but even there they are typical mainly of suburban neighbourhoods, where private nurseries tend to look after this age group.

Primary schools take children in their sixth year. They then proceed to grade VIII, when they are 14. At grade IX students pass into high school. However, this pattern is not universal. Some authorities group grades IX and X in middle school, and reserve XI and XII for high school. Junior high schools are now quite popular. In this case a child will go from I–VI in elementary school, VII–IX in junior high, and X–XII in high school. In Ontario, high school runs on to grade XIII, and there is a I–VI, VII–IX, and X–XIII system. Still other combinations are possible,

---

Ice-hockey is the national sport of Canada. The long and icy winters encourage play on river and canal, but training and professional games are played in ice palaces or stadiums

Canadian football is the main game during the long autumns with their sunny and comparatively dry days. Each college and all the principal cities are involved in highly competitive leagues, culminating in the Grey Cup Final. Here Hamilton Tiger-cats meet the Ottawa Rough Riders at Lansdowne Park, Ottawa

using junior colleges or, as they are now more often called, community colleges, to bridge high school and university.

High school education may be completely comprehensive, vocational or academic: the same city may run all three models. The comprehensive curriculum is aimed at helping the pupil to adjust to society and to take employment not demanding a high level of intellectual or technical attainment. Vocational schools, or vocational streams in general schools, aim really at a sort of apprenticeship training. Academic schools—such as fast stream schools, or academic streams in comprehensive schools—aim at entry to university or colleges of education. Some academic schools offer business or technical courses as a one-year programme after students have finished their academic curriculum. Canadian high schools try to give a broad education, where everyone will take either French or English (or both), history, geography, mathematics and a science. In addition they can take a business course, a technical course, art and music. Students have a good deal of choice in their curriculum.

Toronto, with 3 million people, is now Canada's largest city. It is the hub of finance, industry, the media and the arts. The CN-CP run joint telegraphic and other communication services. The Canadian National Railway has built a communication tower which, at 1,815ft 5in (553.33m), is the world's tallest self-standing structure. On the waterfront it looks inland across the railway yards, Union Station, the Royal York and other hotels, to the towering banks of Bay Street—Canada's 'Wall Street'

Montreal's birth and growth through the church, industry and commerce is illustrated here in this cluster of St James' cathedral, the Royal Bank of Canada complex on the left and the Canadian National Railway station and hotel in the background

G

FURTHER EDUCATION

Entrance to university takes account of the school assessment as well as the matriculation examination: indeed in many instances assessment is used instead of matriculation. Two levels of matriculation occur: the junior certificate is given at the end of grade XI, the senior certificate at the end of grade XII—or grade XIII in the case of Ontario, where high schools provide an extra year of teaching. Junior matriculation is somewhat above the 'O' or Ordinary-level in England; senior matric somewhat below the 'A' or Advanced-level examination. Many provinces now have ceased to provide a formal, comprehensive matriculation exam, but instead are issuing a 'Certificate of completion of secondary school studies'.

Community colleges exist to provide further education, beyond the high school level. They offer a very wide range of courses, both academic and vocational, with or without final examinations. Most of them provide business and technical training for those wanting to go into industry. Arrangements are made with factories for their personnel to study on a day-release basis. Many colleges give students from high school a chance to complete their university entrance requirements. Classes are also offered to citizens for interest and pleasure. Of special interest is the nursing course, begun at a community college or university but finished at a university teaching-hospital. In the provinces of Alberta, Manitoba and Ontario, community colleges are grouped with universities under ministries of advanced education. Elsewhere, they are under the schools education departments.

Colleges (or Institutes) of Technology exist in most provinces; these carry technical training to higher-diploma or degree level. Of special interest are the collèges d'enseignement général et professionel (CEGEPS) in Quebec, of which there are no less than 35, and the 26 colleges of applied arts and technology (CAATS) in Ontario. These serve every major town. They presuppose high school graduation, and offer diplomas that are widely accepted by artisans' and professional associations. In Quebec students leave high school at grade xii, and then study at a CEGEP for two years either for a terminal certificate or to enter university.

Teacher training is carried out mainly in university education departments, except in Nova Scotia, Ontario, and Quebec where it is conducted either in university or in colleges of education. Candidates for an elementary school teacher's certificate must have graduated from high school and taken one year's training at a college; for the secondary school certificate, candidates must take a degree at a university and undergo a year of professional training at either colleges or university departments of education. In Quebec, candidates study for two years at a CEGEP, and then go to a university for their certificate course.

University education as a provincial matter varies very considerably across Canada. Most of the universities established before confederation were private institutions, validating their own staff and degrees. The greater number were set up by the church as liberal arts and divinity colleges: Laval (Quebec) and Loyola (Montreal) were Roman Catholic, Dalhousie (Halifax) and Queen's (Kingston) were Presbyterian, King's (NS) and Trinity (Toronto) were Anglican, Acadia (NS) and McMaster (Ontario) were Baptist, and Mount Allison (NB) and Victoria (Toronto) were Methodist. Today, most of the universities are provincial institutions, and only their theology departments remain under the church. For all that, their boards of governors often continue to have church representatives, though the majority of members represent city hall, regional authorities, industry, business, the professions and the trade unions. Universities receive most of their money from the provincial governments but they also receive income from the federal government, from their municipalities, from private trusts, and from student fees. Private universities are still influential, and are the choice of 15 per cent of Canada's students. University governors are vested with the responsibility of deciding how to spend the budget, upon the advice of the president and deans, and the senate of the university. Senates are usually elected from among staff and students, and there is student participation at faculty and departmental levels. The universities are among Canada's more democratic bodies.

The number of universities in Canada is very large. With 23½ million people it has 65 universities or degree-giving colleges. Britain, with 55 million, only has 40. Canada, then, gives much more opportunity for higher education than most countries: altogether over 350,000 students are enrolled, of which 310,000 are undergraduates. About 40 per cent of these are admitted from junior matriculation, ie after the penultimate year of high school, and receive the equivalent of their last high school year at university: this involves 4 years for a general degree instead of 3. Recently, universities have encouraged would-be students to take the Canadian Scholastic Aptitude Test, to see if they would really benefit from university study.

The geographical concentration of students is very significant. Ontario, Quebec, Alberta and British Columbia lead. Ontario is far ahead of any of the other provinces: with 130,000 undergraduates it has 42·7 per cent of all Canadian students at this level—distinctly ahead of its share of Canadian population, which is 35 per cent. At the postgraduate level Ontario does even better with 17,000 or 47·2 per cent of all the country's postgraduate students. No wonder Ontario has taken the Canadian lead in business and industry; it has by far the most highly educated populace. Quebec is in second position with 61,000 students but this is less than half Ontario's numbers. Alberta is third, but with less than half Quebec's total: British Columbia is a close fourth. Actually on a per capita basis both Alberta and British Columbia fare better than Quebec, a fact that has undoubtedly contributed to their very rapid growth over the last decade. The twelve largest universities in Canada are, from west to east, those of British Columbia (Vancouver), Alberta (Edmonton), Saskatchewan (Saskatoon), Manitoba (Winnipeg), Western Ontario (London), McMaster (Hamilton), Toronto, York (Toronto), Queen's (Kingston) Montreal, McGill (Montreal) and Laval (Quebec).

FEDERAL AID AND PARTICIPATION

Federal participation in education is considerable. In the first place Canada herself is responsible for educating Indians and Eskimos. She now places great emphasis on this, and is operating well-equipped schools, with good teachers and a broad curriculum with a strong vocational bent. She has set up an Educational Branch, which works through the educational department of the Territorial Councils (YT and NWT) in the north, and through provincial education departments in the provinces. Of the 250,000 registered Indians in Canada, 72,000 are at school. They must attend from 6 to 16 years, like all other children. Their schools, if on Indian reserves, are run by Indian school committees and a departmental official; if in town, they are controlled by school boards, of which Indians are members. Thus they have a lot of say in the curriculum they want. Increasingly, Indians want their own teachers, and as a result some of their high school graduates have gone on to the teacher-training colleges where, along with other Canadians, they are trained to be teachers. Indian history, language, music and art are now included in the curriculum, although Indians want the opportunity of schooling in the ordinary matriculation subjects so that they are qualified for industrial, business and other posts in the community at large. Thus their schools are an interesting combination of the traditional and the modern, of looking back at the Indian past, and forward at the Canadian future. Where the Indian reserve is too small to mount a high school programme the Indian students are sent to central Indian Schools, where 12,000 of them live in halls of residence or are boarded out while they finish their education. Increasingly, Indians are being bussed to and taught at integrated public schools, along with whites. Promising students are awarded full grants to attend colleges of further education or the university— and in this respect are better off than other students who only receive a limited grant and, if they are in need of further support, have to take up loans. Eskimos are given similar federal support.

Out of 58 schools in the North West Territories, 30 of them are in Eskimo settlements.

The Federal Education Branch has a continuing and Special Education Division, that gives vocational training beyond high school level, including apprenticeship for all kinds of artisan occupations, and also runs adult education programmes to help older Indians and Eskimos adjust to rapidly changing conditions in the Canadian community.

Federal contributions outside of their responsibility for Indians and Eskimos are also considerable. Under the terms of the Federal-Provincial Fiscal Arrangements Act, the federal government transfers part of its income from nation-wide income tax to the provinces, in aid of education. The federal government also gives direct aid by way of capital grants for buildings and equipment used in special education—schools for the blind and deaf, prison schools and certain vocational training schools—and in colleges of further education and the universities. In all, this now totals over $2 billion, a very substantial contribution. Under the Adult Occupational Training Act the federal government through its Department of Manpower is actively engaged in industrial retraining programmes. Capital expenditure in new buildings and equipment is now an appreciable subsidy to provincial post-secondary education. The federal government also runs the loan scheme under the Canada Students Loan Act of 1970. A full-time student may borrow $1,400 a year to a total of $9,800 over his course of study. Loans are interest free while the student is still at university and for six months thereafter. These loans are made only on receipt from the provincial departments concerned of a 'certificate of eligibility'. All but indigent students are expected to contribute something to their own education; the loan does not cover the full cost of their studies. Thus Canadian students are more personally involved in higher education than their British counterparts, many of whom receive all their tuition, travel, and accommodation at the hand of the government. The federal government also helps substantially in postgraduate studies by providing full grants for PhD courses through awards won from the Canada Council, the National Research Council, the Social Science and the Humanities Research Councils, the Defence Research Board and the Department of Health and Welfare.

Finally, the federal government aids Canadian postgraduate students to go abroad with grants from the Canada Council, and, more than that, assists foreign students to get training and higher degrees in Canada. Also, the Canadian International Development Agency finances post secondary school training in connection with federal technical assistance programmes for developing countries.

EXPRESSION THROUGH THE MEDIA

The media in Canada have always been of the greatest importance in helping to create her national identity. A daughter country of Britain, and a cousin to America, Canada has frequently been dominated by British and American newspapers, magazines, books, films and the theatre. Indeed it has been to resist these that Canadians have tried so hard to develop their own media of public expression. Yet Canada is so large that she has found it difficult to distribute a paper or a programme right across the country. Hence most of her papers, many of her magazines, and a lot of her radio programmes are regional or, indeed, highly local. This has made it difficult for the media to operate nationwide and to create a national image. In this context, the Canadian Broadcasting Corporation and the National Film Board have been of the highest service.

The Canadian Radio Broadcasting Commission was set up in 1932 by the federal government very largely to promote a national radio network to offset the powerful radio corporations in the United States which were flooding Canada with American news, sports broadcasts, plays and music. All the geography of Canada draws it towards the United States and, also, cuts off one region in Canada from another. Hence a strong move was needed to create an internal linkage that would bring and keep the Canadian people together and give them a sense of national identity. The Commission first tried to do this by regulating and, to a certain extent, supervising existing commercial programmes. This was not enough and in 1936 the Canadian Broadcasting Corporation was formed to give a trans-Canada service of its own. It provides regular daily newscasts, with news from all over Canada and the rest of the world and offers a full range of radio drama, music, light entertainment and educational programmes, as well. The CBC is supported by funds from Parliament and from commercial advertising. The head office is in Ottawa, with main sub-centres in Toronto and Montreal, and regional centres across the country. The CBC has 19 English-speaking and 10 French-speaking originating stations, with 108 English and 28 French re-broadcasting stations. Independent television known as CTV, in English-speaking Canada, and TVA, in French-speaking, own 16 originating and 97 re-broadcasting stations. It is estimated that 90 per cent of all Canadian households have one or more TV sets.

Films in Canada have played a powerful part in expressing Canada's view of herself and of the world. In 1921 the Canadian Government Motion Picture Bureau was set up, the purpose of which was 'to introduce one part of the country to another through the medium of film'.[12] This bureau was reconstituted in 1938, under John Grierson, as the National Film Board of Canada, which has been active ever since, to become one of Canada's great institutions. Grierson produced a series of powerful, dramatic, real-life documentaries on fishing, mining, lumbering, wheat farming, railways and aspects of city life. These helped enormously to make Canadians realise how multivariate their life was. The war years were famous for two series in which Grierson tried to get Canadians behind the war effort; these were, 'Canada Carries On' and 'World in Action'. The introduction of television in 1952 gave both the NFB and private film companies in Canada much more scope. Also, Canada started its own magazines of film criticism and information— (the first was *Découpages*, Montreal)—and started to present its own annual Film Awards. Montreal became such an active centre of film-making and film-criticism that the NFB moved there in 1959. In 1967 the government set up the Canada Film Development Corporation to stimulate and subsidise licensed film-making in Canada. This has helped to nurse an independent film industry in Canada, which is a much needed thing, having regard to the fact that 80 per cent of all the films shown in Canada are still American. The private sector is struggling hard against such competition, and has formed the Canadian Film Producers Association, to help further the film industry in Canada.

Telecommunications have improved enormously and this improvement has helped both the CBC and the NFB to reach the people as a whole. In 1969, a crown corporation known as Telesat Canada was created by Parliament to provide satellite transmission of radio and television programmes. It launched the world's first geostationary satellite for microwave transmission. On 9 November 1972 the satellite, ANIK I was shot into space 23,300 miles (37,497km) above the earth's equator, where it rotates with the earth every 24 hours, keeping a fixed point from which radio and TV programmes can be beamed. There are 37 stations across Canada receiving these programmes beamed back with extraordinary speed and clarity from ANIK.

Telegraphic and telephonic communications in Canada assist the media enormously, and other interests as well. Only when the traveller, going between cities over the vast empty spaces, sees the mile upon mile of telephone line does he realise the fantastic network of facilities that has been developed and is needed to keep the far-flung parts of Canada together. Twenty-three telephone and telegraphic companies serving Canada have recently joined to form the Canadian Telecommunications Carriers Association, and in 1969 the federal government recognised the vital role of telecommunications by forming a new Department of Communications. Rapid progress has been made. Most households have a telephone: in fact, there is a telephone for every two Canadians: 85 per cent of Canadian telephones are now hooked up to the direct-dial system. The wide area service (WATS) allows a customer to make or receive calls from all over Canada or from regions within Canada at a flat rate. A hot-line service permits brokers and their business men in Montreal and Toronto to contact their opposite numbers in New York simply by picking up the telephone. The CN-CP telegraphic organisation provides very sophisticated services including telex throughout Canada, the USA and Europe; telepost by which teleprinted messages can go to post offices for delivery; tele-typewriter, a complex order-writing system; teledata for transmitting statistical data over telephone lines; and Vucom, which throws data-graphics on television screens by use of the telephone network.

Newspapers, making use of these many services, are much better able to serve their reading public, which they do over increasingly wide areas. There are few papers that are distributed right across Canada; most newspapers have no more than a provincial or a municipal circulation. However, certain newspapers have been bought up and, in effect, are run as group publications, and the papers in these groups share certain facilities and carry common features. There are 120 papers altogether with a combined circulation of nearly 5 million—or, in statistical terms, 1 paper for every 4 people; 82 per cent are English-language papers, 18 per cent French. Southam Press has the biggest chain of newspapers, 14 dailies, spread across Canada, but with more in Ontario than anywhere else: it has over 25 per cent of Canada's circulation. Thomson Newspapers are the second largest group, with 10 per cent of Canada's readership: many of its papers are county or town weeklies. FP publications control 6 dailies, and 7 per cent of the circulation. However, all these groups and papers use the news and syndicate services of two trans-Canada news-gathering agencies—Canadian Press, and the United Press International. These have offices in the USA and the UK and are linked up with the Associated Press (American), Reuters (British) and Agence France-Presse (French), to collect news and items of interest from all over the world.

Magazine-publishing in Canada is very active. Almost every interest imaginable, from art to welding, is represented. Some more general ones, however, have a wide appeal, with fiction, biography, travel, literary criticism, poetry and reviews in them. It is perhaps invidious to single out a few: of the more academic ones, mention might be made of the *University of Toronto Quarterly*, the *Queen's Quarterly*, and the *Dalhousie Review*—all dealing with contemporary issues in a scholarly way; of the political ones, the *Canadian Forum* has been, and is, outstanding; *Chatelaine* is the leading woman's magazine; the chief family all-purpose journals would include *Macleans, Saturday Night* and the *Weekend*. These have all given Canadian writers, of many kinds, encouragement to publish on main issues and interests in Canada. Of journalists Eggleston, Hutcheson, Nichol, Clark and Berton are outstanding in their interpretation of Canada.

LITERATURE

Playwrights and short-story writers have been encouraged, to a considerable degree, by TV and radio. The rise of a national theatre in Ottawa, and of strong regional centres based on new well-equipped theatres and modern theatre companies, as for example in Montreal, Toronto, Winnipeg and Vancouver, has also given an immense stimulus. The annual festival of plays at Stratford, Ontario, encourages Canadian talent, as well as doing homage to Shakespeare. Canada has no longer had to rely, as it used to, on visiting theatre companies from Britain and the USA bringing with them British and American plays and actors (although these still do come). Instead, Canada can give scope to its own creative talent. Script-writers of some note have been associated with the National Film Board and with independent film-making companies; some of their work has been published, though most of it is expressed in films. Five of the early writers for the NFB made an international reputation; Clement Perron in his dry, witty, humorous and yet tragic, very moving story, *Mon Oncle Antoine*, about a boy growing up in the family of a storekeeper-cum-undertaker. This was a description of life in a small Quebec mining community on the edge of pioneer farming and the bush. Charles Cohen's *The Drylanders* earned him instant fame; he told the story in crisp stark realism, but with real tenderness, of the struggles and joy of western pioneer farming, afflicted as it was by drought and hail. Pierre Perrault wrote for Crawley Films, Montreal, producing a series of dramatic sketches of hardship and humanity among farmers and village-dwellers on marginal farmland along the edge of cut-over or second-growth bush on the Quebec north shore—

Pour la Suite du Monde. Later he wrote *Le Règne du Jour* and *Les Voitures d'Eau*, making a trilogy on the old rural scene in Quebec of great force and beauty. But Canada's main life lay in the cities. This was recognised in a series of scripts on Toronto life by Don Owen, the best known of which concerns the bafflement, doubt, despair and yet courage of youth in *Nobody Waved Goodbye*. Gilles Groulx did much the same thing for Montreal, where a young Roman Catholic French girl meets up with a Jewish English-speaking boy in scenes tense with cultural conflict and personal drama in *Le Chat dans le Sac*.

Some stage-play writers have adapted their plays for the TV. Notable among these are Bill Fruet, with his *Wedding in White*, a family story of the Prairies; he heads a young playwriting group at Toronto: John Herbert, with *Fortune and Men's Eyes;* and Ted Allan, with *Lies My Father Told Me*, a very moving story about growing up among the Jewish, Protestant, Catholic loyalties of Montreal.

Stage playwrights have not been numerous in Canada, largely because of the British and American dominance of the Canadian stage until very recently.[13] Canadians are of course members of a worldwide literary community, and are extremely well read in, and like to see plays from, the drama of England, the USA and France. Consequently, playwrights have to face a lot of competition. Merely to dramatise Canadian life is not enough, one must do it with the literary skill and force to admit comparison with mainstream writing in English or French. Much of Canadian playwriting has been sectional, for one part of Canada or another; also it has depended a great deal on local amateur dramatics. Notwithstanding all this, four or five writers of national impact have arisen. Gratien Gélinas is perhaps the most notable of these, since he not only writes for stage and screen but also acts, produces plays and films, and is deeply involved in Canadian culture, especially French-Canadian culture. He began his career writing skits about and acting the part of a character, *Fridolin*, by now famous as the 'little man' in the community, tough, shrewd, humorous and sentimental. He then wrote a play *Tit-Coq* (the Li'l Rooster) which shows this man in war and peace. In Ontario, Robertson Davies has proved himself a sophisticated, controversial, scintillating writer whose humour has a keen edge. As Samuel Marchbanks he gained fame for his satirical wit, publishing his comments on Canadian society in the form of a diary. His 'disrespect for sacred cows' was then carried to the stage in a series of one-act comedies. His earliest full-length play, *Fortune, My Foe*, is still in many respects his best, where he describes the state of a bright young intellectual in Canada 'overlaid by a stultifying home atmosphere and cultural malnutrition'. Again, this was a recognisable Canadian situation and as such it struck home.

James Reaney, much younger than Davies or Gélinas, has developed a wide reputation for his unusual not to say grotesque twists to events that suddenly show up the hidden but real issues in life. A small town (Stratford) person though educated in a metropolis (Toronto), Reaney is interested, as he says in *Colours in the Dark*, in the 'person growing up, leaving home, going to big cities, getting rather mixed up and then not coming home again but making home and identity come to him wherever he is'. He has written three plays on the Donnely family, a violent group, at the centre of much controversy in Ontario. More recently Ryga has made his mark with *The Ecstasy of Rita Joe*.

Short-story writers[14] have been a feature of Canada because they have been able to evoke the local scene in a country where people first think locally. The Canadian story itself is like a collection of short stories, each about a different region. The regional element is supreme. Morley Callaghan, for example, writes about the Canadian metropolis—the clash of black and white, Protestant and Catholic, in Montreal; of rich and poor, materialist and idealist in Toronto.

Ethel Wilson is also concerned to bring out community traits in her respect for self-respect. She has a controlled intensity which one sees in those who have to endure the long winter and still maintain the summer mind. Mavis Gallant along with Alice Munro, produce stories that are marvellously fresh, true vignettes of the Canadian small town or city, but, more than that, open windows into the Canadian interior, into the struggle for Canadian identity. David Helweg sees the confusions of life in Yorkville, at one time the 'hippyville' of Canada, as part of this identity-confusion between well-meaning tenderness and humanity (always typical of a people who have had to face up to so much hardness) and the rectitude by which, nevertheless, they have measured their ways. Part of the confusion is due to rapid social change which is faster than mental adaptation. Hugh Garner's stories are full of the challenge of change. Anne Hebert's are about the abiding things like suffering, prejudice, and injustice that show through change. Hers is an old Quebec in agonising contrast with the new.

The novelists of Canada are now too numerous to list and discuss in a short book. And yet they are certainly an important part both of living and of the expression of life in Canada. Perhaps the three most widely read are Lucy Montgomery, author of *Anne of Green Gables*; Mazo de la Roche, of the Whiteoaks saga; and Louis Hemon, of *Maria Chapdelaine*. These are all in William Rose Benet's *The Reader's Encyclopedia*, a standard reference book of world literature. Though the authors are very different they have this in common, their concern with the family. And this is very much a Canadian feature, since the family was for long the basis of pioneer living in countryside and town.

Stephen Leacock is also an internationally known Canadian writer, mainly as an author of humorous sketches. His most famous book *Sunshine Sketches of a Little Town* scarcely has the structure of a novel, but is a presentation, in a highly ironic way, of a group of shrewd, self-centred, self-important, small-town people, the epitome of Ontario provincial life. Its appeal is that these people could be found in any small British, French, or American town: very Canadian yet they are universal.

Modern writers have stretched the grasp of Canadian life enormously—still concerned with the family, but more with its tensions, still with the small town but more with its demise, centering themselves mainly on the city, and on the city problems of anonymity, exploitation, confusion, conflict, the clash of race, 'women's lib', the generation gap between father and son, and the split with which sectionalism threatens the nation. In Woodcock's excellent *The Canadian Novel in the Twentieth Century* he selects essays written about 20 living novelists, but these only represent the English-speaking stream.[15] French-Canadian literature is also very strong. Among living authors, Woodcock's list includes Ethel Wilson, Morley Callaghan, Hugh MacLennan, Sinclair Ross, Robertson Davis, W. O. Mitchell, Mavis Gallant, Margaret Lawrence, Hugh Hood, Mordecai Richler, Robert Kroetsch, Leonard Cohen, and Margaret Atwood. The late Malcolm Lowry is also discussed: his work has a powerful contemporary influence.

It is obviously an invidious distinction to single out any of these, but some have an international as well as a Canadian following. Callaghan's best-known work, *Such is My Beloved,* is about the Great Depression in Canada and the social ills it deepened. A country like Canada, then so dependent on primary production and the export of fish, wheat, lumber and metals, was particularly susceptible to economic breakdown, and felt the depression more than most countries. Irene Baird's *Waste Heritage* brings this out in a powerful way, following the misfortunes of a group of young hoboes. World War II ended depression with a boom—but created new problems, not least of which was the intensification of the differences felt between British and French in Canada. Most people of British stock supported the war, many French Canadians did not. Long a theme of Canadian writers, the difference between the French and British traditions received new attention. It was the subject of several of Hugh MacLennan's works, particularly of *The Two Solitudes, The Watch that Ends the Night,* and *The Return of the Sphinx.* As Cockburn had said of *The Two Solitudes* 'it has passed into the language as a common descriptive phrase of Canadians', as a summation of the Canadian situation, a land divided into two systems that hardly communicate with each other.

Mordecai Richler and Leonard Cohen are products of yet another solitude, the world of the Jew, that is far older and far other than Canada. The war everywhere sharpened men's consciousness of the Jewish problem, and the rise of Israel afterwards posed for Jews the crucial question of their loyalty. Both Richler and Cohen are Canadian and chose to write about Canadian themes, but they have done so in a way that has caught up

life in Canada into universal issues—not just the conflict of Jew
and Gentile, but conflict itself, between classes, between sexes,
between persons. Richler's early novel *The Apprenticeship of
Duddy Kravitz* follows a young Jew from the ghetto of Montreal
to the success admired among the Anglo-Canadians who dominate affairs, but success is won at the cost of bitter conflict with
friends and traditions. Cohen's *Beautiful Losers* may perhaps best
be summarised in its cry, 'Undress, Undress . . . let's look at
each other. Let's have education.' Out of the intense confusion
of the times only the most direct confrontation of people and
ideas can bring us to a knowledge of ourselves. This is important
for a nation struggling to find its identity.

Margaret Lawrence and Margaret Atwood are very individual thinkers, albeit in a distinctly Canadian context. Lawrence describes the Prairie sense of immenseness, isolation,
freedom, self-reliance and determination almost as though this
was itself a character, as in the *Jest of God*. As for Margaret Atwood she is swimming up out of *Surfacing*, like a deep diver coming to light again: from Canada's depths in the water and the
wood—those essentials of the Canadian nature where Miss Atwood has her characters plunge—the country emerges to its
identity: in seeking the basic things of its past it can move into a
future more true to itself.

French-Canadian novelists have also sought to express the
Canadian dilemma—a nation split in two trying to make one
country. This has been difficult, because loyalties have been
different. Traditionally the French have had an inward-looking
and homogeneous culture; British culture has rested on variety,
if not division.

However, the hand of tradition is loosening in Quebec, and
people have the freedom to grasp at the different and the new.
A quiet revolution has occurred largely led by the writers, who
are distinctly 'forward looking, sophisticated and cosmopolitan'.
The new writing has 'emphasised poverty, unemployment,
crime, urbanisation and industrialisation'. As Gerard Tougas
has said, contemporary French Canadian novelists have 'begun
to shake the pillars of their society, namely religion and family'.[16]
Joan Simard became openly critical, especially of those who

carried on their old ways in the trapping of the new. Langevin has been frankly anti-clerical and Filiatrault anti-filial. Even Roger Lemalin's famous story of *The Plouffe Family* set in old-town Quebec, while filled with forgiving understanding of the old order, needles people into an awareness of change.

Gabrielle Roy best expresses this crisis of transition in her novels *Alexandre Chenevert, The Tin Flute* and *The Cashier*. In the first, she describes the mental confusion and social conflicts of men caught up in the complications of large-city life, which is highly secular and impersonal. These themes are carried on in *The Tin Flute* where the insufficiencies of the old French order are brought out in face of the competitiveness and materialism of the Anglo-American régime. *The Cashier* shows a humble bewildered individual trapped by a brazen, indifferent system. These are all situations relevant to present-day changes in Quebec, now dominated by big business, and big American business at that. This has led certain younger novelists, like Marie-Claire Blais, to look back with longing, but others, like Jacques Godbout, look forward with grim intensity to the day of confrontation, if not independence. His *Knife on the Table* is a fierce probe into the problem of Quebec identity, showing all the indeterminism and confusion of the young French-Canadian facing the affluence and assumed superiority of the Anglo-American way. Even more searching is Hubert Aquin's *Prochain Episode*, (The Next Step), dealing with the spiritual drive but mental uncertainties of a young terrorist, who is caught up in this international situation. Gilles Vigneault, the writer most associated with the disturbance of mind and spirit known as '*l'octobre québécois*', represents the French pride and anguish.

Canadian poetry has always been very active in giving a voice to Canadian hopes and problems. Confederation was met with a burst of creative enthusiasm, and towards the end of the nineteenth century poets like Bliss Carmen, Archibald Lampman, and Duncan Campbell Scott had earned an international reputation.[17] Like the romantics of England and America they were full of the love of nature and concern for people, their emotions and ideals. As the critic Malcolm Ross says, they were peculiarly Canadian, not in gilding the maple, though they

H

were very patriotic, but in making the pattern of Canadian life apparent—'a pattern of opposites in tension'.

This tension, and the attempt to resolve, or at least contain it, saw in the depression and in the two world wars young Canadian poets giving active expression to Canadian aspirations. Among the poets of this period, E. J. Pratt towered above the rest in the many majestic themes he treated and in the heroic spirit he fostered: a Newfoundlander used to hardship and storm, his works were of great events like the sinking of the *Titanic*, or of challenging experiences like hunting *The Cachalot*. By no means a nationalist—one of his finest poems was on the epic British story of *Dunkirk*—he nevertheless wrote in *Brébeuf* one of the ringing poems about Canada, celebrating the courage and fidelity of the great French missionary burned at the stake in the Indian wars of Huronia.

Of contemporary poets, Earle Birney stands out in his power to handle great Canadian themes with an almost glacier-like strength and austerity. In his poem *David* he shows man matching himself against the wilderness, a basic feature of Canadian life which, as we have seen, with its rugged relief and bleak climate, is always on the razor's edge between success and failure. The young David and his friend are challenged by an unclimbed peak, the 'Finger' but, in the very moment of triumph meet with tragedy, as one of the climbers falls to his death. Birney then goes on to other Canadian themes, like exploitation, and the pollution of the landscape in his shock-filled *what's so big about green?* But though intensely conscious of the raw edge of Canada's problems, Birney has a deep faith in the people. Indeed, this concentration on man has focused more and more of his writing on mankind as a whole, making the poet a great internationalist. Canada's problems, because she is so dependent on other nations, can only be solved in terms of the world. F. R. Scott and A. M. Klein, other noted Canadian poets, express this humanistic and cosmopolitan view even more—a view that is now so important in Canada's vision of herself. Scott's biting sarcasm at parochialism in his famous poem *The Canadian Authors Meet*, shows his concern that Canadians should mature as world citizens. Klein has felt this too, both as a Jew and Canadian, his poems extending the Canadian experience to all the oppressed.

A. J. M. Smith, eminently cosmopolitan, has written a notably Canadian—and probably the best—poem on Canada in his *The Lonely Land* where, describing the heartland of Canada, the great, rocky, rugged, ice-torn and wind-harried Shield, he cries,

> This is the beauty
> of strength
> broken by strength
> and still strong

Smith has edited quite the best anthology of Canadian verse, made all the more serviceable by his very penetrating and distinguished introduction.[18]

Again, it is an invidious task to say how Canadians express themselves by selecting only a few poets, but this is inevitable in a short summary. Among the most recent of the writers one might mention Margaret Atwood and Leonard Cohen, already referred to as novelists but whose poetry is singularly fresh and provoking; Al Purdy, Raymond Souster, and Irving Layton, very forthright, at times bawdy, at times bitter, always very concerned; and Alden Nowland, John Newlove, Nicol, and Onondaatje often disenchanted but determined to strive for a Canada recognising social justice and equality as its living base.

Both the geography and history of Canada emerge very strongly in her writers. Time and again there is the appeal to one or the other—or both. That this occurs among French-speaking as well as English-speaking Canadians, must show the pervading source, for all her dwellers, of Canada's especial inspiration.[19] Paul Chamberland, the poet of the Quebec revolt, claims this sort of inspiration. 'I restore my eyes, my head and bare fists to the natural freedom of the close-cropped wind . . .' For André Major, 'the landscape's in me'—and it's in him cruel, with all the asperity of the Canadian winter, yet 'his words are green', the human message is that of a nation which, struggling against difficulty outside and division within, has always come up with the growth of new ideas, and new hope. In

Anne Hebert's *Poèmes*, she is concerned with 'le coeur de la terre', not merely a French-Canadian heart in French Canada, although that is essential, but with the human situation in which the earth plays its continuing part. This is very much the French-Canadian message. Paul-Emile Borduas returns to it again and again, the greater world in the world of the heart: as Gaston Miron puts it, pithily, '*l'avenir dégagé, l'avenir engagé*'— withdrawal is a commitment, the French-Canadian wish to be separate goes with a will to embrace the universal. At the end of the day Canada will, as Marie-Claire Blais affirms in her simple statement, *Life*, 'continue her work in the fields', in a history of unstinting effort that will sustain the nation's growth.

7

Their Art and Music

Art is a nationwide activity in Canada. In city squares, amateur art shows attract thousands; in libraries or art galleries, thousands of children gather on Saturday mornings to participate; art classes in school and in evening class are packed; art associations have sprung up in small towns and townships; radio and TV take art programmes into every home.

Part of this is because of increased leisure and income, part of it because of a better education in the arts. As a result there has been a general flowering of artistic interest and effort that is changing the image of the country. Good indications of this may be seen in the art histories by Colgate, or Lord.

One of the best ways of seeing this is to go into the art galleries.[20] The traveller will find these in each major city, and in each region of Canada. Each specialises in the work of its own area, yet each tries to represent Canada as a whole.

CANADA'S GALLERIES

Galleries in Canada have at least a two-fold role. First they are anxious to preserve for Canadians their rich cultural heritage in Britain, France and other parts of Europe. Second they are the treasure-house of Canada's own development in the arts. Until the Canadian renaissance of the 1930s, galleries emphasised the European antecedents, but after that, gave increasing space to the Canadian achievement. Both policies are important, for Canada. While she is still very European, she is at the same time progressively North American. Of the art galleries in the major cities, some have grown to national importance.

The Beaverbrook Art Gallery at Fredericton, New Brunswick, as might be expected from its benefactor, and from the Loyalist Province, has the most British of collections in Canada, but there is also a very good Canadian section. Whereas many other galleries have mainly embraced the French strand of European tradition, the Beaverbrook gallery maintains the British connection. This is important not only because many Canadians studied art in Britain, or, during the wars, as war artists in a Commonwealth nation, got to know their counterparts in the home country, but because the British element in Canada, ever threatened by the dominance of American culture on the continent, seeks to maintain its ancient but still vital tie with Britain.

Most of the British works in the Beaverbrook collection are the moderns. Sickert and Sargent introduce them with powerful portraits and interiors, then come Peploe, Spencer, Lowry, Nash and Freud with their searching, disciplined ways, pared down to the essentials, trying to get at the truth. A magnificent series of portraits by Graham Sutherland, including some forceful studies of Churchill, show this concern of the modern Briton for the essentials. The Canadian section, which includes some fine winter scenes by Krieghoff and Horatio Walker, and some more than usually fine landscapes by Thomson and Carmichael, moves on to the fierce intensity of Emily Carr in her pulsing *Woods and Blue Sky*, the portraits of Cosgrove with the dignity of simplicity, scenes by Muhlstock and Hughes getting at the essence of woods and the sea, and the explosive urban scenes of Riopelle. The high realism of Colville is also very impressive.

Moving on to the central provinces, the traveller should pay a visit to the Montreal Museum of Fine Arts. This arose from efforts by the Montreal Society of Artists, founded in 1847, and the Art Association of Montreal, created in 1860, to persuade citizens and the city to establish a library and gallery of art. The Montreal Museum carries forward the older French and other European traditions up to the French Impressionists and indeed to contemporary French art, so that Canadians may realise that the roots from which they sprang have continued to flourish and produce new and vigorous growth. In fact, many Canadians have been affected by that growth, through study in Paris and London. At no time have they really been separated from their European origins. The museum also has a very fine collection of eminently Canadian paintings and sculptures, showing how strongly and also how differently the Canadian offshoots grew. Here are the early Canadian painters like Plamondon, portrayer of the religious base to settlement; Kane, interpreter of the Indian; and Krieghoff, mirror of pioneer life, where white and Indian were closely in touch with each other. Brymner, Cullen, Suzor-Côté, and Morrice are there, picturing the emergence of a distinctively Canadian landscape, first represented in relation to village or small town. Nature became the theme of the famous Group of Seven including Harris, Thomson, Jackson, Lismer, Casson, Macdonald and Varley. Symbolic or non-objective painting then arose, as Canadians got away from a narrow and perhaps too agressive Canadianism, to their heritage as sons of men, and became cosmopolites. Pellan, Borduas, Riopelle, and Tonnancour seem to express this new world-consciousness in Canadian life and art.

The Art Gallery of Ontario, formed in 1900, was, like its forerunners in Quebec, out to demonstrate the wide and rich background of Canadian life in European civilisation, and the development from that of an identifiable Canadian culture. There is a nice progression of works from the Italian Renaissance through the French and Flemish artists to those of Britain, recalling the 'Westward march of empire' which was to carry the great Graeco-Roman traditions through France and England to Canada. At the stage when the French and the British were celebrating a highly manmade world of great town houses, fashionable ladies, eminent proconsuls, and idyllic countrysides steeped in peace and plenty, it is a bit of a shock to see Canadian painters, like Kane, depicting a Huron encampment which he himself saw; Krieghoff showing us a settler's log cabin almost buried in the snow; and Plamondon presenting three young lads spending their Saturday, not at the races, but a wildfowl shoot, on the edge of the primeval marsh. O'Brien gives a water-

colour sketch of a prospector's camp high up in the lonely
mountains; and then, a group of late nineteenth-century painters, Beatty, Walker, and Morrice, depict the woods of Canada,
from which the settler has wrested his farm, and the street of the
market town with its make-do humble architecture. However,
although these artists portrayed a Canada that was still largely
a frontier country, they tended to romanticise it.

It was really left to the Group of Seven to discover in the
'wild', the distinctiveness, indeed the soul of Canada. Here is
something new—here is a starkness and simplicity unknown in
Europe, here is the power of a people pitted against—and yet at
one with—nature. To look at Renoir's *Le Concert*, with its
richly clad artistes in a Paris dressing room where a Louis
Quinze table is heaped with gorgeous roses in a glowing vase, as
fine as the finest Sèvres ware (a setting where the sadness if not
despondency of a Europe at the fin de siècle reigns), and put all
this beside Lawren Harris's *Above Lake Superior* with its vibrant
simplicity and stark grandeur, is not merely to put the romanti-
cist and the realist together, it is to contrast two views of the
world.

The McMichael Collection near Toronto is without question
the supreme home of the Canadian Renaissance. Set amidst the
bucking and pitching boulder-broken landscape of the great
Oak Ridge moraine (dumped by the ice between the Lake Ontario and Simcoe basins), it is a fitting place to show off the
Group of Seven in all their brutal ruggedness, aseptic clarity and
awesome strength. Here are Tom Thomson's passion for wood
and water, storm-lashed trees, ice-sliced rivers, frost-cracked
rocks and wind-torn skies; A. Y. Jackson's rolling and surging
landscapes, splashed with sun, and streaked with shade, where
villages sprawl with the gullied slopes, and telegraph poles are
splayed with the burden of ice; J. E. H. Macdonald's aura of
mysticism in an array of mists shot through with a flame of colour; Harris's sheer austerity of skeletal rock honed down by the
elements, yet still stern within the waters; Varley's twisted and
wind-stripped pines in crannies of ice-fractured granite; Lismer's sun after rain, lighting the chaos of tortured stumps on
fused and twisted rock; Carmichael's huge sweeps of hunch-

backed and rough-shouldered hills cut into strips by glacier-breached gorges; and Casson's bitter rock and rumpled sky tied to each other by broken trees.

Winnipeg Art Gallery, situated near the heart of that city, was the earliest in the West, founded in 1912, when three members of the Royal Canadian Academy, Watson, Cullen and Challoner, were at the opening. The new building is itself a striking work, in the contemporary style. The Gort collection of Medieval religious painting again stresses Canada's European tie. This leads to what one can only describe as 'Canadian primitive'—early Canadian painters faithfully translating the terms of their rough and ready life into pictures: the portraits are notable for the severity of a people who eschewed bows and furbelows and lived by the Bible and hard work. Then are shown what the gallery calls the Canadian Classics, mostly the Group of Seven, with Emily Carr. From these Milne, with his emphasis on landscape in terms of finesse rather than mass, and on the impact of man rather than the control of nature—(as for example in his *Clearing on the Hill*), leads into the moderns. Using the townscape for inspiration, they, like Fitzgerald in his *Garages in Winter*, or Varvarande, in his *Construction* (a tearing down and building up of the city), are concerned with the environs of the contemporary Canadian, whose life is lived in a forest of concrete and glass. Richards' *Tree of Life* features man and woman, not the wild wood; Kahane's *Rain* is a concourse of umbrellas, not clouds towering over the Prairie; Archpenko's rugged beauty deals not with the struggle of root and rock, but with *The Boxers*; Ivan Eyre typifies the Prairies in a group of wheat elevators seen from the *Underpass* of a super-highway going over a railroad. The contemporary concern is with economic problems and social conflicts: moving to affluence has meant moving to economic gulfs and social chasms which Canada must learn to bridge. Affluence has also brought a new sophistication, presented in the Nitikman collection of modern graphics, an exercise in lines, masses, and planes.

For the traveller who starts or ends his tour of Canada at Victoria or Vancouver, BC, there are the twin galleries, run as a joint enterprise; the Art Gallery of Greater Victoria and the

Vancouver Art Gallery. Begun in 1945–58, youth dominates. At Victoria, an old Victorian home with a modern wing again emphasises the duality of Canadian art, with one foot in Europe and the other in North America. The galleries 'envisage the acquisition of the work of many periods and civilisations, special emphasis being put on the arts of seventeenth–nineteenth-century Europe (the colonial era in Canada when it was so dependent on its mother country), oriental art and Canadian art'. Of particular interest, because of the many Asians on the Pacific Coast, is the oriental section of paintings, carvings and porcelain from China and Japan. These have not yet had much influence on Canadian art, but it is as well to be reminded that they too are part of the past for a growing section of Canada.

Not unnaturally, emphasis is laid on the great West Coast painter, Emily Carr, whose electrifying paintings of the forests of giant cedar and fir, on the Pacific shore, are full of the flow of light between the spear-like trees. The luminosity of her pictures captures the West Coast air, moist off the ocean, and turbulent with winds that carry shine and shade sweeping across the landscape. Milne's nervously fine perception leads on to Shadbolt's scenes full, simultaneously, of the delicacy and tension of the woods. Jock Macdonald represents the dramatic turn from the outer to the inner world, from his early landscapes, reminiscent of the Group of Seven and of what the natural environment meant to Canada, to his later abstractions and designs, which are highly personal *Contemplations* of the forces of change in Canada. At Vancouver, a 'cultural explosion' of the younger artists has seized on the contemporary urban confusion as its milieu. A mixture of plastics, wire, neon lights and other aspects of modern technology, with painting that focuses on stress-lines and planes of discord, has created a dynamic representation of life today—life in the exploding metropolis.

The National Gallery in Ottawa draws together all the trends that have emerged in the different parts of the country. It was organised in 1880 to provide a viewing place for the newly established Royal Canadian Academy. By Canadian standards it is a quite venerable institution and, indeed, it was founded 56 years before the National Gallery of Art in Washington. Its inception was to help create a national concern for the arts across Canada —a country still without the Provinces of Saskatchewan and Alberta (which were then part of the North-west Territories), and a country still not connected from coast to coast by road or railway. This is significant. It means that when Canada was concerned about the basic economic and administrative framework of the developing nation, it still felt constrained to nourish the arts. Canadians have a deep sense of spiritual values even if they are at the same time level-headed pragmatists. The development of their country has always been thought of in terms of human as well as natural resources.

At its commencement, the National Gallery had few Canadian painters to choose from: its main task was to commemorate the spirit from which the Canadian image grew. The deep religious fervour of the French, the British love of the countryside, French and British respect for the elegance of life (especially as centred in the court), French rationalism, British romanticism, the French and British revival of classicism and particularly of the Vitruvian tradition in city planning, the French love of glory, the British eye to profit, the French and British interest in science—all these, and more, are there, reminding Canadians of how far they had been carried in colonial days before they started out on their own.

The Canadian tradition, once it began to shape itself, tried to represent the clash of cultures, between Indian and White, and between French and British; the conquest of the environment; the way of life of the people, as they began to develop their country; and the struggle for identity.

In her publication on the National Gallery, Jean Boggs[21] has shown each of these phases through her selection of the Canadian artists represented there. First is Plamondon with his painting of the nun, *Sister Sainte-Alphonse*, showing the deep concern of the French Canadian for religion, and for the simplicity and dignity of life—still important virtues in Quebec; then comes O'Brien with his British love of nature and his romanticisation of its scope and power in *Sunrise on the Saguenay* where, however, man is the focus, with his questing ships; next is Leduc with his concern for the home, and the arts and crafts of pioneer living, in his *Still Life—Study by the Light of a Candle*; this is followed by Tom Thomson's magnificent *Jack Pine* where he gets back beyond French, British, the pioneer, indeed beyond man, to nature itself in all its wildness, solemnity, and beauty; Milne's work, *Billboards*, is in strong contrast, underlining, through the advertisements that dominate the whole façade of a Canadian city street, the rise of a manmade environment, finally, Borduas appears with his untitled 'oil on canvas' that seems to have nothing to do with Canada, except a play on light and dark (which feature in the strong contrasts of Canadian history and geography alike). Here the Canadian is trying to find himself as Man.

Perhaps this began in the Great War; it continued to foment through the Great Depression, and was brought to a head in World War II. Canada then had to find out which values she most cherished. The awe-inspiring salon in the National Gallery on the war experience forms a great insight into Canadian character. Varley's blasted graveyard on the Western Front, Jackson's blown-up homes around Ypres queried two of the root ideals, the place of religion and the family in life. Comfort's seering scene of *Ferentino, Italy*, shows, in pieces, the whole Graeco-Roman world that was soil to the Canadian roots. Jack Nichols's *Men on HMS Iroquois at Action Stations* appears to ask, from the look on the men's faces, action for what? This is still a major question in Canadian life and art.

Sculpture, pottery, weaving and tapestry are usually represented in Canadian galleries. As a multi-cultural country Canada has inherited many traditions in the full range of handicrafts. Many of these have been kept on at the sort of peasant level at which they were brought over, and are shown at folk fairs throughout the country. Others have been developed to very sophisticated levels of artistry, giving rise to noted schools of sculpting, pottery, and other manual arts, principally in Montreal and Toronto.

Native sculpture among the Eskimos has bloomed tremendously in the last fifteen years. It is featured in the National Gallery, in the National Museum of Man, Ottawa, the Royal Ontario Museum, Toronto, and in the Eskimo Museum, Churchill. Significant displays also occur in Montreal, Winnipeg, Edmonton, and Vancouver.

FOLK SONGS

Canadians are a singing people. Indeed, according to Kallman, 'Jacques Cartier and his hardy mariners greeted the new-found land by singing a mass'.[22] The *coureurs des bois* of the French régime sang songs as they paddled up the St Lawrence and Great Lakes; the British seamen sang their shanties as they weighed anchor and set sail for Canada; English and Scottish mothers crooned their ancient lullabies as they put their children to sleep, and later immigrants brought over the songs of their homelands too. Then Canadians of all types began to make their own folk ballads, the ballads of sea and forest, mines and Prairie, cattle trails and railway lines—with occasional Indian songs echoing through.

Folk songs form a rich part of Canada's heritage. Pioneers in collecting them were Herbert La Rue, with his *Le Foyer canadien* (1863) and Ernest Gagnon, with *Chansons populaires du Canada* (1865). In this century, Maurice Barbeau has spent a lifetime collecting folk tales, and folk songs; first, from his fellow French Canadians, and then from Indians, both from east and west. Another famous collector has been Sir Ernest MacMillan who arranged many folk tunes for piano. MacMillan and Barbeau jointly made a trip in 1927 up the Pacific Coast of Canada to visit the Kwatkiutl, Tsimshan, Bella Coola, Haida and Alaska Indians. Sir Ernest transcribed and arranged the Indian songs, many of which he published. Other collections of Canadian folk songs have appeared and school editions have made folk singing very popular among the young. Folk singers appear regularly on CBC and on independent radio and TV, while folk-singing festivals draw enthusiastic crowds. Recordings now make it possible for people outside of Canada to appreciate the wealth of Canadian folk song.

Edith Fowke offers an excellent assemblage of both the old European folk songs, carried over and preserved in Canada, and the Canadian folk songs that began to arise out of New World conditions and ways of living.[23] A record of these, 'Canada's Story in Song', Folkways Record Album No FW 3000 (sung by Alan Mills) forms a marvellous cross-section of history and geography, with Indian and Eskimo songs, sea shanties, war songs, national songs and work songs.

THE EUROPEAN TRADITION

Most musicians came with their French or British training and sought to make use of this in what was essentially a transplanted France or Britain. Thus although Marc Lescarbot, who was probably the first composer in Canada, transcribed four songs from the Micmacs, his chief work was a very French masque, *The Theatre of Neptune*. This was performed in 1606 at Port Royal, a year after that first (white) settlement on the Canadian mainland was established.

Pioneer life did not mean a downgrading of the civilised arts. Men fiddled as the forest was cleared. In a surprisingly short time they built churches, theatres and concert halls, and sang their masses, oratorios and operas. In 1632, fourteen years after Quebec was founded, Father le Jeune was teaching 'the elements of Gregorian chant' to boys sent by their parents to his school. In 1664, an organ was installed in Quebec Cathedral; in 1705 another at Montreal. Choirs were trained, and the great masses of Europe were heard within bow-shot of the woods. The oldest preserved composition in Canada was by Chas-Amador Martin (1648–1711) who wrote a plain chant for his choir while organist at the Cathedral in Quebec (1665–85).

In 1769, only twenty years after Halifax was laid out, the newly formed philharmonic society there performed an oratorio in St Paul's Church. Thirty-two years after its foundation, Halifax boasted an orchestra and a year later, 1782, had enough singers and players to mount an opera in the Theatre Royal. Meanwhile, in Quebec, Joseph Quesnel had written the first opera in Canada, *Colas et Colinette*, first performed in Montreal in 1790. Toronto, founded in 1793, started within seven years to build its great Anglican cathedral, and then invited a first-rate British musician, Edward Hodges, to be its organist and choirmaster. In the West, even more rapid progress in music was made. Victoria, the only town in the West in 1850, had a philharmonic society in 1859. Vancouver, established in 1885, had its philharmonic in 1890. Regina, although not incorporated as a town until 1903, started its choral society in 1889.

The music of these early and pioneer days consisted of choir and solo singing, organ recitals and chamber concerts. It was dominated by church organists, most of whom played and conducted European music. However, Father Brébeuf is credited with America's first Christmas carol, in 1641—*Jesus Ahatonhia*: the Christmas story in Iroquoian, in terms of the Huron way of life. The first music published in Canada, in 1801, was a hymn book, *British America's Sacred Vocal Musick*, edited by Stephen Humber, choirmaster in New Brunswick. Antoine Dessaine (1826–73) is often called 'the father of Canadian music'. A Parisian, and friend of César Franck, he succeeded as organist in Quebec from 1849–65. He started the Société Harmonique de Quebec in 1849. Later, in 1857, he founded a chamber music group, the 'Septette Club', and helped to organise Quebec's Union Musicale, 1866. In Montreal, R. J. Fowler, an organist from England, started the Montreal Philharmonic Society in 1848, dedicated to both English and French music. C. W. Sabatier, who came from Paris to Montreal, founded Canada's first musical journal, *L'Artiste*, in 1860. Another Montreal choirmaster, Labelle, helped to start the Société de Ste Cecile de Montreal, 1860. Meanwhile, in Toronto, John McCaul from Dublin who was to become President of King's College (the precursor of the University of Toronto) in 1845 started the Toronto Choral Society. The Toronto Philharmonic was established the next year: this was conducted by G. W. Strathy, first Professor of Music. Healey Willan, one of Canada's greatest composers of choral music, likewise had a great and formative influence.

CONTEMPORARY MUSIC

Contemporary music in Canada has thus had a lot to count on. Two main streams occur, the national and the cosmopolitan. The national tradition has been fostered mainly through the use of Canadian folk song and Canadian poetry as themes in, or as the inspiration of, modern choral or orchestral work. Earlier work stemmed from Calixa Lavallée, composer of the Canadian national anthem, *O Canada*, written in 1880. Amédée Tremblay followed on, weaving Canadian folk songs into his work. About the same time William Reed, in Toronto, made use of Canadian motifs in his sacred chorals. These people lived until the late 1940s and prepared the way for even stronger national sentiment in Canadian music. Murray Adaskin, for example, has written an *Algonquin Symphony*, exploiting bird calls in the forest, and also the *Saskatchewan Symphony* evocative of the open wind-swept prairie. Violet Archer has produced variations on French-Canadian folk songs and has also set Arthur S. Bourinot's poems to music. Similarly we find John Beckwith with his *Great Lakes Suite* celebrating the majesty and variety of Canada's oldest and greatest region: he has also put to music some poems of that most individual yet most Canadian of poets, James Reaney. Claude Champagne's first major work, the *Suite Canadienne* worked in French-Canadian folklore. The music critic, Archer, has said of Champagne's *Danse Villageoise*, that 'it has put into terms of art music a scene immortalised in French Canada of the lively fiddler and the dancing couples, which may be seen in hundreds of parish halls through generations of winters . . .' Jean Coulthard has transcribed Haida Indian songs and also set to music the poetry of Duncan Campbell Scott and other Canadian writers. Robert Fleming, the music director of the National Film Board, has written the scores for over a hundred films and, in addition, created his symphonic studies of *Red River Country* and *The Awakening Mackenzie*. J. Freedman's work has been described as 'an example of Canadianism in music', where he has tried to catch the nuances of wind and water, the movement of trees, and the immensity of skies in his tone studies. M. Perrault says frankly 'I like a folk tune and the harmony that goes with it' and has written two ballets, *Sea Gallows* and *Canadiana* based on Nova Scotian and other folk songs. J. Weinzweig is perhaps the best-known composer for ballet, and again was at his best in a Canadian theme, *The Red Ear of Corn*, based on both Red Indian and French-Canadian folk music. His best-known symphony, *Our Canada*, strives to show the sweep and ruggedness, the severity and beauty of the Canadian landscape. However, he is an internationalist, and in *Wine of Peace* he uses a poem written by a seventeenth-century Spanish poet, Calderon, for inspiration.

The cosmopolitan stream of writing, though concerned with general human themes or with music for its own sake, is none the less Canadian in that it expresses the desire to be part of a greater world which is a lively force in the country. Many composers are of course immigrants whose heritage is of the world, and they continue to write in their own cultural script. Istran Anhalt, from Budapest, Gramatté-Eckhardt, from Moscow, and Otto Joachim, of Dusseldorf, are good examples, bringing with them the modern European concern with serial and chance music, or with electronic music and other experimental forms. They are matched by some native-born Canadians, who are also of this non-national, non-cultural bias, trying to write music for its own sake. Of these mention could be made of the avant-garde French-Canadian composer, S. Garant, for whom serial music is a 'true and timely reflection of our age', an age more interested in the essence than in the form; P. Percure the TV music producer in Montreal, concerned with objectivism in music, and Barbara Pentland who was one of the first Canadians to introduce Schoenberg's serial technique to composing, and who has an austere style that goes well with her expressed aim 'to write as much meaningful music using as few notes as possible'. She is very forward-looking. 'Our civilisation is dynamic and constantly changing' she asserts, 'so the arts as a reflection of life must inevitably follow. The creative force should be such that the laws necessary for its expression ought to be continually challenged.' C. Pépin is also very much the modern man: 'I am

I

interested in the contemporary arts', he declares 'of astronomy, space, light, time. Serial music opens the way to a new vaster world. We might make a parallel between man going into space and escaping from gravity.'

8

Sport and Recreation

CANADIANS are a sports loving nation. From pioneer times they
have loved outdoor life. Sports featured at the very birth of Canada. As Henry Roxborough shows, 'on the first Dominion Day,
(1st July, 1867) every civic oration was but a prelude to an
athletic afternoon. The programme was sure to include throwing the hammer, sack races, and sprints.'[24] Canada Day is still
everywhere characterised by sports fairs.

INDIGENOUS SPORT

Indigenous sports, learned from the Eskimos and Indians, are
widespread. They echo the marked differences between winter
and summer, a distinction that runs through all Canadian sport.
Racing dog-sleds against each other, which was the chief winter
sport among natives, particularly the Eskimo, has become very
popular. Snow-shoe racing is another winter contest, held in
every province. In summer, the rivers of Canada become un-
locked from ice and are at once alive with trade and sport. The
geography of the Canadian river systems, and especially of the
low portages between them following old glacial meltwater
channels, has provided a remarkable network of natural routes,
now used extensively for watersports. The handling of the Eskimo kayak and the Indian canoe is learned by boys and girls in
thousands of summer camps, run by private clubs, or by the
State, wherever woodland and lakeland come together. Canoeing was of course a business amongst the French fur-traders, and
for this reason Quebec has often been called 'the cradle of Can-

adian canoeing'. It is still a major centre of the sport, but youths all over the country today go in groups on trips by canoes lasting for several days or even weeks, thus returning to the pioneer spirit of Canada.

Camping is a major form of recreation in Canada, and is associated with canoeing, swimming, walking, back-packing, ski-ing, hunting and fishing and many other sports. It has a very strong hold on Canadians. In the French régime the *coureurs des bois* camped with the Indians, who were their guides and companions. Many whites took to fur-trapping, and lived under canvas while they were chopping down the trees with which to build their cabins, and it was common for the men and boys to go off hunting for deer or bear to supplement the diet. Thus living out in camp became such a tradition that even after most Canadians came to be city dwellers they seized the opportunity to go camping: to get back to nature is a constant theme in Canadian life.

Hunting and fishing clubs are common across Canada as men band themselves together, in the appropriate season, to go out into the bush and hunt deer and moose, or camp by Prairie sloughs to shoot wild duck and geese, or climb into the mountains after bear and goats. Indeed, the white man now vies with the Indian in hunting skills. Fishing is even more popular than hunting or shooting. Salmon fishing in the Atlantic and Pacific rivers, and trout fishing up the rivers off the Great Lakes and Lake Winnipeg are favourite invitations to camp out.

Lacrosse is a more specific gift of the Indians to Canadian sport. They invented it to develop group discipline and personal ingenuity. As such it appealed to lovers of team games, and has become a truly Canadian sport. The first lacrosse club to be formed anywhere was that at Montreal in 1839, after Indians from the Caughnawaga reserve, opposite the city, had made it popular, playing with the whites. A famous Indian-White contest was held in 1861 before the then Prince of Wales during his visit to Canada. In 1867 the National Lacrosse Association of Canada was formed, the first nationwide sports organisation in the country.

SPORT FROM THE OLD WORLD

Introduced sports brought by the European immigrants, have become the mainstay of the sporting world. The British, who were the chief immigrants and also the ruling power in Canada, happened to be a very sports-loving people. They brought with them their passion for horse racing, their love of football, their keenness on ice shinty, their skill at bowling, their enjoyment of tennis and golf and their pleasure in yachting. Their experience of winter in the old country with its frozen ponds and canals made them great skaters and curlers. Thus, as the Howells's show us, a very wide variety of sporting activities, using both summer and winter, soon took root in Canada.[25] Some of these were kept on in the same form, others like football and shinty were modified into Canadian rugby and ice-hockey which are now the great national games.

Horse racing, it is claimed, was at first 'the most common out-door amusement'. Shortly after the British established themselves in Quebec, the Quebec Turf Club was organised in 1789. This is one of the oldest continuing race clubs in the western world. The French too were, and still are, great horse lovers. Here French and British could mix, a good example of the power of sport to create national goodwill and co-operation. In 1860, Canada's main prize in horse racing known as the Queen's Plate, in honour of Queen Victoria, was founded by the Ontario Jockey Club. The Queen's Plate held at Toronto, is a major sporting event today, attracting American as well as Canadian entrants.

Tennis and golf were early carried to Canada by the British. Both of these games led to 'a greater acceptance of women in the fields of physical endeavour'. Both man and wife, indeed whole families, could play them together, which strengthened their popularity. Tennis especially 'was one of the "proper" sports for women and many girls participated'. It became particularly popular in the strongly British provinces of Ontario and British

Columbia and among English-speaking Montrealers. By the end
of the nineteenth century most schools and colleges across Canada had their tennis courts. The Canadian Championship
match, held at the Toronto Lawn Tennis Club with very substantial prize money for the winner of the Rothman Cup, attracts international players of note. However, the short season of
summer play, and the strong competition of winter sports,
have never made tennis a leading Canadian sport.

Golf might be thought to suffer from the same limitations, but
in some curious way it early became a 'prestige' game for the
Canadian élite, and as such it has had an enormous importance
in Canada. Golf and Country Clubs are found at the edge of
every major city, whose splendid club houses are used as much
for dinner parties, dances, bridge clubs, and even wedding-re-
ceptions as for 'a drink after the game'. These clubs are private
social organisations and charge both a high initial fee to join and
also a high playing fee. Their wealth attracts professional golfers
of distinction, and enables them, backed by handsome prizes
donated by rich members, to put on tournaments of international note. The Royal Montreal Golf Club, founded in 1873,
was the continent's first golf club. The Royal Quebec Club
opened in 1874. As Kavanagh records, 'The first inter-club
match ever played on this continent was between the Montreal
and Quebec clubs in 1876.[26] Toronto established its club in
1876. After this event, matches were regularly played between
the Royal Montreal and the Toronto golf clubs and they were
the matches of the year.' The first Canadian Open was held in
1904; in that year too, a Canadian, George Lyon, won the Gold
Medal at the Olympic Games Golf Championship. Canadian
golf had come into its own: it has been prominent ever since. In
1927, the then Governor-General, Lord Willingdon, a keen
golfer, established the Willingdon Cup for amateur players at
the interprovincial level. The notable event in Canadian professional golf is the Seagram Cup tournament, attracting top
world players. Canadian business in this way is taking a bigger
and bigger part in fostering high-quality sport in Canada.

Yachting is another summer sport introduced by the British.
It proved extremely attractive in the great bays and broad in-

lets of the Atlantic Provinces, during the ice-free season of the
year. Here people got about mainly by sea; much of their living
came from the sea, or through trading across it. Thus the sea
was in their blood. The Royal Nova Scotia Yacht Squadron
was established at Halifax in 1839, and at once organised important regattas. In 1862 this club became the first in Canada to
display the blue ensign with the crown on the fly, a highly
prized warrant from the Royal Navy.

Most provinces of Canada are well suited to summer yachting. Quebec has the Gulf of St Lawrence; Ontario, the Great
Lakes; Manitoba, Lake Winnipeg; and British Columbia, the
magnificent Inner Passage to Alaska. The country, as we have
seen, is swept by cyclonic wind systems following broad belts
from the Mackenzie to Cabot straits. Magnificent sailing is
assured. Toronto established the Royal Canadian Yacht Club in
1852, and the Great Lakes regatta became an annual event. The
Royal Vancouver Yacht Club was set up in 1904 and developed a
series of international races with American yacht clubs across
the border. In 1912 Lieutenant-Governor Cameron of Manitoba presented the Lake of the Woods International Challenge
Cup, which has become an institution.

Curling takes over from yachting when the waters freeze. It is
today a major winter sport in Canada and, as winter is a large
part of Canada's life, it is not surprising that 'the roaring sport'
brought from Scotland soon became prominent. Curling is a
sport for both men and women, and is often played as a family
game, whole households vying with each other in weekly competitions. In 1807 the Montreal Curling Club was founded by
the many Scots with standing there. Games were played in the
open on the frozen surface of the St Lawrence river. Its members
met 'every fortnight at 4 o'clock [it was getting dark by then] to
dine on salt beef and greens . . . the dinner not to exceed 7s 6d a
head'. During those early years of curling in Canada the majority of curlers were Scots, and their antics on the ice were looked
upon with some dismay by the older Canadian settlers. French
Canadians did not know what to think of these activities. One of
them related, 'Today I saw a band of Scotchmen, who were
throwing large balls like tea kettles on the ice, after which they

cried "Soop! Soop!" and then laughed like fools. I really believe they *are* fools!'

Today the cry of soop, soop (sweep, sweep) may be heard in so-called Granite Clubs across Canada in a sport that has attracted the fervour of all immigrants. It generates a nation-wide winter fever! International competition is well supported. In 1908–9, Canada and Scotland met for the first of a continuing series of contests to win the highly prized Strathcona Cup, donated by Lord Strathcona, a Scotsman eminent in Canadian affairs. The Dominion Championship, set up in 1927, is marked by the award of the Macdonald Trophy. Curling Societies are now present in most high schools and a Curling Colts League has many eager competitors. Interestingly, most of the players wear the traditional Tam o' Shanter cap, from Scotland.

Ski-ing is another winter sport introduced from Europe that has a tremendous vogue. Canada offers the ideal environment for this, with its long snowy winters, with its uplands, like the Canadian Shield, and its mountains such as the Appalachians and the Rockies. Good ski slopes can be reached from most of the major cities, such as the Nova Scotia uplands from Halifax, the Shield from Quebec, both the Shield and the Appalachians (in the Eastern Townships) from Montreal, the Shield and the Niagara Escarpment from Toronto, the Shield and the Manitoba Escarpment from Winnipeg, the Rockies from Edmonton and Calgary, and Canada's magnificent Coastal Mountains from Vancouver. Ski trains and buses, as well as thousands of private cars, go out every winter weekend to well-known ski-resorts, while a great number of people have their own ski chalets to which they and their friends retreat each weekend between mid-October and the end of March. Indeed at that time the winterscape quivers with lines of intense movement as the ski commuters rush out into the country or crawl back to town.

As early as 1904 the Montreal Ski Club set itself up, with professional instructors from Scandinavia. It used the sharp edge of the Laurentides for its outings. Almost immediately ski clubs were formed in Vancouver and Calgary, and in 1907 a western ski-championship meet was organised at Rossland, BC. Two years later, in 1909, a nationwide Ski Championship was established, patronised by the Governor General, Earl Grey.

Mechanised ski-ing, in the form of skidooing, is now becoming extremely popular. The skidoo has two skis in front and a fast revolving caterpillar track behind. It is a modification of the snowmobile, itself a modification of the caterpillar tractor. It travels at 50mph (80km ph) or more, and gives a new spaciousness and speed to winter sports.

Other activities introduced by the Europeans were the ancient outdoor sports of archery and riding; and fencing, badminton and squash, played indoors. These have a relatively small following. Not so the track and field sports that the early British brought over, which Canadians have adopted and developed.

Track and field sports have been popular principally because their emphasis is on individual attainment. Competition at an individual level has long been a part of the Canadian tradition. (A recent directive from a provincial Department of Education reminded teachers that their main duty was to provide a means by which 'each student could achieve a sense of uniqueness through personal success'.) Team games do not instil this sense as well as track sports. In many schools team games are on the decline in favour of individual sports like running, jogging, jumping, throwing and vaulting. Hannon avers that 'The Olympic Club of Montreal . . . was formed for foot-running and summer outdoor sports in 1842, and it is probably the oldest Athletic Club in the British Empire, since it was organised eight years before the Exeter Club in England, which claims to be the oldest one in that country.'[27]

The Grand Annual Gathering of the Caledonian Society in Montreal, 1857, which established Highland Games in Canada, also pre-dated Confederation. At this, the following sports were performed—throwing the hammer, tossing the caber, putting the shot, the highjump, the longjump, vaulting, the short race 'won by an Indian of Caughnawaga', the sack race, and the barrow race. Here were 'track and field' in full swing.

Since then every high school and college, YMCA, town and city has put aside land and laid it out as a sports track and held annual track meets. To set national standards in these, to recognise national records, to organise interprovincial and national championships, the Amateur Athletic Union of Canada was formed in 1895.

THE NEW WORLD'S GAMES

Naturalised new-world sports grew out of the North American environment, either modifying European forms of sport, or developing new ones. These too showed marked summer and winter differences. American baseball was a summertime sport played in the Thirteen Colonies in a crude sort of way, but became organised in 1869 when the Cincinnati Red Stockings took it up as a competitive commercial venture. In Canada it started up in Hamilton, about the same time, when one of the effects of the Buffalo–Hamilton–Toronto railway was to bring American workers into the Canadian cities near the borders. Hamilton keeps up the tradition with its baseball 'Hall of Fame' for great Canadian players. The strong link between Montreal and New York, using the Champlain–Hudson gap, led to an early flourishing of baseball there, at least among English-speaking citizens. Montreal rivalled Cincinnati with a club in 1869, and in 1870 opened its first of a continuing series of challenge games with New York. By 1900 every town and village in Canada had its baseball park, with professional players in the larger cities. After World War II these cities mounted teams that could attract American professionals. Montreal Expos in particular moved into the big league class, and now form part of the National League (of America).

Basketball is another American game that has spread widely in Canada, perhaps mainly through the YMCAs who make a lot of it. Basketball is also popular as a high school game. It has not yet become the highly commercialised spectator sport that it is in America. Its effectiveness is that it can be played indoors, during the long Canadian winter.

Canadian football is a modification of American football, both resembling a very sophisticated type of rugby league play in Britain. The field is marked off in ten-yard lines, and the team must make at least ten yards in three attempts, or surrender the ball to the other side. Major differences from English rugby are that team mates can deliberately obstruct attacks on the ball-holder and thus prevent him from being tackled, and that the forward pass is a main feature of the play. English rugby is still played in the Maritimes and British Columbia, but virtually everywhere else it has given way to Canadian football. Huge football stadiums, lit by batteries of floodlights, are familiar landmarks on the Canadian scene. The game is played ubiquitously at the high school level; it is somewhat more concentrated at the college level, important only in the big universities, and it is narrowed down still further at the municipal level. Here it is divided into two major leagues—an eastern one including Montreal, Toronto, Hamilton and Ottawa; and a western one, of Winnipeg, Saskatoon, Edmonton, Calgary and Vancouver. This division between east and west underlines the strong regionality that exists in Canada. The winners of the eastern and western leagues meet each year to fight for the Grey Cup, one of Canada's supreme sports awards.

'This trophy was donated in 1909 for "the amateur rugby football championship of Canada" by Earl Grey [a great proponent of rugby and its virtues], one of Canada's most popular governors-general. Albert Henry George Grey, the fourth earl, liked to slip away from his chores at Government House to watch rugbyfootball at Ottawa's Varsity Oval, and it was his fancy to leave in Canada some memento of his love of the game.'[28]

Ice-hockey has its equivalent of this in the Stanley Cup. It is often regarded as the supremely Canadian game, even though it may have started from English hurling, or from Scottish shinty, played in winter on the ice. However, it was also played by the French-Canadians, and some people hold that the name derives from the French *hoquet* (a shepherd's crook) referring to the hooked staff with which the game was played. Brian Conacher, one of the great Canadian players, writing about a lifetime in the game, says ' . . . I can easily see the ingredients that have made hockey a national pastime. Our climate with its long cold winter has provided the media—ice, and the French Canadian temperament has given the game its robust and colourful flair. Before a youngster becomes very old, playing hockey becomes a part of every winter, and the characteristic he is developing as he jostles with his opponent for the puck, is—individualism. As soon as school is out every youngster on the street will race home, get his skates and stick, and join in the game that ends only when he can no longer see the puck.'[29] Flooded and frozen fields in every park make neighbourhood hockey pitches: from these the children graduate to ice-hockey arenas in school. Better players then move on to the huge arenas in almost every college, while it is the dream of many a college hero to become a professional in the enormous ice-hockey palaces of Canada's big cities. No other sport is so widely played by so many aspirants for so much honour. 'For more than fifty years now the pinnacle of organised hockey has been the National Hockey League. For decade after decade this league has drawn the dreams and focused the fancies of sports-minded boys and young men.' The League was set up in 1917 to standardise rules, organise competitions and generally foster good sportsmanship through hockey playing. It was initiated in the east by Montreal, Toronto, and Ottawa. In the west, another organisation, starting out as the Pacific Coast Hockey association, was formed in Vancouver, Edmonton, and Winnipeg. These groupings whipped up professional interest in hockey, making it a career as well as a sport, and Canadian professionals stocked American and British teams. At the international level, and particularly in the Olympic Games they reigned supreme until the 1960s when they were challenged by Russia.

This supremacy was to a large extent the result of the keen competition to win the Stanley Cup—'today the symbol of the hockey championship of the world, the oldest professional sports trophy in North America'. The Stanley Cup was donated for the promotion of hockey in Canada in 1892 by Governor-General Lord Stanley. 'Lord Stanley, like many English noblemen of his time, was a great sportsman. Lord Stanley became a hockey fan. Not only that but his two sons, Arthur and Algie, became so enamoured with the game, they equipped themselves with skates and sticks and became devout puck-chasers. The staff at Rideau Hall, [the Governor-General's mansion, in Ottawa] flooded an outdoor rink and . . . got up a team!'[30] The attempt to win the cup creates one of the great sporting and social events of Canada and brings out fans by the scores of thousands, many from the remote ends of the country, to the host city in which the game is played. Television and newspapers put virtually all other interests aside to concentrate on the game, and the victory is a national celebration.

SPORT AS A NATIONAL INFLUENCE

Both at an amateur and at a professional level, sport is a major feature of Canadian life. National interest in sport came to a head in the 1960s in attempts to create a truly national games programme to be known as The Canada Games. In 1966, federal, provincial and municipal support of a Canada Games Society was given, and in 1967 the first Canada Winter Games were held in Quebec City. In 1969 the Canada Summer Games had a spectacularly successful meet at Halifax. It included, in addition to all the running, jumping, vaulting and throwing events of track and field, baseball, bowling (lawn), box lacrosse, canoeing, cycling, fencing, field-hockey, rowing, soccer, softball, swimming, water-polo, water-ski-ing and tennis. The Canadian Prime Minister himself, three premiers and seven senior cabinet ministers from the ten provinces of Canada and senior representatives from the federal government attended, thus giving sport in Canada unique public recognition.

Perhaps the height of these developments occurred in the holding of the Olympic Games in Canada, in 1976. Appropriately, these took place at Montreal, one of the great sportsminded cities of the world, and the first community in Canada to have an Olympics Club. Indeed it was the first to establish many of the major sports clubs or associations in the country. With the hosting of the Olympic Games, Canada really came of age, in terms of sport. The decision to hold the world's greatest sporting event in Canada was a recognition of the high place

sports have in Canadian life, and the significant contribution
Canada has made to the life of sport.

NATIONAL AND PROVINCIAL PARKS

To meet the needs for an outdoor life Canada has developed
no less than twenty-eight national parks, covering over 50,000
sq miles (129,500sq km). Provincial parks are also very important; those in Quebec, with 75,000sq miles (194,250sq km) are
bigger than the whole of England. Canada has reserved a great
deal of its land for national recreation. Indeed she was one of the
first nations to establish national parks as a means of setting
aside relatively untamed land as a lasting heritage for people
profoundly influenced by and attached to the wilderness. In
1885, Canada maintained some of the hot sulphur springs at
Banff for public use in what is now Banff National Park. The
superb mountain scenery of the Coast Ranges, Selkirks, and
Rockies, in British Columbia and Alberta, with the presence of
ice-fields and active glaciers, and with an abundance of wapiti
mountain goat, grizzly bear, and mountain lion, led to the
formation of the Pacific Rim Glacier, Yoho, Waterton, Jasper,
Kootenay, and Revelstoke parks. The need to protect wild life
for people to study and enjoy lay behind Wood Buffalo, Elk
Island, and Riding Mountain (buffalo) parks in the Prairies.
The Georgian Bay Islands were reserved in a recreation park
for boating and canoeing in Ontario. La Mauricie and Forillon
in Quebec preserved large areas of native forest before this was
cut down or altered by second growth. The Atlantic provinces
have striking coastal scenery to offer—maintained for public
pleasure at Fundy Bay, Cape Breton Highlands, Prince Edward
Island, and Terra Nova (Newfoundland). Thus national and
provincial parks play an ever more important part in Canadian
life and landscape.

9

Hints to Travellers

THE chief routes to Canada are now by air from Europe or Asia, and by car, bus or train from the United States. Passenger boats no longer run from Britain or France, though a passage may be booked on Polish and Russian boats plying to Montreal which call at London. The main airports of arrival are Montreal and Toronto, from which connections are made elsewhere. However, there is a more limited schedule of direct flights to Halifax, Winnipeg, Edmonton and Vancouver. Tourist flights at a substantially reduced rate are usually prescribed for twenty-one or forty-five days. Even cheaper flights by charter plane may be obtained, but usually only upon joining a 'charter group'. Package-deal holidays can be arranged which include the flight, travel in Canada, and hotel accommodation.

HOW TO TRAVEL

Rail travel within Canada is still important, though the number of passenger services has been cut back appreciably. The Canadian Pacific Railway and the Canadian National Railway have special observation passenger trains, with individual cabins for one or two people, a good dining car, a cocktail bar and excellent observation saloons from which one can view the spectacular scenery of the country.

Special tourist trains are worth taking. The Polar Bear express from Toronto to Moosone on James Bay (a great re-entrant of Hudson Bay) is well worth patronising, since it takes one from Canada's greatest city to the edge of the tundra. A similar trip, requiring four days there and back, can be made from Winnipeg to Churchill. Again this gives a complete cross-section from the highly developed wheatlands of the Prairies, through the forests of the Shield, up to the muskeg and tundra of the Hudson Bay Lowlands. At Churchill there is the great grain terminal, the Hudson's Bay Company post and other stores, the rocket range, an Eskimo village and a very good Eskimo museum. A short train excursion from Sault Ste Marie on the Great Lakes, into the heart of the Algoma country, a spectacular section of the Canadian Shield, is a popular tourist attraction in summer.

Summer cruises are a magnificent way of seeing small sections of Canada. Of these, the most scenic is the cruise up the Saguenay, a long arm of the sea penetrating deep into the Canadian Shield between rocky cliffs, from the Gulf of St Lawrence. Several companies put on very fine cruises of the Thousand Islands, near Kingston, where the Great Lakes empty by way of the broad St Lawrence river across an arm of the Shield: the granites and gneisses of the Shield stand up in closely forested islands out of the strong currents of the river. The 30,000 Island cruise of Georgian Bay is an even more fascinating spectacle, leaving Midland, Ontario, for the rock-studded waters of Lake Huron. Ferries also offer passengers lovely views of different parts of Canada: some of these journeys, like those from Nova Scotia to Newfoundland, or from mainland BC to Vancouver Island, are quite long, and form veritable cruises, passing through very fine scenery, where sea and land penetrate each other. Good dining facilities and passenger saloons make travel comfortable and interesting. The longest ferry service traverses the Inner Passage from Vancouver or Prince Rupert to Alaska. A number of large general-purpose coastal ships ply this really scenic route, where stops are made to load or offload cargo at many small ports, and the traveller can see fishing, lumbering, mining communities and Indian settlements, to get a marvellous impression of the Pacific north.

Private cruising is a very popular tourist activity in many parts of Canada. Those tourists who have their own yachts and cruisers will find that the Bay of Fundy, the St Lawrence–Great

Lakes system, the Red River and Lake Winnipeg, and the San Juan and Georgia Straits from Vancouver all offer an amazing range of cruising conditions. Particularly attractive to Americans are the cruises from harbours on the south shore of Lake Ontario across that lake and then up two systems of canals: the Rideau system from Kingston to Ottawa, or the Trent system from Trenton past Peterborough to Georgian Bay. Visitors can hire houseboats to cruise up and down the Rideau and Trent canals.

Air travel is widespread in Canada. The nationwide carriers are Air Canada, with services from coast to coast. Canadian Pacific Air Lines are also major carriers, especially in the west and north, where they operate Western Canada Airways, Prairie Airways and the Yukon and Mackenzie Services. Pacific Western Airlines have a great number of small subsidiaries flying planes out to Queen Charlotte Isles, Vancouver Island, Skeena and Whitehorse. Nordair specialises in flights to northern Quebec and Labrador and also runs the Maritimes Central Airways. Transair out of Winnipeg has flights up north, especially through Arctic Wings, and to the west, through Midwest Airways. Finally Quebecair is a company dealing with flights to Rimouski at the head of the Saguenay and, through Gulf-Aviation, to the north-shore towns of the Gulf of St Lawrence. All these companies are very reliable, have well-trained crews and keep their planes in first-class condition. Canada has one of the most envied reputations in the world for accident-free flights.

Bus services are good between cities, but poor within them. Long-distance bus trips, run by the Voyageur, Colonial and Greyhound bus lines are quite frequent, are fast and comfortable. These buses have tip-back seats for night travel, and also toilets. They connect all of Canada's major cities and compete with passenger trains by offering cheaper prices. They are most widely used for medium-distance travel for overnight or one-day distances, but connections can ensure a traveller of a transcontinental journey. By contrast, bus services in most cities suffer such competition from taxis and the private car that, by European standards at least, they are slow and infrequent. However, the underground trains, as in Montreal and Toronto, are

K

fast and frequent: midtown and downtown stations usually provide elevator or escalator services direct to major shopping centres. This is a great convenience in winter, when it may be bitterly cold on the streets.

Car-hire services are available everywhere. A few of these are run by companies with nationwide connections, such as Hertz, Avis, Tilden, Host, and Budget, and are to be found both at every major airport, and in the downtown area of every major city. In addition, however, there are many regional or district car-hirers, especially for trippers who want to do a day or two's visit of city sights and of the surrounding countryside. These often provide special rates which can be worked out on a customer basis and may be cheaper than the standard rates. They are listed in the Yellow Pages of the local telephone book. Travellers should note the habit of many car-hire firms of charging a quite considerable 'dropping-off' fee, if the car is dropped off at any other city than the point of origin.

Combinations of rail, air, bus, and car-hire trips are often a useful way of arranging a tour. Both the Canadian National and the Canadian Pacific railways have excellent information and ticket services to provide the traveller with complete bookings, especially since they run auxiliary airlines, lake and sea ferries, and have close links with bus or car-hire facilities.

Touring with trailer and picnic trips are very popular. Excellent municipal, provincial and national parks offer grounds and facilities for camping at a low rate. In the months of July and August it is essential to phone ahead of time to see if the campsite has any vacant places for tents or trailers and at any time it is advisable to move into a camp early in the day. Much trouble is caused by people arriving late, finding the camp full and then having to move on, perhaps over a considerable distance to a less popular camp, or to private accommodation. Most public camping grounds provide individual lay-bys for each trailer, separate tenting grounds, running water, showers, toilets and barbecue grills. Some also have shops at which one can buy charcoal, calor gas, food and other supplies. Larger camps often have indoor cooking and laundry facilities.

Tourist information bureaux and camp headquarters supply

a great deal of literature and may help out by giving phone numbers and addresses of motels, tourist homes, camps, etc. In every case, as the traveller passes a provincial boundary, he will see a nearby provincial information office. He should make use of the maps, brochures and other aids provided: all the beauty spots, good eating places, and sites of historic interest are listed. These are usually marked by provincial or private signs on the road side. In addition, most counties and municipalities run separate bureaux which are well worth stopping at. Canada is quite unusual in providing so much free information about itself: it does this because it is so dependent on tourism, which is now its largest industry.

CLIMATE

Climate is a factor that must be considered by the traveller. Winter predominates in Canada, and snow can be expected even in the southern parts between the end of October and the end of March. The main exceptions are the extreme maritime regions, especially coastal BC—though even here strong falls of snow do occur every January and February. Snow is something to enjoy, but something to be careful about. As already indicated, snow sports are a marked feature of Canadian life, and many sports enthusiasts motor up or fly into Canada to enjoy ski-ing, snow-shoeing, sledding, ice-yachting, skidooing and dog-sled racing. At all the winter-sports centres there are good hotels and motels: roads in and out of them are kept clear by snow plough. The traveller should, however, phone the weather bureau, or various motoring organisations, to find out about the road conditions before embarking on his trip. To be snowed-in en route can spoil the whole event. Make sure that cars have adequate anti-freeze in their radiators, and that their heaters are working. Car trouble, even without running into a snow storm, can cause a lot of distress.

It is assumed that the traveller in winter likely to expose himself will have a fur hat, or a cap with ear-flaps, or will wear ear muffs; that he will wear a fur coat or heavy top coat, wind-proof trousers, fur-lined boots, or weather-proof overshoes and fur-backed or wool-lined gloves. Remember, that wind-chill can considerably reduce the outside temperature, and low temperatures that can be tolerated on a calm day, become quite unbearable on days with a breeze or wind.

In spite of these warnings about cold, travellers should not *normally* wear heavy suits or dresses, or a lot of underwear, since all public transportation, public buildings, hotels, theatres, cafés and other commercial places are centrally heated to give temperatures of between 70°–80°F (21–26·7C) indoors. Thus, once heavy outer wear is shed, the traveller will feel quite comfortable indoors going round in light winter, or summer clothing.

Summers in most of Canada are hot. As has been shown, tropical air floods into Canada from the Gulf of Mexico, or from the hot deserts of the American southwest, every June, and dominates the weather through July and August. Since most parts of Canada are close to the sea or to great lakes, they are very humid. Thus a hot, humid climate prevails that demands light tropical clothes, at least until one gets into northern resorts: there cool evenings and nights require a sweater or stole.

Spring is ever beautiful to Canadians after the long months of winter, and indeed few sights are more thrilling than the break-up of winter ice on river and lake. However, spring has its problems. Thaw by day and freezing by night can develop boils, bumps or pot-holes in the roads that must be watched for by the driver. Thaws can turn many places very muddy and bog down a car or trailer at a camp site. In early spring clouds of black-fly and mosquito swarm into the air and can make camping a misery, especially in wooded camp sites, all through May and well into June. Warm air temperatures may tempt people to swim when the water is still very cold: drowning by cramps and heart attacks in ice-cold waters on hot May days is an annual tragedy.

Autumn is often the loveliest time in Canada. Days are still sunny and warm, humidity drops, and nights, no longer muggy and close, are crisp, cool and comfortable. The woods turn a glorious colour, maples and sumachs are flaming red, oaks change to a deep brown, and poplar and birch are a vivid gold.

No time is better for walks in the woods, or picnics by the lake. The traveller who can choose this time of year for his holiday, through September to mid-October, has the choice of the year.

Housing varies with the seasons. In winter most houses are centrally heated. This means they are hermetically sealed. Storm windows and storm doors are put up outside the permanent ones and every effort is made to seal out draughts. Visitors must learn that warm air can be 'fresh' air and not seek to ruin the heating system by opening windows.

In summer, houses have to be kept cool. The traditional way of doing this is to open the windows and doors at night to let in the cool, night air, then at sunrise close everything down, pulling the blinds, to keep out the heat of the day. This keeps the house reasonably cool, but at the expense of light. Many middle- and upper-class homes are now fitted with air-conditioning, which is a welcome relief from the heat outside. But once again visitors must resist opening doors and windows if this is to function properly.

Clothing is a difficult thing to decide about, because of this marked difference between outdoors and indoors. Since houses, cars, trains, buses, offices, hotels and other closed spaces are generally warm in winter and cool in summer, they demand nothing more than medium- or light-weight clothing: most men never wear a waistcoat or cardigan, and few women a stole or heavy woollens. Going from a heated or air-conditioned house, to a car, to an office, or to a public building, which are warm or cool as the season requires, one can go about most of the year in light woollens. But if one has to walk quite a distance from car park to theatre on a cold windy wintry evening, one could suffer extreme chilling, if not well and warmly clothed. The visitor must use his discretion. In summer outer wear is reduced to a minimum. In suburbs and at resorts boys and girls go round in swim suits and women in shorts with a halter-top; men go about in an open-necked shirt and shorts, and discard socks. But it should be mentioned that fuller wear is traditional in downtown areas, women would not be proper there in abbreviated two-piece beach-wear, nor men in bare legs and sandals. Canadians have a very delicate sense of what is right in one place and wrong in another, and visitors, welcomed to be free and easy in the suburbs, would be frowned on downtown unless they were properly clothed.

FOOD

Food varies tremendously across Canada, since each ethnic group has continued the tastes it inherited. French food in Quebec, British food in most parts of Canada, Jewish, Italian, and Chinese foods in all the major cities, have become part of the flavour of Canadian life. Traditionally cooked meals in the winter and cold plates and salads in the summer have been the norm, but increasingly, with Canada's ability to import fresh greens and fruit from tropical zones, winter meals are livened up with salads, and the old seasonal contrasts are not so marked. European visitors may be embarrassed by the very large helpings Canadians serve. Canadians eat more than Europeans, and both in public places and at home give very large portions, especially of meat. Quite often Europeans after taking their soup and meat course find they cannot manage a sweet—which is a shame if one is a lover of desserts: Canadian desserts are very sumptuous! It is advisable in restaurants to ask for the smaller sizes in steaks, otherwise one may be surprised by a 12–16oz (340–453gr) steak on one's plate.

Because helpings are so generous, meal prices are very high. Indeed, food prices as a whole are high, particularly in winter, when most vegetables and fruits have to be imported long distances from Texas and California. Even customarily cheap foods like breads and cereals are now expensive because of the strong demand for Canadian wheat in countries like Russia and China. Meat too is expensive since it can be sold at very good profit to the United States: Americans are great meat eaters and pay well for Grade A meat.

MANNERS

Manners are a matter of some importance to Canadians. Without being fastidious they are careful to observe good manners. This goes for all they do. They eat in a mannerly way. They show good manners in public places. British visitors who have grown accustomed to smoking in cafés or cinemas, or on public transport, should observe with care the no-smoking tradition of Canadians where smoke could cause general offence. Mention has already been made about propriety in clothes, at least on the occasions and in the places where Canadians expect public good taste. Special concern should be felt in rural Quebec not to cause offence, since the Quebecois of the small town and countryside are conservative in their tastes.

Canadians are the kindest and most generous of people. Always remember to thank them for any act of interest or help. Canadians are an extremely courteous and warm-hearted people, often repeating their thanks for courtesies received to the point where Europeans might think them over-demonstrative. This makes the reserved Englishman seem to be cold. During the last war, evacuees from Britain were advised to say 'thank you twice' in response to Canadian hospitality. Without being gushing, one should be positive in showing one's appreciation.

Perhaps because of their warmth and generosity, Canadians are sensitive to criticism. No visitor is welcome who spends his time comparing Canada unfavourably with Britain or America. Remember that Canada's history has been one of trying to escape from the shadow of Britain, and of standing up against America. Try to understand if not sympathise with this: a new national spirit is rising in Canada, where Canadians are breaking away from age-old colonialism, to become strongly independent. This is exemplified in the playing of *O Canada* in place of *God save the Queen* as their national anthem, and in the flying of the Maple Leaf instead of the Union Jack. However, one should not gather from this that because Canadians do not regard themselves as British any more, they think of themselves as Americans. They are of course North Americans and to that extent their way of life is very American. But Canadians bristle when they are taken for American. They themselves see—and hold to—many differences which give them a separate identity on the continent. Developed from France and Britain, constituted under the British North American Act, yet growing side by side with America and powerfully influenced by the American way, Canada has none the less forged its own destiny and has its own character and ideals.[31] This is something always to be appreciated.

Notes and References

1 *Canada, 1867–1967* (Queen's Printer, Ottawa, 1967), p 64; *Encyclopedia Canadiana*, Vol 5, p 260

2 Battle, G., in *Canada, 1867–1967*, op cit, p 65

3 *Canada, 1975, Official Handbook* (Queen's Printer, 1975), p 55

4 Watson, J. W., *North America, its countries and regions* (Longman, 2nd ed, 1968), p 385 ff

5 Trudeau, P. E., *Federalism and the French Canadians* (Macmillan, 1968), p 29

6 Forsey, E., 'Canadian Federalism: the Federal Point of View,' in Wolfe, N. (ed) *Federalism: Central/Regional Relations* (Edin Centre of Canadian Studies, 1975), p 2

7 Ibid, p 9

8 Roberts, G. D., *A History of Canada* (Kegan Paul, 1898), p 76

9 Tyman, J. L., *By Section, Township, and Range* (Assiniboine Hist Soc, 1972), p 3

10 Rotstein, A. and Lax, G., *Independence, the Canadian challenge* (McClelland and Stewart, 1973)

11 Lawr, D. A., and Gidney, R. D., *Educating Canadians: a documentary history of Canadian Education* (Van Nostrand, 1973)

12 Beattie, E., *A Handbook of Canadian Film* (Martin, 1973), p 5

13 Moore, M., *Four Canadian Playwrights* (Holt, Rinehart and Winston, 1973)

14 Stevens, J., *Modern Canadian Stories* (Bantam Books, 1975)

15 Woodcock, G., *The Canadian Novel in the Twentieth Century* (McClelland and Stewart, 1975)

16 Tougas, G., *L'Histoire de la littérature canadienne–française* (Presses Univ de France, 1969); also Robert, G., *Littérature du Québec* (UL Pr, 1970)

17 Ross, M., *Poets of the Confederation* (McClelland and Stewart, 1960)

18 Smith, A. J. M., *Modern Canadian verse in French and English* (Oxford, 1967)

19 Sylvestre, G., *Anthologie de la poésie canadienne—française* (Quebec, 1966)
20 Colgate, W., *Canadian Art, 1820–1940* (McGraw, 1967); Lord, B., *The History of Painting in Canada* (NC Pr, 1974)
21 Boggs, Jean, *The National Gallery of Canada* (OUP, 1971)
22 Kallman, H., *A History of Music in Canada* (U of Tor Pr, 1970)
23 Fowke, E., *Penguin Book of Canadian Folk Songs* (Penguin, 1973)
24 Roxborough, H., *Great days in Canadian sport* (Ryerson, 1957)
25 Howells, N. and Howells, M. L., *Sports and Games in Canadian Life* (Macmillan, 1974)
26 Kavanagh, L. V., *The History of golf in Canada* (Fitzhenry and Whiteside, 1973)
27 Hannon, L. F., *Maclean's Canada, portrait of a country* (McClelland and Stewart, 1960) (Note: Maclean's is a national magazine)
28 Sullivan, J., *The Grey Cup Story* (Pagurian Prd, 1970)
29 Conacher, B., quoted in Howells and Howells, op cit, p 33
30 Macfarlane, B., *The Story of the Stanley Cup* (Greywood, 1972)
31 Morton, W. L., *The Canadian Identity* (U of Tor Pr, 2nd edn, 1975)

Bibliography

A GOOD introduction to reading about Canada is in Granatstein, J. L. and Stevens, P., *Canada since 1867, a bibliographical guide* (Hakkert, Toronto, 1974).

Ready reference books are also of great help. *Quick Canadian Facts* is a most useful compendium and can be obtained at most bookstalls. It is revised annually. The Bank of Montreal issues a more compact guide in *Canada Today*. The *Annual Directory and Almanac of Canada* is a much bigger book, published by Corpus, Toronto, but is absolutely indispensable for those wanting to make contact with government offices at all levels, with business and labour-union headquarters, and with societies and associations of all kinds. The Canadian government publish two ready-reference books, *Canada, the Annual Handbook* of present conditions and recent progress, and *The Canada Yearbook*, a statistical review. Of special value is the handbook *Canada One Hundred, 1867–1967*, a unique survey of the growth of Canada during its first hundred years after confederation.

The geography, history, economics and social conditions of Canada have been well written up. Helpful general texts are: **geography**—*Canada's natural environment, essays in applied geography*, McBoyle, G. R. and Sommerville, E. (Methuen, 1975); *Canada, the land and its people*, Tomkins, D. M., et al (Gage, 1975); *Canada, a geographical interpretation*, Warkentin, J. (Methuen, 1970); *Canada, problems and prospects*, Watson, J. W. (Longman, 1968): **history**—*Canada, a modern study*, Cook, R. (Clarke-Irwin, 1972); *From Sea to Sea*, Hardy, W.G. (Doubleday, 1970); *Canada, an outline history*, Lower, J. A. (McGraw, 1973); *Canada, a political and social history*, McInnis, E. W. (Holt, 1969); *The Pelican History* *of Canada*, McNaught, K. (Penguin, 1975): **economics—** *Canada's economic problems and policies*, Archer, M. (Macmillan, 1975); *Economics, contemporary issues in Canada*, Auld, D. (Holt, 1972); *Economics Canada, selected readings*, Kierstead, B. S., et al (Macmillan, 1974); *Canada's energy crisis*, Laxer, J. (Lorimer, 2nd edn, 1975): **politics and society—***Canadian Society*, Blishen, B. B., et al (Macmillan, 3rd edn, 1973); *Canada's Indians, contemporary conflicts*, Frideres, J. S. (Prentice, 1974); *Population issues in Canada*, Grindstaff, et al (Holt, 1971); *Canadian political parties*, Heggie, G. (Macmillan, 1976); *The Canadian family*, Ishwaran, K. (Holt, 1976); *Le Canada français d'aujourd'hui*, Lamontagne, L. (UTP, 1970); *Canada, a socio-political report*, Manzer, R. A. (McGraw, 1974); *Canadian settlement patterns*, Radley-Walters, M. and Cook, S. A. (Nelson, 1973).

The arts, education and recreation are well represented in Canadian writing. Only a few general titles are given; more specific ones are mentioned in the Notes and Reference section: **art—***Three Hundred Years of Canadian Art*, Hubbard, R. H. (National Gallery of Can pubn, 1967); *Canadian artists in exhibition* (Roundstone Council for the Arts, annual pubn); *A Canadian art movement, the story of the Group of Seven*, Housser, F. B. (Macmillan, 1974): **literature—***Canadian literature, beginnings to twentieth century*, McLay, C. (McClelland & Stewart, 1974); *Creative Writing in Canada*, Pacey, D. (McGraw, 1968); *Selections from Major Canadian Writers*, Pacey, D. (McGraw, 1974); *Canadian Writing Today*, Richler, M. (Penguin, 1970): **education—** *Educational administration in Canada*, Giles, T. E. (Detselig (Calgary) 1974); *The Best of Times—The Worst of Times, Contemporary issues in Canadian education*, Stevenson, H. A., et al (Holt, 1972); *Canadian education, a history*, Wilson, J. D., et al (Prentice, 1970): **recreation—***Recreation Canada* (annual publication of the Canadian Parks and Recreation Assoc); *Recreation Land Use Planning in Canada*, Pearson, N., Guelph, U. (Centre for Resources Dev Bul, 1972); *The Canadian National Parks, today and tomorrow*, Nelson, J. G. and Scace, R. C. (Univ Calgary Pr, 1969).

General books about Canada are legion. Amongst the better known are: *The National Dream*, Berton, P. (McClelland, 1970);

The Canadians, Careless, J. M. S. and Brown, R. C. (Macmillan, 1968); *The Unknown Country*, Hutchison, B. (McClelland & Stewart, 2nd ed, 1965); *The Canadian Identity*, Morton, W. L. (Univ Tor Pr, 2nd ed, 1972); *Canada and the Canadians*, Woodcock, G. (Macmillan, 1973). A most interesting book on what Canadians say about themselves is R. M. Hamilton's, *Canadian quotations and phrases* (McClelland & Stewart, 1965).

Index